THE VOTING WARS

Kelly de la Vega

Richard L. Hasen

The
Voting
Wars

From Florida 2000 to the
Next Election Meltdown

Yale university press

new haven & london

Yale University Press books may be purchased in quantity for
educational, business, or promotional use. For information, please e-mail
sales.press@yale.edu (U.S. office) or sales@yaleup.co.uk (U.K. office).

Set in Scala & Scala Sans type by Integrated Publishing Solutions,
Grand Rapids, Michigan.
Printed in the United States of America.

Library of Congress Cataloging-in-Publication Data

Hasen, Richard L.
The voting wars : from Florida 2000 to the next election meltdown / Richard L. Hasen.
p. cm.
Includes bibliographical references and index.
ISBN 978-0-300-18203-3 (clothbound : alk. paper)   1. Election law—United
States.   2. Elections—United States—Corrupt practices.   3. Contested elections—
United States.   I. Title.
KF4886.H39 2012
342.73'07—dc23   2012000703

A catalogue record for this book is available from the British Library.

This paper meets the requirements of ANSI/NISO Z39.48–1992
(Permanence of Paper).

10 9 8 7 6 5 4 3 2

For Deborah, Shana, and Jared,
the lights of my life,
who deserve better than
the voting system they are inheriting

CONTENTS

PREFACE

Belief in the integrity of elections is essential to any democracy. As nations such as Iraq move from dictatorial rule to democracy, outside election observers play a critical role. Until these observers verify that the elections are free and fair—that those who are eligible are allowed to vote for the candidates of their choice, free of intimidation and bribery, and that neither election officials nor voters have improperly altered the tallies—election losers will doubt the results and will hold back support for the new government. The legitimacy of democratic government itself thus depends on faith in the rules for casting and counting votes, and in the fairness with which these rules are followed and enforced.

When belief in election integrity is lacking, bad consequences follow: people think their leaders do not serve the popular will or common good but the interests of some faction; they doubt their leaders' legitimacy and thus the legitimacy of their laws and executive actions; and they are apt to believe that if one group is working to fix elections, it's not only acceptable but necessary for others to do so as well. A lack of faith in elections becomes a self-fulfilling prophecy that undermines faith in democratic governance itself.

Belief in electoral integrity is crucial not only in emerging democracies but in all of them, including long-established ones such as the United States. In recent decades it became common for US voters to view stolen elections as a thing of the past—a relic of the era of machine politics, and even then something largely confined to big cities and a few corrupt bosses. In our day, those who questioned the casting and counting of votes have increasingly been seen as part of a political fringe.

Over the past decade, however, this has begun to change. In our hyperpartisan political atmosphere, where people with of an opposing ideology are not to be merely disagreed with but denounced as malevolent and unhinged, the conduct of elections has become one more accusation to throw in opponents' faces. We have entered a vicious cycle: continued questioning of the integrity of our elections encourages gaming of the electoral process by political insiders, agitation by political hacks aimed at undermining the legitimacy of the election of those on the opposing side, and a dangerous corrosion of public faith in electoral outcomes.

The shift in attitudes about election fairness began with the 2000 presidential election between Republican George W. Bush and Democrat Al Gore, in which the ultimate victory depended on a virtually tied vote in the critical state of Florida. The thirty-six-day dispute over who really won the state, and was therefore entitled to be president, altered American elections and put great stress on the public's faith in electoral integrity.

The problems revealed by the 2000 election are twofold. First are the actual defects in how we run our elections, and second are efforts by various factions to focus on the wrong issues for self-interested ideological reasons. It is the confluence of these two that creates the potential for a major crisis. And should we face another virtual tie in a presidential race, the rise of social media in the years since 2000 has the potential to make things much worse.

Our elections are plagued by technological, organizational, and political difficulties. Before 2000, few understood how inaccurate some of our vote casting and counting equipment really is. People took it on faith that the numbers of votes reported in the media accurately reflected voter preferences. But these inaccuracies extended well beyond the notorious "punch card" voting machines with their hanging chads, which played such a prominent role in the 2000 election dispute. Election officials often lack the resources and training to effectively manage the complexity of a large modern election. For example, the lists of eligible voters are sometimes wildly inaccurate, and the procedures put in place to clean up the rolls sometimes lead to the disenfranchisement of eligible voters. Election officials need to roll out election equipment on election day to a large number of polling places staffed by volunteers or poorly paid workers, many of whom lack adequate training or formal expertise. Some jurisdictions handle elections well; many don't.

Procedures and equipment vary from county to county, with the result that voters' chances of casting a vote in a statewide election that will actually be counted are wildly unequal. In our hyper-decentralized system, state and federal election officials have very little control over election decisions made at the local level.

On top of the localism issue is the problem of partisanship. Many state and local election officials are either elected in partisan elections as Democrats or Republicans, or are appointed and supervised by partisans. The United States is almost alone among mature democracies in allowing the foxes to guard the henhouse. Even ignoring those election officials who consciously manipulate election rules to achieve partisan advantage, there's no question that Democrats and Republicans, acting from their own views of the public interest, tend to administer elections differently. Democrats, for example, are much less likely to be interested in purging voter rolls of potentially ineligible voters than Republicans are. Democrats worry about disenfranchising eligible voters; Republicans worry about the potential for fraud from bloated voter rolls.

Aside from the real problems with running our elections, since 2000 we have seen political insiders become increasingly aggressive in undermining the legitimacy of the electoral process by making unsupported claims about election integrity. Key elements in the Republican Party have pushed the false belief that voter fraud is a major influence in our elections and that it tends to benefit Democratic candidates. In response, Democrats have attacked Republican anti-fraud efforts, such as voter identification laws, as means of suppressing the Democratic vote, the new Jim Crow. While some Democratic claims of voter suppression are legitimate, others are not, and even genuine voter suppression efforts seem unlikely to be effective in suppressing Democratic turnout.

Some will view this book as harsher on Republicans than Democrats. My aim was neither to favor one side or another nor to impose a false even-handedness on the narrative in the name of objectivity. Republicans may have been more blameworthy in the years since Florida 2000, but support-ers of Democrats should not delude themselves into thinking that Demo-crats have been faultless. Each side is guilty of manipulating the political and legal processes to partisan advantage, and each side entertains con-spiracy theories that at some point lose contact with reality.

Many of the partisan fights over election rules have ended in court, lead-ing judges further into the political thicket. Judges have tended to divide on party lines in resolving many of these disputes. Republican judges seem more concerned about fraud; Democratic judges more concerned about disenfranchisement. Thus the threat to the legitimacy of our elections also threatens the perception of judicial impartiality.

The soldiers in the Voting Wars are harming the body politic. Partisans on both sides now buy into the rhetoric of electoral unfairness, and the ex-plosion of social media such as Twitter, Facebook, and instant messaging allow pernicious messages to be amplified, repeated, and distorted in an echo-chamber of like-minded voters. Should another presidential election go into overtime, these social media may not only heat political tensions to the boiling point. Recent experience from Egypt to London shows that the new media also provide the organizational tool for the kind of mass politi-cal protests that, for the most part, did not materialize in 2000.

The United States has done far too little to cure the problems that led to the Florida breakdown. The main barriers to reform are political, not tech-nical. To stop the Voting Wars we need greater uniformity and nonpartisan-ship in our election rules and procedures. These changes would be achiev-able and uncontroversial, but for the Voting Wars themselves.

ACKNOWLEDGMENTS

All good scholarship depends upon the sharing of ideas by others with greater or different experiences, perspectives, and knowledge. In this work I have relied more on the generosity of friends, family, and colleagues in sharing their ideas than I have in any of my other work. If this book succeeds, it is due in large part to them. However none of my readers and commenters bears responsibility for my ideas or errors. I benefited most when I was pushed on my arguments and forced to justify the claims I make by those who disagree with me.

This book began as a grant proposal for an academic work with a grander title and an intended narrow academic audience. In crafting that proposal I relied upon the sage advice of Ellen Aprill, Lori Klein, and Michael Waterstone, and the support of Richard Briffault, Bruce Cain, Heather Gerken, and Dan Lowenstein.

Very helpful conversations with David Pervin convinced me to write a very different book, one which would be accessible to the general reader without sacrificing intellectual rigor. Adam Winkler convinced me of the value and joy of writing for a wider audience. My spouse, Lori Klein, was indispensable in these early stages, reading my book proposal and draft Introduction with an eye toward what would be interesting and relevant beyond the world of election geeks. I hope the book as written has both contemporary relevance and historical value.

David Ettinger, Ned Foley, Davina Klein, Justin Levitt, Lori Minnite, Rick Pildes, Charles Stewart, Abigail Thernstrom, and Dan Tokaji read and provided detailed comments on significant portions of the manuscript. Many others read portions of the manuscript or provided important information or feedback, including: Bob Bauer, John Berger, Bruce Cain, Doug Chapin, Erwin Chemerinsky, Michael Conover, Mary Dudziak, Marc Elias, Deborah Gershenowitz, Ben Ginsberg, Ken Gross, Joe Hall, Lisa Hauser, Michael Herron, Candice Hoke, Brett Kappel, Michael Kerns, Alex Keyssar, David Kimball, Beth Kingsley, Morgan Kousser, Ethan Leib, Vince Leibowitz, Brian Leiter, Ray Martinez, David McBride, Jeff Milyo, Lynn Nesbit, Larry Norden, Frank Partnoy, Bob Pastor, Trevor Potter, Tony Reese, Gail Ross, Jennifer Rothman, Mark Scarberry, Roy Schotland, Jim Sleeper, Larry Solum, Matt Streb, John Tanner, Steve Wasserman, Jay Weiner, and Jeff Wice.

Law students Denny Chan and Joy Kim provided exemplary research assistance, and they were joined by Leanna Constanini and Ryan Graham for meticulous cite-checking work. Joy Shoemaker, the Head of Research Services at UC Irvine's law library tracked down a very important 1984 grand jury report from Brooklyn, New York and led a team of outstanding law librarians including Ellen Augustiniak, Jeremy Hufton, Dianna Sahhar, and Christina Tsou who assisted me with many arcane research queries. UC Irvine School of Law and Dean Erwin Chemerinsky generously supported my scholarship. Kazumo Washizuka, Andrew Campbell, and Angie Middleton provided cheerful and professional administrative support.

At Yale University Press, Bill Frucht made this a considerably better book, with suggestions on both the larger ideas in the book and the means of expressing them. Of his many treasured qualities, I value most his good judgment about how to think through and present a cogent and persuasive argument. Jaya Chatterjee graciously eased the way for my manuscript to sail through review and editing. Laura Jones Dooley kept my prose clean and clear. Jennifer Doerr runs a mean publicity machine.

Finally, I owe a great debt to my spouse, Lori, and children, Deborah, Shana, and Jared. Lori's support, encouragement, and love made this book possible; I could not have written it without her. The entire family sacrificed as I spent many nights and weekends finishing this manuscript.

I dedicate this book to Deborah, Shana, and Jared. My love for them exceeds my capacity to express in words. They are part of the next generation, which will inherit the mess of an election system we and generations before us have created. My children—and yours—deserve better.

THE VOTING WARS

Introduction

THE NEXT MELTDOWN

*E*lection Day. Another presidential election goes down to the wire. It all hinges on the battleground state of Wisconsin, which has erupted recently in partisan rancor as the governor tried to break the power of public sector unions. As the polling places close, election returns begin to trickle in from the various counties.[1]

The lead between the Democratic and Republican candidates seesaws all night as returns roll in. Some counties report quickly, others slowly, and the candidates remain within a few hundred votes of each other. In the middle of the night, when it appears that all the returns are in aside from some uncounted absentee and questioned ballots, the Democrat has eked out a come-from-behind lead of about two hundred votes.

The Wall Street Journal's John Fund leads a parade of conservative bloggers and Twitter users charging that voter fraud was responsible for the Democrat's lead. On a Wall Street Journal "Opinion Journal" webcast, Fund points to "bizarre" voting patterns in liberal-leaning Dane County, cites Wisconsin's laws that allow Election Day registration, and references a controversial Milwaukee police report from a few years back suggesting voter fraud in Democratic areas. There is much to build on. Republicans have been crying "voter fraud" for years, clamor-

ing for voter identification requirements, tough voter registration rules, and other laws that could depress turnout of Democrats.[2]

The next morning, the head election official in Waukesha County, Wisconsin, Republican Kathy Nickolaus, announces that she had been storing her county's election results on her personal laptop computer, and when she reported votes on election night she had inadvertently failed to include 14,315 votes from the City of Brookfield. With those votes included, the Republican candidate jumps to a 7,300-vote lead statewide, and he appears to be the winner.[3]

Republicans quickly drop their cries of voter fraud, and Fund goes silent on the Dane County vote, but Democrats and their allies immediately suggest chicanery by Nickolaus, who had previously been chastised for lax security with ballots and for using her laptop to store official vote totals. The influential liberal blog "Think Progress" says that "critics" suggest the result must be from foul play or incompetence: "All of this evidence raises a cloud of uncertainty over any vote counts, and it raises disturbing questions about the legitimacy of this election." The URL for the blog post is a more pointed. It reads in part: "kathy-nickolaus-crook-or-idiot."[4]

Ramona Kitzinger, the Democrat on the local elections board, vouches for Nickolaus, but the next day she issues a statement posted on a local Democratic Party website: "I am 80 years old and I don't understand anything about computers. I don't know where the numbers Kathy was showing me ultimately came from, but they seemed to add up. I am still very, very confused." The Democratic candidate demands a recount and an investigation. Partisans on both sides gear up for a long and bitter fight.[5]

Aside from one crucial fact, the story you've just read is true. It happened not in a presidential election but in a 2011 race for the Wisconsin Supreme Court between incumbent David Prosser, a former Republican state legislator, and challenger JoAnne Kloppenburg, a Democrat and assistant state attorney general. The race gained national prominence because of the toxic political atmosphere in Wisconsin at the time. Scott Walker, the new Republican governor, urged the legislature to pass a law taking away collective bargaining rights from some public sector unions. Democratic lawmakers fled the state to try to deprive the Republican-dominated legislature of a quorum to pass the antiunion law. Republican legislators used a procedural maneuver to pass the law anyway, and Democrats then started campaigns to recall some of the Republican state senators who had supported the proposal.

The state supreme court race, which would determine the ideological balance of the court, became larger than life. Some saw it as a referendum on Walker and the union controversy, and the court itself was poised to rule on the legality of the legislative vote against the unions. The court, at the time, was mired in a partisan spat unconnected to Walker. Someone had leaked an internal court email from a few years earlier in which Prosser called Wisconsin chief justice Shirley Abrahamson, a well-respected liberal jurist, "a total bitch," a claim repeated in anti-Prosser television ads. A few weeks before the election, federal judge William M. Conley, in an opinion upholding Wisconsin's rules for publicly financing its state supreme court elections, lamented the decline of what he said was once one of the most respected courts in the country. Such public criticism of another court was highly unusual.[6]

After Nickolaus announced her mistake the day after the election, Kloppenburg exercised her right to demand a recount, to be funded by the state because the margin between the candidates was so close. The odds against Kloppenburg's prevailing were high: in a state like Wisconsin, which has relatively few "provisional ballots" to check for possible counting after Election Day, it is really hard to make up a seven-thousand-vote shortfall without proof of a major error (like finding another fourteen thousand votes) or criminal activity. Still, Kloppenburg went forward with the recount, insisting that there were "anomalies" in how the election was conducted, especially in Waukesha County. Tammy Baldwin, a Democratic member of Congress from Madison, called for a federal investigation, but after it became clear there was no proof of intentional wrongdoing by Nickolaus, the election appeared to be beyond what insiders call the "margin of litigation," and the issue faded from the national radar screen. Prosser was declared the winner and Kloppenburg conceded.[7]

How much worse would things have been had the fate of a presidential election depended on Wisconsin and had the vote margin been only a bit closer? It would be an echo of 2000. Then, the U.S. presidential election went into overtime as just a few hundred votes, out of millions cast, separated Republican George W. Bush from Democrat Al Gore in the state of

Florida, whose twenty-five electoral votes would decide the nation's next president. For thirty-six days, the nation was riveted and divided between Democrats and Republicans as the election morphed into a sequence of challenges, recounts, and lawsuits before culminating in one of the most controversial Supreme Court decisions in American history, *Bush v. Gore,* the case stopping the recount and giving Bush the victory. Everything related to the election controversy went under the microscope: the varieties of election machinery; the method for culling people who had moved, died, or become ineligible from the lists of registered voters: the rules for vote-counting; the poor drafting of Florida's election statutes; the partisan officials involved in the recount; and the role of the courts in resolving election disputes. Calls for reform came from everywhere, including the Supreme Court.

If you think that a dozen years later the country would have fixed its problems with how we run our elections, you'd be dead wrong.

Just look at Wisconsin. Why would a county clerk keep official voting records on her personal laptop? Why do we even allow local partisan officials to run statewide elections? How could it be that the one check on the power of the local partisan election administrator responsible for supervising the computerized reporting of thousands of votes is an eighty-year-old election board member who claims no familiarity with computers? And why were Republicans so quick to yell "voter fraud" on election night and Democrats so quick to suspect Nickolaus of malfeasance?

In the years since the Florida debacle of 2000 we have witnessed a partisan war over election rules. The number of election-related lawsuits has more than doubled compared to the previous decade, and election time invariably brings out partisan accusations of voter fraud and voter suppression. These allegations have shaken public confidence, as campaigns deploy armies of lawyers and the partisan press revs up whenever high-stakes elections are expected to be close. All this is much worse in presidential election years. We are just one more razor-thin presidential election away from chaos and an undermining of the rule of law.

The next overtime will be much more partisan and nastier than 2000, full of acrimony and unsubstantiated allegations of fraud or official wrongdoing. The rancor will be amplified as partisan tweets, instant messages, blog posts, and Facebook messages reach people instantaneously over their smartphones, laptops, and tablets. The controversy could threaten the very legitimacy of the next president, as well as the courts, which almost certainly would be called upon as the final arbiters of a postelection controversy.

How did we get here? Why haven't things improved since the meltdown in 2000? Why has the situation in fact grown worse? This book is the story of lessons not learned.

It begins with the 2000 Florida debacle. That story has been told many times before, but always from the perspective of the lawyers and the courts, culminating in the Supreme Court's controversial decision in *Bush v. Gore,* which handed the election to Bush over Gore. I retell the story from the point of view of the real losers in Florida, the voters. Just about every problem we've seen in the past decade over election disputes—bad machinery, partisan hacks turning up on cable news, turf wars among election officials, dueling courts and judges, and spurious allegations of fraud—has its origins in Florida.

Florida served as a wake-up call, but not in the way many people think. Though there was some effort to improve the ways the country casts and counts votes, and especially to get rid of the worst-performing pieces of voting machinery like those "punch card" voting machines, Florida mainly taught political operatives the benefits of manipulating the rules, controlling election machinery, and litigating early and often. Election law has become part of a political strategy.

Chapter 2 starts with the decade's most cynical attempts to manipulate election rules for political gain: spurious claims of "voter fraud" made by Republican lawyers, conservative columnists such as John Fund, and others as a means of passing voter identification laws and other restrictive legislation. The late judge Terence Evans of the United States Court of Appeals for the Seventh Circuit explained the motive for such laws in a dissent to his court's decision upholding Indiana's voter identification law: "Let's not beat around the bush: The Indiana voter photo ID law is a not-too-thinly-veiled attempt to discourage election-day turnout by certain folks believed to skew Democratic." Chapter 2 also looks at the activities of the now defunct ACORN voter registration group and shows that the voter registration fraud committed by some ACORN workers did not lead to actual fraud affecting our elections.[8]

Just as Republicans are quick to yell "voter fraud," Democrats turn frequently to cries of voter suppression, comparing election changes proposed or passed by Republicans to poll taxes and other discriminatory laws of the pre–Civil Rights era South. Although some claims of voter suppression are legitimate, others are exaggerated or imagined, and even some of real efforts at vote suppression seem unlikely to be effective.

During the 2010 midterm elections, a Massachusetts Tea Party group put up a billboard in a predominantly Latino neighborhood that read: "Protect the Integrity of the Vote: Show ID." The group did not put up billboards elsewhere, and state law did not require voters to show any identification. That same year, a group named Latinos for Reform ran television ads on Spanish-language television in Nevada urging Latinos "Don't Vote." The message was particularly important in the U.S. Senate campaign, as Senate Majority Leader Harry Reid, a Democrat, was in a close election race with Republican challenger Sharon Angle. Latinos for Reform turned out to be an organization backed by Republicans and apparently funded by non-Latino conservatives.[9]

In chapter 3 I look at efforts to suppress the vote, particularly those aimed at minority communities, which tend to vote for Democratic candidates. The newer methods follow earlier attempts to spread misinformation through flyers, such as those telling Democrats to vote the day after Election Day or to choose a convenient polling place rather than the only one where they would be permitted to vote. Though there is ample evidence that these heavy-handed voter suppression methods are still occasionally used to target minority communities, there is little indication that the methods actually work. In recent years the attempts themselves have been used by Democrats and minority activists to boost voter turnout. Fallout from the Latinos for Reform controversy could well have boosted turnout for Democrats and helped Reid survive a tough reelection battle.

More effective means of voter suppression include restrictive registration and vote-counting rules as well as sloppy efforts to purge the rolls of ineligible voters. But it is hard to tell when such efforts are intended to suppress the vote and when they are simply misguided antifraud measures. I conclude the chapter with a look at the paranoid left's unsubstantiated claims of hacked voting machines and at conservative claims (heavily promoted by

Fox News) of voter suppression stemming from an isolated incident at a Philadelphia polling place in 2008 involving the New Black Panthers.

Chapter 4 looks more closely at who counts the votes, focusing on the battleground state of Ohio, which has seen more than its share of election controversies. The United States is unique among mature democracies in using local, partisan officials to run national elections, and the results have not been pretty. Localism brings varied levels of competence as well as turf wars. Much of what gets described as partisan manipulation often looks more like lack of training, inadequate resources, or failure to follow proper procedures. Yale law professor Heather Gerken suggests applying "Hanlon's razor," the computer scientist's maxim that "one should never attribute to malice that which can be adequately explained by stupidity." The Washington State election officials who sent voter registration materials to ineligible felons in 2004 created a mess in the postelection dispute between Dino Rossi and Christine Gregoire over who would serve as that state's governor. The errors in sending the materials to felons could have cost Rossi the election (though that's far from certain). But the election officials' action came from inadequate registration procedures, not some underhanded conspiracy.[10]

State and local election officials, fighting to keep their share of power, have also rejected attempts to impose nationwide standards (such as a uniform federal ballot for presidential elections). After Florida 2000, Congress took a baby step toward uniformity by creating the U.S. Election Assistance Commission. Though the agency was given almost no power—aside from the power to dole out money to get rid of bad voting machines—state and local election officials have fought since its inception to have it shut down as a threat to their autonomy, and Republicans in the House passed a measure to cut off funding for it (a measure that is unlikely to go anywhere in the Democrat-controlled Senate).

Partisanship also matters in vote counting, a fact evident from Florida. Since 2000, however, not one state with partisan administration of elections has removed authority from partisan officials.[11]

In Ohio, Democrats saw Republican secretary of state Ken Blackwell's decisions in the 2004 presidential election as a deliberate attempt to help Republicans, and Republicans saw Democratic secretary of state Jennifer

Brunner's decisions in the 2008 election as a deliberate attempt to help Democrats. Blackwell decided that voter registration forms submitted on paper that was thinner than required by state law were unacceptable. Brunner decided not to accept absentee ballot request forms created by the Republican McCain campaign when voters returning the forms did not check a box affirming that the voter was qualified to vote—a box not required by state or federal law.

Whether or not the partisanship actually motivates election officials' decisions, there is no question that Democratic and Republican election officials administer elections differently. Democrats often aim for greater inclusiveness (even if it raises the potential for fraud), and Republicans (in the name of preventing fraud) often aim to make voting harder (except for military voters, who tend to vote Republican). So long as partisans administer our elections, suspicions of their motives are inevitable.

It should be no surprise that these issues often end up in court. When the United States Supreme Court held, in *Bush v. Gore*, that the Constitution required an end to the 2000 Florida recount, some election law professors told a "lemonade from lemons" story. It was true, they said, that there was much to criticize about the Supreme Court's decision to take the case, its rationale, and its controversial decision to end the recount rather than send the case back for a recount complying with (brand-spanking-new) standards. But the opinion could usher in an era when courts would use the principle of the case to fix fundamental inequalities in our country's hyperdecentralized election system.[12]

So far, these dreams have not materialized. In the twelve years since the decision, the Supreme Court has never even cited *Bush v. Gore*, much less relied on it for any legal principle, and lower courts have mostly failed to force the fixing of our election problems through constitutional litigation. On issues such as the constitutionality of voter ID laws, many courts have divided along Democratic-Republican lines.

This is not to say that courts have played no role in the story of Florida's aftermath. We've seen an explosion of election litigation. Since 2000, campaigns are more willing to use election law as a political strategy. The problems in how elections are administered mean that any razor-thin election will be within the "margin of litigation" and allow lawyers to put election results in doubt as they attempt to overturn them. In chapter 5 I tell the story of the major postelection recounts and contests since 2000, including the 2004 Rossi-Gregoire gubernatorial contest in Washington State, the 2008 Coleman-Franken U.S. Senate race in Minnesota, and the 2010 Murkowksi-Miller U.S. Senate dispute in Alaska. It remains very hard to overturn even a very close vote. But it is easy to cast doubt on the fairness of the electoral process and the legitimacy of the winner. The distrust feeds into existing partisan divisions and corrodes our faith in elections and government.

The distrust of people has translated into a distrust of technology. Chapter 6 looks at voting technology since 2000. Gone are the pregnant and hanging chads, but what has replaced them is a mixed bag. Florida was one of the first states to move toward electronic voting, and one of the first to abandon that technology when eighteen thousand votes appeared to go missing from electronic voting machines in a 2006 congressional election in Sarasota County.[13]

The problem turned out to be poor ballot design and not a problem with the machines themselves, but distrust of electronic means of casting and counting votes persists. Concerns about whether electronic voting machines could be hacked or manipulated were only magnified when Walden O'Dell, the chief executive of the voting machine manufacturer Diebold, wrote a fundraising letter in 2003 stating that he was "committed to helping Ohio deliver its electoral votes to the president next year." Given the widespread distrust of high-tech voting technology, Internet voting, which could be a great help for military and other overseas voters, seems off the table, as least for now, as too vulnerable to hackers.[14]

Voting technology has improved a great deal since 2000, but it is still bought from private companies, programmed, and used on the local level, often by partisan officials with little technical expertise or training. No national election goes by without at least one story of a technology goof, security issue, or design problem. It is only a matter of time before such a dispute arises again in a presidential election.

When the Supreme Court decided *Bush v. Gore*, the Internet was in its relative infancy. During the thirty-six days between the election and that decision, it was hard to get the relevant facts or keep up with the multiple lawsuits. Once the Supreme Court issued its decision in the case, it took the

Washington Post more than thirty minutes to post the opinion on the Internet, and many hours passed before anyone besides television commentators could effectively disseminate views about the decision and about Gore's potential options.

In the final chapter, I argue that a Florida debacle today would be much nastier and more confrontational because of the rise of social media. Because anyone with a cell phone or internet connection can now spread information (and misinformation), and because people tend to get their information and spread their ideas through partisan websites, every fact, statement, and argument during a postelection presidential contest would be quickly disseminated, analyzed, and critiqued by those questioning the motives of the political opposition. It has become common to accuse the other side of criminality at the drop of a hat. Having watched reactions in real time in the Twitterverse to recent Wisconsin election disputes, I shudder to think at how the country would have reacted to the Waukesha County snafu had the fate of the presidency rested on it.

A meltdown in the next tight presidential election is not inevitable. I conclude by describing how we could modernize our elections and minimize the chances of a catastrophe. The chances of such a change happening are thin, given the partisanship under which all election reform proposals are viewed these days as well as the steps state and local election officials have taken to protect their turf under the cover of promoting "federalism."

The unfortunately less figurative meltdown at Japan's Fukushima Daiichi nuclear plant in 2011 was also preventable: the plant should have been built to withstand a stronger earthquake and tsunami. In the same way, our election system should have been built to withstand Florida 2000. But even after the Florida debacle, not much has improved. While Japan is taking steps to prevent the next nuclear meltdown, we have not learned the lessons of Florida 2000. We are not building a higher sea wall or rethinking fundamental design questions. Either we or our children will likely pay the price of the next election meltdown.

1

All I Really Need to Know
I Learned in Florida

"Well, why isn't the standard the one that voters are instructed to follow, for goodness sakes? I mean, it couldn't be clearer. I mean, why don't we go to that standard?" United States Supreme Court Justice Sandra Day O'Connor sounded exasperated, her voice rising.[1]

Al Gore's attorney, David Boies, was patiently trying to explain to Justice O'Connor and the other justices at the oral argument in *Bush v. Gore* how the Palm Beach County canvassing board decided which votes to count for Gore, George W. Bush, or the other eight presidential candidates in the November 2000 election when the board manually recounted some of the ballots. Fewer than two thousand votes separated Bush from Gore on election night in Florida, and over the next few weeks, as Gore succeeded in getting some Florida ballots recounted by hand, the number fell below two hundred votes. Now, a month after the election, with the winner still undetermined, the Supreme Court was deciding whether to allow a further statewide recount of certain ballots, as ordered by the Florida Supreme Court. Gore was hoping that recount would finally give him the lead, Florida's electoral votes, and eventually the presidency.[2]

The justices fired questions about the arcane world of voting machines and about Florida's byzantine laws and county-based system for hand re-counts and contesting election results. Palm Beach County, like fourteen other Florida counties including its five largest, used "punch card" voting machines for casting ballots. Voters slid cardboard cards with pre-scored, numbered rectangles into a slot in a machine. The voter then flipped through a list of candidate names for each office that sat over the part of the machine holding the punch card. The list lined up with a set of circular openings next to the names of each candidate. The circle was the gateway to one of the pre-scored rectangles on the loaded punch card. The voter was instructed to use a metal pin, or "stylus," to punch through the rectangle, thereby releasing the perforated paper rectangle, or "chad," corresponding to a vote for the candidate.[3]

At the end of the voting, election officials would feed the punch cards into another machine, which quickly counted the punched-out rectangular holes and produced vote totals for each candidate. The punch card system was, in technological terms, an antique: IBM had developed it for use with its accounting machines before World War II. By 2000, voting was one of its last remaining uses.

The reason for this longevity was not the system's reliability. The punch card technology was flawed: sometimes the chad was only partially detached or just indented; sometimes the voter did not load the card correctly into the machine; the machines used to count the punch cards missed some ballots or failed to count all the holes. Some of these machines were so stuffed with old chads that there was no place for a newly punched chad to go, leaving the chad partially attached to the ballot. My wife bought me a punch card voting machine from Lee County, Florida, on eBay after the controversy ended. Years later, whenever I carried it to class to show it off to my students, I would leave a trail of chads falling from the machine.

The vote in Florida was so close—on election night, Bush led Gore by only 1,784 votes out of almost 6 million votes cast—that state law provided for a machine recount. The votes were fed again into the same machines that counted them originally. When Gore was still behind after that ma-chine recount, he asked for a hand recount of ballots in Democratic coun-ties, where a large number of recovered votes were likely to be for him.

There was much squabbling about when, how, and whether to do such hand recounts. One law firm alone eventually handled forty election-related lawsuits for the Florida secretary of state.[4]

Palm Beach County was one of the heavily Democratic areas that conducted a partial hand recount, the nature of which came under close Supreme Court scrutiny at the *Bush v. Gore* oral argument. Florida law required that when the county canvassing board, the body in charge of resolving election disputes, conducted hand recounts, the board had to judge the "intent of the voter," as evident from the physical condition of the ballot, in deciding how to count a ballot.[5]

Boies explained to the justices how the Palm Beach board treated "dimpled" and "hanging" chads—punch cards with indented or partially separated chads in the location corresponding to votes for a particular candidate. He said that the chairman of the canvassing board testified in a Florida trial court that to determine the intent of the voter, "you looked at the entire ballot, . . . if you found something that was punched through all the way in many races, but just indented in one race, you didn't count that indentation, because you saw that the voter could punch it through when the voter wanted to. On the other hand, if you found a ballot that was indented all the way through, you counted that as the intent of the voter."

What got Justice O'Connor so worked up was Boies's statement that the "other thing that they counted was he said they discerned what voters sometimes did was instead of properly putting the ballot into the slot where it was supposed to be, they laid it on top, and then what you would do is you would find the punches went not through the so-called chad, but through the number."

Justice O'Connor's exasperation with Florida voters was understandable. Few people then realized that using a punch card machine to cast a vote that would actually count was not straightforward. Chief Justice William Rehnquist, in his later concurring opinion in the Supreme Court's *Bush v. Gore* decision, highlighted the instructions given to Florida voters about using punch card voting machines: "AFTER VOTING CHECK YOUR BALLOT CARD TO BE SURE YOUR VOTING SELECTIONS ARE CLEARLY AND CLEANLY PUNCHED AND THERE ARE NO CHIPS LEFT HANGING ON THE BACK OF THE CARD."[6]

The Palm Beach County voters were not alone. A study conducted by the Caltech-MIT Voting Technology Project determined that up to a million ballots cast nationwide in the 2000 election (out of about 105 million total ballots) did not record a valid vote for president. A small number were from people who intentionally did not cast votes for president. But these deliberate "undervoters" were few. How many people would go to the polls on Election Day and choose not to cast a vote in the marquee race, the one that got far more media and public attention than any other?[7]

Consider this: In October 2003, Californians went to the polls to decide whether to recall Democratic governor Gray Davis. They ousted Davis and installed bodybuilder-turned-actor Arnold Schwarzenegger as California governor. The recall was a media circus, with 135 candidates on the ballot, including former child actor Gary Coleman, the watermelon-smashing co-median Gallagher, and a porn star.[8] The ballot in that special election contained only four questions. Two were "Should Davis be recalled?" and "If he is recalled, who should replace him?" The other two were ballot propositions. In Los Angeles County, where I live, we voted on punch card machines. I filed a legal brief in the United States Court of Appeal for the Ninth Circuit supporting efforts by the ACLU to force a delay in the election until more-reliable voting machines could be put in place, but with no luck.

According to official statistics, an astonishing 9 percent of Los Angeles voters cast a ballot that day that did not include a valid "yes" or "no" vote on the recall question. In contrast, in Alameda County, which is demographically similar to Los Angeles but used electronic voting machines, the undervote on that "yes" or "no" question was less than 1 percent. The only plausible explanation for this disparity was the voting technology. Whatever might have caused a 9 percent undervote in L.A. County, it wasn't that massive number of voters in Los Angeles—but not in Alameda—were turning out at the polls only to not cast a vote on the most important question on the ballot.

In 2003, the memory of Florida 2000 was still fresh. When Angelenos went to the polling places in the recall election, they found signs everywhere urging them to check for hanging chads. Poll workers helped them check their ballots. Still, 9 percent of those ballots did not record a vote.

If it is hard to blame Los Angeles voters for this undercount, it is even harder to blame Florida voters in 2000. At that time, virtually no one had heard of chad, and people assumed that the votes they cast at the polling place, on machinery they had used for years, would be counted accurately and fairly. In retrospect, who could blame the voters of Palm Beach County for casting their ballots incorrectly?

Not that voter error in Florida in 2000 was always excusable. Putting the punch card *on top of* the machine rather than in the slot and poking holes in the numbers looks like a bone-headed move—though maybe not for a new voter who had never seen one of these machines before and perhaps could not read the English-language instructions. But most of the ballots that went uncounted in Palm Beach County had a more conventional problem, such as a dimpled or hanging chad.

The overall statistics showed that voters using punch card voting machines were many times more likely to cast a ballot that would not be counted than voters using other technologies, such as an optically scanned ballot. Punch card voters were not stupid voters; they were voters stuck with bad technology.

Throughout Florida in 2000, about 180,000 ballots, cast on several different types of voting machines, did not record a valid vote for president. Punch cards, which performed the worst of all these types, were about five times more likely than optical scanners to fail to record a valid vote. The problems ran the gamut from no vote recorded to more than one vote recorded for president to marking the ballots with pen and to writing in a candidate whose name was already printed on the ballot. On some over-voted ballots the voter's intent was clear, such as when voters marked a vote for Gore and also wrote "Gore" on the line for write-in votes. But the machines were programmed not to count such votes.[9]

If Palm Beach County voters deserve little blame for the voting failures on Election Day, others are not so innocent. The Palm Beach machines were not the usual bad Votomatic punch card machines but an even worse knock-off brand known as Data-Punch. On tests run just before the November 2000 election, the *Miami Herald* found that the Data-Punch machines had an error rate of over 20 percent. Some machines recorded no valid votes at all.[10]

Not only did these voters use especially bad punch card machines, but they were also the victims of a particularly bad ballot design: the infamous "butterfly ballot." Most Floridians voting on punch card machines saw the list of all presidential candidates on the left side of the ballot; a hole to the right of each candidate's name allowed voters to use the stylus to punch out the chad on the ballot beneath. Palm Beach had a different design: the candidates' names appeared to both the right and the left of the holes, with arrows pointing toward the center.[11] The problem with this layout was how the holes lined up with the candidate information. The designation for Bush and his vice presidential candidate, Dick Cheney, appeared on the top left, with Gore and his running mate, Joe Lieberman, listed just below Bush on the left. But on the top right, staggered between Bush and Gore on the left, were Reform Party candidate Pat Buchanan and his running mate, Ezola Foster.

The ballot design was very confusing, especially to many of the elderly voters who populate Palm Beach County. Some who wanted to vote for Gore punched out the chad corresponding to Buchanan; to the left of the hole for a Buchanan vote was the word "(DEMOCRATIC)," which appeared as part of the ballot designation for the Gore-Lieberman ticket. Other voters punched both Buchanan's hole *and* Gore's hole. One hole was roughly across from Gore's name, and the other was roughly across from his running mate, Lieberman. These voters probably meant to vote for the Democratic presidential candidate and his vice presidential running mate, but a ballot with more than one vote was an invalid overvote.

This design was calamitous from the point of view of Palm Beach County voters. Pat Buchanan was no friend of Israel or Jews; yet in heavily Jewish Palm Beach County he received 3,407 votes, about 2,800 more than political scientists calculated he would have received (based on his votes elsewhere) had the butterfly ballot not been used. The *Miami Herald* quoted one Israeli-American Palm Beach County voter as saying that "Yasser Arafat could have gotten more votes here." Even Buchanan agreed that most of those "Jews for Buchanan" voters were trying to vote for Gore.[12]

Ironically, this design was a conscious and well-intentioned choice by Palm Beach County election official Theresa LePore. Florida made it relatively easy for third party and independent candidates for president to get

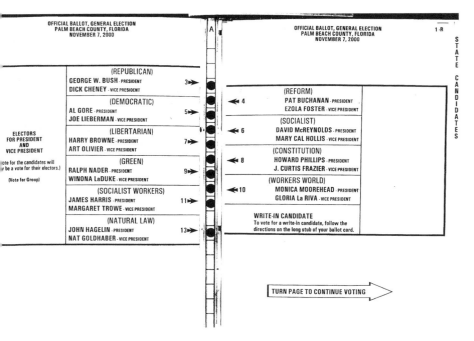

Palm Beach County "butterfly ballot," November 2000
(Courtesy Election Data Services, Inc.)

on the ballot, and a total of ten candidates were running for president that day. LePore thought that keeping all the candidates on one ballot page would require using a font so small that elderly Palm Beach voters would have trouble reading it.

But of course the design did not help voters in heavily Democratic Palm Beach County. LePore's life became "hell" after Election Day as Democrats sent hate mail accusing her of being a "closet Republican" who cost Gore the election. Though some press reports described LePore as a die-hard Democrat, others said she had no use for either major party and just fancied herself a bureaucrat. Whatever her true political leanings, there was no evidence that LePore had some kind of secret plan to help Bush.[13]

Palm Beach was not the only county with serious ballot design problems. Though it got much less national attention, the problem was as bad if not worse in Duval County. There, election officials threw out more than 26,000 ballots, most of them with more than one vote for president. A *New York Times* analysis showed that "nearly 9000 of the votes were thrown out in the predominantly African-American community around Jacksonville, where Gore scored 10-to-1 ratios of victory." Duval's presidential ballot went onto a second page to fit Florida's ten candidates, and it looks as though many voters voted once on each page, casting two votes for president and thus invalidating their ballots.[14]

Why would they do this? "Democratic Party workers instructed voters, many persuaded to go to the polls for the first time, to cast ballots in every race and 'be sure to punch a hole on every page,'" a lawyer for Duval Democrats told the *Times*. A sample ballot printed in the local paper (which by law had to accurately represent the final ballot) also told voters to vote on "every page." The actual ballot contradicted these instructions, saying to vote on "appropriate pages." Local election officials pledged never to use the two-page design again.

Democrats sued over what happened in Palm Beach County but not over Duval, which looked at least partially like a self-inflicted wound. But what could a court do about the problems in Palm Beach County? Constitutional scholar Erwin Chemerinsky came to Florida and argued in state court for a "do over" in Palm Beach County, under the theory that these voters were deprived of their constitutional right to equal protection when they cast a ballot with less chance of being counted accurately.[15]

This was a legal Hail Mary pass. The constitutional guarantee of equal protection under the law had been used in other cases to create the one person, one vote rule and to bar the use of poll taxes in state elections. But the principle had never been extended to create an equality of voters in the nuts-and-bolts running of our election system. At the time I told the *Los Angeles Times* legal reporter Henry Weinstein that I could not imagine many courts, especially not the conservative Supreme Court, accepting such an expansion of equal protection law. (Ironically, that's the same equal protection theory that later won the day in *Bush v. Gore*.)

Even tougher for Chemerinksy than the question of right was one of remedy: from at least one perspective, a partial "do over" in a presidential election seemed unfair. Voters would be free to change their votes. All of the Palm Beach County voters who had voted for Green Party candidate Ralph Nader, the consumer activist who ran as a presidential candidate to the left of Gore in 2000, could switch their votes to Gore. Nader, echoing

George Wallace from 1968, had said there was "not a dime's worth of difference" between the Democrats and Republicans. Applied to Bush and Gore, this sentiment seems not to have stood the test of time. (Would Al Gore have invaded Iraq?) But Nader had attracted nearly 3 million votes nationwide, including over 97,000 votes in Florida. Seeing with hindsight that a vote for Nader was a vote for Bush, these Palm Beach voters, if allowed a revote, could well have chosen to vote for Gore, their strong second choice, rather than cast a second, quixotic vote for Nader.[16]

The trial court judge said that a revote would be unconstitutional, because the Constitution allowed only a single national Election Day for president. This has always struck me as a questionable ruling. Should Florida voters be excluded from voting for president if, say, the state's polling places were closed because of a Category 5 hurricane on Election Day? In extreme cases, such as the New York City primary that was held on September 11, 2001, courts have ordered revotes in elections. But they have never done so in a presidential election.[17]

On appeal, the Florida supreme court didn't address the "do over" issue, holding that there was nothing illegal under state law about the use of the butterfly ballot. The format, the court said, "substantially complied" with Florida's voting laws. The Palm Beach voters never got their revote. The closest they came was in 2004, when they voted LePore out as their supervisor of elections.

When the Supreme Court heard oral argument in *Bush v. Gore,* the legality of the butterfly ballot was not before the Court, but it added to Democrats' sense of injustice. Republicans sensed deep injustice, too, as we will see, but they had a different set of villains. The two sides could not be farther apart on who was to blame for the Florida mess.

The driving force behind the Democrats' legal push was their belief that more Florida voters preferred Gore to Bush, and for that reason he deserved to be the next president. Even conservative judge Richard Posner, who sits on the United States Court of Appeals for the Seventh Circuit and wrote a 2001 book about the controversy, agreed that more Florida voters likely *intended* to vote for Gore than Bush. (Posner's book defended the

Supreme Court's decision in *Bush v. Gore* to end the recount as a way of averting a constitutional crisis.)[18]

The problem for Democrats was that intent did not matter, only the legally counted ballots. Neither canvassing boards nor the courts could do a Vulcan mind meld with Florida voters to determine who really "won." Nor did it matter legally (though it mattered morally to many Democrats) that Gore had won the popular vote nationwide. About half a million more votes were recorded for Gore than for Bush nationwide, but with Florida in his column, Bush would win the only vote that counted, the one in the Electoral College. In the end, Florida's electoral votes gave Bush a 271–266 victory in the Electoral College and the presidency.[19]

But Democrats' sense of unfairness stemmed from more than their view that Gore deserved to win. They saw Republicans as manipulating the process from the beginning. Bush's brother Jeb was Florida's governor, the individual responsible for certifying the winner of the state's Electoral College votes. Throughout the thirty-six days of controversy, Jeb Bush provided his brother's campaign with strategic advice and helped round up lawyers and strategists. The Republican-dominated Florida legislature worried Democrats, too. It threatened to choose its own set of presidential electors, pledged to George W. Bush, to be sent for Jeb Bush's signature and on to Congress.[20]

But no one was more hated and mistrusted by Democrats during those thirty-six days than Florida secretary of state Katherine Harris. Florida's laws governing the recount process were unclear and contradictory, and Harris stepped in during crucial moments to interpret and implement the laws. Some Democrats derisively referred to Harris, with her long dark hair, heavy makeup, and high cheekbones, as "Cruella de Vil," after the puppy-killing villain from *One Hundred and One Dalmatians*. Harris's own self-image was rosier; she fancied herself a modern-day Queen Esther, the biblical heroine who saved the Jews from destruction at the hands of the evil government minister Haman. She did not say whether Democrats represented Haman.[21]

When the Florida mess hit, Harris found herself with an irreconcilable conflict of interest. On one hand, as the Florida secretary of state, her job was to run Florida's elections impartially. On the other hand, she was a loyal Republican.

It is worth pausing on this point. Other modern democracies, such as

Australia, Canada, and the United Kingdom, put nonpartisan officials in charge of their elections. That's not the norm in the United States, and it certainly was not in Florida in 2000. What would be especially shocking to someone outside the United States is that while supervising Florida's 2000 election, Harris also served as the cochair of the Bush for President election committee in Florida.[22]

Even if Harris were scrupulously fair in handling the postelection dispute, Democrats would never believe it. Telephone records later revealed that on election night, as it was becoming clear that the election would hinge on Florida's vote, a call was placed from Harris's cell phone to the Bush headquarters in Texas. Harris later insisted that she did not make the call but that Florida Republican Party chair Al Cardenas borrowed her phone when they were together on election night. Even if that's true, why would the state's chief election officer be sitting with the head of one of the political parties on election night, and not huddled with the staff in her office managing the returns?[23]

Though Harris was Florida's chief election officer, it is wrong to think she had some kind of plenary power over the state's election rules and procedures. She actually possessed very little authority when it came to conducting recounts and resolving local issues. The United States has what Vermont political scientist Alec Ewald has called a "hyperfederalized" system of election administration, with more than ten thousand separate jurisdictions (often at the county level) having the power to decide what equipment to buy, whether and how to conduct recounts, and many other questions. These counties also differ in their budgets, which are set locally, and the training and education of their election officials. As we'll see, much of the Republican distrust was aimed at the county canvassing boards in Democratic counties.[24]

Still, Harris exercised significant power at key points in the election dispute, and each time she made a decision, it benefited the Bush team. It was not hard to figure out which decisions would favor which candidate. Gore was behind, so he wanted as many votes recounted as possible in Democratic counties, where he was likely to find more votes. "Count every vote" was the Democrats' mantra. The Republican strategy was to try to prevent the recount and to delay things as much as possible. The recounts were painted as unreliable and manipulated for partisan reasons.[25]

Delay helped Bush in two ways. First, psychologically, the longer Bush was ahead, the more Gore could be pressured to give up his recount fight and concede. Second, federal statutes provided dates for the different steps that needed to be taken for Congress to formally count the Electoral College votes. Under one of those statutes, the so-called safe harbor provision, a state's Electoral College votes could not be challenged in Congress if they were sent in by December 12, 2000. Congress was to count the votes on December 18. Bush's team wanted to delay any further recounts until the calendar reached the safe harbor day, at which point Florida election officials would certify the vote totals as they stood.

Though Harris insisted she did not consult regularly with the Bush election team during the crisis, she didn't have to. Longtime Republican operative J. M. "Mac" Stipanovich stepped into Harris's inner circle, as urged by Bush loyalists, and advised the inexperienced Harris throughout the process. During marathon meetings, Harris appeared more interested in clearing the pizza boxes from around the table than in making tough judgment calls. But guided by Stipanovich, her decisions helped Bush at just about every turn.[26]

One of the first such decisions involved hand recounts. Harris asked her director of elections, Clay Roberts, to advise whether hand recounts of disputed ballots would be proper under Florida law. Gore wanted them in Democratic counties. Florida courts had said that it was up to individual county canvassing boards to decide whether to conduct such recounts. Still, Harris was in a position to issue guidance.

Harris's office took the position that Florida's election statutes allowed a hand recount only in the case of a failure of the election machinery. At issue was language allowing such recounts when there was an "error in the vote tabulation." It was certainly plausible to read this sentence as barring a hand recount when the problem was something other than a breakdown of the ballot counting machines. The three most conservative justices on the Supreme Court—William Rehnquist, Antonin Scalia, and Clarence Thomas— ultimately interpreted the statute that way when the Court decided *Bush v. Gore* and ended the recounts.[27]

But this reading was not inevitable. Under another reasonable reading, an "error" in "vote tabulation" can occur if the voters' intent was not properly recorded by the machines, whether the problem stemmed from a breakdown of the machines or voter error. In any event, it was reasonable to conclude that there was an election machinery failure. It was widely known that machine counts were not always accurate, especially with punch card ballots. Even the expert hired by the Bush team for the later election contest to dispute the Democratic claims of the machines' inaccuracy had applied for a patent on a new type of machine, pointing to the accuracy problems with the existing punch card voting and vote tabulation systems. What a great fact for Democrats to use on cross-examination![28]

Hanging chads were a fact of life in Florida and everywhere else these machines were used. It was certainly plausible to claim that when machines failed to count a hanging chad, there was an "error in the vote tabulation." And there was a history of leaving it to election boards to decide under the statute whether to conduct a hand recount.

Perhaps most important, Florida courts, like many state courts, had long had a rule that if an election statute was unclear, it should be interpreted to enfranchise voters. If one reading of the statute would disenfranchise many voters and the other would not, Florida courts traditionally favored the interpretation enfranchising voters. This "Democracy Canon" of interpretation goes back at least to Texas cases in the 1800s, and it makes sense if you believe that voters have the right not only to vote but to have that vote counted. Harris, however, adopted a hypertechnical reading of the statute that left Democrats fuming and Republicans elated.[29]

Not to be outdone, the Florida attorney general, Bob Butterworth, issued his own opinion on the question: hand recounts were allowed if the county canvassing boards wanted to go through with them. Butterworth, the chief law enforcement officer of the state, was hardly an objective observer. He was Harris's political mirror image. Elected as a Democrat, he served as the chair of the Gore election committee in Florida. He also had no jurisdiction over the interpretation of election rules, which fell to the secretary of state's office. But none of this stopped him from acting as a counterweight to Harris.[30]

Harris's decision was consequential and influential. The canvassing boards were under intense political pressure and wanted guidance from her office. Some boards delayed counting while waiting for Harris's assistance, and her opinion influenced many of their decisions on whether to conduct hand recounts.

Eventually, the Florida Supreme Court said that hand recounts could go forward, and some counties resumed their counting. Bush's team tried to stop the hand recounts by going to federal court, raising an equal protection claim similar to Chemerinsky's claim in the Palm Beach suit. Selective hand recounts, in only some counties, with unclear and shifting standards treated some voters unfairly.

It was not odd for someone like Chemerinsky to push a broad reading of the Constitution's equal protection clause to expand voting rights. But it was incongruous for conservative Republican lawyers to do so, because they generally did not favor expanding individual legal rights through broad readings of the equal protection clause. There was pushback within the Bush camp over whether to make the equal protection argument. One of Bush's lawyers, Tim Flanigan, "thought the claim extremely weak." Another, Michael Carvin, considered it "fairly lame."[31]

Bush got no immediate relief from the federal courts on his equal protection theory or otherwise, and Gore pressed ahead with hand recounts in four heavily Democratic counties: Broward, Miami-Dade, Palm Beach, and Volusia. Just as Willie Sutton robbed banks "because that's where the money is," Gore pushed for recounts where he expected to harvest the most votes the fastest.

It was a risky strategy. Florida's convoluted election laws allowed for challenges to election results at two stages in the process. First, Gore could ask for hand recounts during a "protest" phase, which had to come before the election results were certified by the secretary of state, and then during a postcertification "contest" phase, in which he could claim that legal votes were not counted that would change the outcome of the election. The longer Gore spent on the protest phase, the less time he would have for the contest phase. Both phases were pushing up against the Electoral College safe harbor day.[32]

The Gore lawyers later defended their strategy of extending the protest phase. Despite the delays caused by Harris and the decisions of some of the county canvassing boards, Gore picked up the most votes during this phase. Also, it was psychologically important for the campaign, the courts, and public opinion for Gore to be close to Bush when later bringing his election contest. By the time the U.S. Supreme Court heard *Bush v. Gore*, the machinations, recounts, and lawsuits had reduced Bush's advantage from 1,784 votes to fewer than 200.

While Gore was doing his best to extend the protest period, Harris was trying to prevent recounts from going forward before she was scheduled to certify the election results. At first she announced that she had no discretion to extend the deadline for the submission of any revised vote totals absent a catastrophic event, like a hurricane, or a machine breakdown. Democrats took Harris to court over the question of her discretion, and Harris appeared to lose. Judge Terry Lewis, one of the few judges whose reputation emerged stronger rather than weaker after the Florida controversy, ruled that Harris was wrong and that she actually had discretion to decide whether to accept late-arriving vote totals.

Judge Lewis's decision wasn't much of a loss for Harris. She exercised her discretion: she told the counties that were conducting hand recounts that they'd have to provide her with a good-enough reason to accept late returns, and of course no reason turned out to be good enough. Palm Beach County, where the canvassing board worked thirty-six hours straight trying to get a recount done in time, asked for a few extra hours to complete the counting. Harris said no.

The Florida Supreme Court would later say that Harris was wrong in not extending the protest period and allowing the inclusion of late returns in the vote totals, but the delay itself helped Republicans greatly. Had the counties cherry-picked by Gore actually conducted full hand recounts of the ballots before Harris was ready to certify the results, it could have been Bush, not Gore, who was behind in the count and filing the postcertification election contest.

Harris's two decisions—to not allow hand recounts absent machine malfunction and to not accept late returns—have in common a strict reading of Florida's election statutes. So you might think it is just a coincidence that the legal opinions Harris issued and the discretion she exercised happened to help Bush. Strictly following the rules was in line with Republican rhetoric. But consider how Harris handled overseas absentee ballots, many of which came from members of the military, who tend to vote Republican.

If you think it was hard for the Palm Beach County voters to vote using a butterfly ballot, it was even worse for some voters in the military. Not only did they have to obtain the right ballot with all the federal, state, and local races (there was a special federal ballot available if you wanted to vote only the federal races), but they then had to get it back to the right county office in time. It's sad irony that a soldier fighting to defend the democratic ideals of the United States can have one of the hardest times of any voter casting a ballot that will actually be counted.

Under a consent decree with the federal government, which had earlier gone after Florida for its ineffectual handling of overseas ballots, Florida agreed to accept and count overseas ballots mailed from a foreign country by Election Day and arriving at Florida county election offices within ten days after the election. Under the agreement and state law, which were in place before 2000, those ballots had to have a foreign postmark showing mailing by Election Day in order to be counted.

If Harris were philosophically committed to following the rules to the letter, she would have confirmed this prior practice of handling the overseas ballots. Doing so would have made it clear that there would be no changing of the rules after Election Day to benefit either candidate. It also would have ensured against fraud: soon after Election Day, there were rumors that military voters were mailing in their votes late for Bush and that Jewish-American voters living in Israel were going to send in their votes for Gore.[33]

But Harris-the-stickler became Harris-the-lax when it came to overseas ballots. She issued an interpretation of state law, four days after Election Day, saying that it was enough for a ballot to have a foreign postmark and to be received within the ten-day window: proof of mailing before Election Day was not required.[34] Democrats were very unhappy, because the conventional thinking was that most overseas ballots were from military voters—which was not true. Though the Democrats' public mantra was "count every vote," privately the Gore lawyers challenged overseas absentee ballots that did not have a postmark showing proof of mailing by Election Day. For most overseas voters, satisfying the postmark date requirement would not be a problem, unless the voter waited until the last minute to vote.[35]

Word got out about the Democrats' strategy through a leaked memo, and in the hyperpartisan postelection environment it was quickly painted by Republicans as antimilitary. Retired general H. Norman Schwarzkopf called it a "very sad day in our country" when members of the military find "that because of some technicality out of their control they are denied the right to vote for the president of the United States, who will be their commander in chief."[36] Democrats asked vice presidential candidate Joe Lieberman to put the controversy to rest, but he did so in a way that undercut the Democrats' strategy. He said on the NBC news program *Meet the Press* that military ballots received by county canvassing boards should be given the benefit of the doubt.[37]

It was a momentous statement. At that point, Democrats abandoned their strategy of challenging overseas ballots without a dated postmark. The Duval County canvassing board, made up of three Republicans, had initially rejected overseas ballots without the dated postmark. But when Democrats gave up the fight after Lieberman's statement, the board reexamined those ballots and counted the vast majority of them. The *Washington Post* concluded that if the canvassing boards hadn't revisited the overseas ballots, "Bush would have fallen behind. Gore would have had a lead of 22 votes—a lead that could have changed the entire public relations dynamic."[38]

Bush's lawyers had gone even further than Harris did in advancing a lax standard for dealing with overseas ballots, filing suit against thirteen Florida counties in an effort to get them to accept ballots with "a postmark after Election Day, a postmark of domestic origin, or no postmark at all." But when it looked like the judge in the case might rule that all overseas ballots *received* after Election Day would have to be thrown out under Florida law, the Bush lawyers quickly dropped their suit.[39]

A study of the Florida 2000 overseas ballots found a huge surge of absentee ballots beginning on the seventh day after Election Day. Given the patterns of mail delivery, this was consistent with these voters' having mailed their ballots after Election Day. Some military personnel even admitted to the *New York Times* that they had voted days after Election Day.[40] This was real voter fraud, and thanks to Harris's rulings, some of those fraudulent votes were counted.

In the end, the canvassing boards threw all the rules out the window. As Diane Mazur, who comprehensively studied the military ballot situation in Florida 2000, writes, "Additional overseas absentee ballots were accepted even though they were postmarked within the United States, postmarked after Election Day, or not postmarked at all. Some ballots were accepted from purported voters who were not registered to vote or who had not requested an absentee ballot. Other ballots were accepted even though they lacked the required witness certification or arrived after the close of the ten-day window. Some voters were permitted to vote twice. In perhaps the most blatant disregard of election law, Clay County counted two ballots sent from a fax machine in Maryland as valid overseas votes."[41]

Harris's decisions over the thirty-six days of Bush against Gore slowed the hand recounts, excluded some of the recounted ballots in vote totals, and paved the way for the very lax counting of overseas votes, including some cast after Election Day. But perhaps just as important for the outcome was a decision made well before the election and supervised by Harris—a decision that was not fully understood until long after Gore conceded: the 2000 Florida felon "voter purge."

Purging sounds unpleasant no matter what the context, and voter purges are no different. The United States government does not keep a list of eligible voters for national elections; the rules for who is eligible to vote are set by each state, subject to the limits of the Constitution. For example, most states bar felons from voting, and there are various procedures for restoring felons' voting rights. In some states, they can never have these rights restored. In others, restoration may be automatic at the end of parole.

Because there is no national standard for who is eligible to vote, each state historically has kept its own voter rolls, and the quality of voter registration data varies greatly. Registration forms may contain wrong information, or someone might input it incorrectly into a voter database. People have similar names, and it is more common than one might expect for people to share both a name and a birth date. Each time a voter dies or moves, the lists need to be updated.[42]

States have their own procedures for purging the names of ineligible voters on the lists, though federal law limits how and when these purges can be done. Under Harris's watch, Florida undertook a purge of ineligible felon voters before Election Day. The purge was done badly: at least two thousand eligible voters were removed from the rolls. Some of these voters showed up to vote on Election Day and were turned away as ineligible. For these voters, too, there was no "do over."

To this day, Democrats contend that there was a deliberate effort at vote suppression by Harris and Governor Jeb Bush through the purge effort. They claim that Republicans wanted to remove likely Democratic voters from the rolls so as to tip the 2000 election to George W. Bush. Repu cans claim that it was all about preventing fraud and cleaning up bad c Whatever the real motive (which we will probably never know), Harr.. .. office was at least reckless in how it let a private company conduct the purge.

What we know about the incident comes mainly from a controversial report by the United States Commission on Civil Rights. In response to fraud in a 1997 Miami mayor's race, including absentee ballot fraud and ineligible voters voting in that race, Florida hired an outside company, DBT Online, at a cost of several million dollars to manage the voter rolls and purge ineligible felons from those rolls.[43]

DBT's job was to compare the names on Florida's voter rolls with sources of ineligible voters, by looking at such items as death records and databases of felony convictions both within and outside Florida. After performing the matches under instructions from Florida election officials, the company sent a list of more than forty-two thousand possible felons to the sixty-seven supervisors of elections in Florida.

DBT officials knew that the list contained a number of "false positives," people who came up as potential matches for ineligible felons but were not the same person or who were felons but had had their voting rights restored. Many of the supposed "matches" were people of different sexes. Among the false positives were a judge and the father of a county election supervisor.

DBT's list went out anyway.

How did this happen? There were a number of problems, but it is clear that DBT used loose criteria for matches because that's what Florida officials required. The company had recommended that Florida require an exact match of first and middle names, so that a Floridian named "Deborah Ann" would not match with an "Ann Deborah. "But the Division of Elections favored more inclusive criteria and chose to 'make it go both ways,'" the DBT official testified to the civil rights commission. State officials believed that a partial match was good enough. "The state dictated to us that they wanted to go broader, and we did it in the fashion that they requested."

There were also flat-out errors. DBT used a list of eight thousand people convicted of misdemeanors in Texas (and who remained eligible to vote if they were Florida residents and had no felony convictions) as a basis for purging voters. In 2001, the *Washington Post* estimated that at least two thousand felons whose voting rights had been restored were kept off the rolls and in some cases denied the right to vote. Even some voters with clean records were erroneously identified as felons and were unable to clear their names by Election Day; some of these voters faced an administrative process in which they bore the burden of proving they were not ineligible felons.

Though the Division of Elections said that it was expecting each county's elections supervisor to ferret out the errors, no one instructed the supervisors to do so. The DBT official in charge of the program said that he did not believe all the supervisors knew that the lists were intentionally overinclusive.

Some election officials used the DBT lists while others did not. The choice was not random. A study by Guy Stuart found that fifteen of nineteen Republican elections supervisors used the list in some way, but only twenty-six of forty-four Democratic supervisors did so. Therese LePore, the Democratic supervisor of elections in Palm Beach County and the hapless creator of the butterfly ballot, was one of the supervisors who decided not to use the felon list to purge voters. She said she found errors on it and did not trust the verification process. "I decided to err on the side of the voter."[44]

Erring on the side of the voter had its costs, too. A *Palm Beach Post* investigative report later found that the DBT list included more than sixty-five hundred felons who likely would not have been declared ineligible but for the list. They had been convicted of felonies in other Florida counties and yet were registered to vote.[45]

Which brings us to Republican complaints about the process. We've been looking at the Florida controversy through Democratic eyes, but the picture looks very different from the Republican perspective.

Consider the eighteen Florida counties with Democratic supervisors of elections who decided not to use the DBT list even as a starting point for undertaking a felon purge. As Guy Stuart explains, "If the 2000 list was accurate, one could only characterize the behavior of the Democratic county

supervisors as a cynical attempt to protect their political base in a close election. An accurate felons list also meant a list of low-income white and minority men who would be more likely to vote Democratic. By not using the
exclusion list, a county supervisor was creating the opportunity for these
people to vote."[46]

The list wasn't accurate, but Republicans could legitimately question the
motives of Democratic supervisors who would not even use the list as a
starting point for purges of ineligible voters. A *Miami Herald* investigation
found that, for whatever reason, thousands of ineligible voters participated
in the 2000 election: felons were sent voter registration cards, and unregistered voters were sometimes allowed to vote. There was no proof that
most of these voters were trying to break the law; many did not know they
were ineligible. But their votes were illegal nonetheless.[47]

Republicans could question Bob Butterworth's motives, too. Why was the
Democratic attorney general, an honorary chair of Gore's election campaign,
offering an interpretation of Florida's standards for conducting hand recounts that conflicted with the opinion of the state's chief election officer—
especially when Florida law gave him no official role in interpreting election statutes?

Partisanship may have started at the top in Florida, but it went all the way
to the bottom, to the local election supervisors and county canvassing boards
that had to make discretionary decisions over how to handle requests for
recounts, determine the intent of the voter on ballots, and judge the post-
marks on overseas absentee ballots. The three-member county canvassing
boards, composed of the supervisor of elections, a local judge, and the chair
of the county commission, tended to be dominated by one party. In the four
counties where Gore sought hand recounts, three of the boards (Broward,
Palm Beach, and Volusia) were dominated by Democrats. In Miami-Dade,
the election supervisor was nonpartisan and one of the members of the
commission was apparently not a committed Democrat.[48]

If the Democrats' mantra during the Florida controversy was "count every
vote," the Republicans' was about the "rule of law": A fundamental principle of democratic elections is that the rules for conducting the election and
counting the votes cannot be changed after the fact. Not only would doing
so be arbitrary, upsetting the expectations of the parties about how the elec-

tion could be conducted, but it would also leave room for partisan manipulation of the counting. As the head of Bush's Florida team, former secretary
of state James Baker, said: "Machines are neither Republicans nor Democrats, and therefore can be neither consciously nor unconsciously biased."[49]

Three factors came together to convince Republicans that any recount of
the presidential votes would be both arbitrary and subject to partisan manipulation. The theme was that Democrats were trying to steal the election.
First, Gore was cherry-picking the counties where he wanted hand recounts.
There was no requirement in the Florida code that the recount be conducted
statewide, and decisions on whether to allow a recount were left to each
county canvassing board. If the goal of a recount was to get an accurate
count of the ballots actually cast in the election and to determine if Gore got
more votes than Bush, only a statewide recount seemed fair.[50]

Second, Florida had no set standard for judging the intent of the voter
from punch card ballots. Other states using the ballots had better-defined
standards, such as a two-corner rule, which said that a chad not detached in
at least two corners could not be counted. (Election attorney Fred Woocher
spoke to my election law class in the late 1990s about recounts of punch
card ballots in California. I remember the students' eyes glazing over when
he described the number of tiny paper connections that a chad might have
to the ballot. Who knew then that hanging chads would become a national
obsession?) In Florida, no such standard existed.

Third and most important, the decisions of whether to conduct a hand
recount and, under the recount, of how to judge the intent of the voter, were
being made by partisan officials. Gore was targeting the large Democratic
counties for recounts, and in those counties the county canvassing boards
were headed by Democrats. Gore's lawyers pushed these boards to use a
very generous standard in judging voters' intent.

To Republicans, the shifting and conflicting actions of the canvassing
boards did not look like the rule of law. The boards changed their minds on
whether to conduct recounts and how to conduct them. The Miami-Dade
board, after going back and forth, considered recounting just the ten thousand undervotes, because they believed they could not do a full hand recount in time to meet Harris's deadlines.[51]

The board gave up the partial recount after its the offices were swarmed by Republican protesters, in what Democrats later referred to as the "Brooks Brothers riot." Republicans flew down House staffers from Washington, D.C., to protest, yelling "Stop the fraud" and "Let us in." Whether the board was actually intimidated by the protesters or just tired of the ongoing controversy and unable to meet Harris's deadlines is unclear.[52]

In Palm Beach County, the board went from a hanging chad rule to a looser "sunshine" rule (could you see light shining through the hole for Bush or Gore when the punch card was held up to the light?) and back to a rule counting the number of detached corners of the chad. The boards voted to start and stop and start counting again. There was inconsistency between counting teams in the same county and across counties. The U.S. Supreme Court later noted that Broward County seemed to use a more forgiving standard for judging the intent of the voter than Palm Beach, finding a valid vote on three times as many ballots as Palm Beach.[53]

Why was Broward more forgiving than Palm Beach? The Broward board in the past had been advised on election matters by an assistant county attorney named Norman Ostrau. Ostrau had advised the board to use a narrow hanging chad standard in conducting its recount. But Andrew Meyers, an appellate lawyer who also worked as a county attorney, thought Ostrau was wrong, "and without consulting Ostrau, Meyers drafted a brief for the Florida Supreme Court urging Justices" to adopt a more liberal standard. He also showed up at a Broward canvassing board session and told members both publicly and privately to adopt a broader standard. They did.

At the time, Meyers did not mention that his wife was a lawyer for one of the firms working with the Gore legal team. He later told the *Washington Post:* "In a legal sense there was no conflict . . . but in hindsight, I probably should have mentioned it earlier."[54]

Were the county boards deliberately biased to help Gore? Republicans thought so, just as Democrats suspected Harris's motives. But even if there was no conscious bias, it seemed inevitable that Democratic board members and counting team members might help Gore. As evidence, consider what happened after the Florida controversy ended and a consortium of media organizations had the University of Chicago's National Opinion Research Center (NORC) hire people to count the uncounted ballots in Florida. Counters were to determine whether an uncounted ballot had a legal vote, and if so, for which candidate. Each ballot was judged by multiple counters.

The counters agreed 96 percent of the time, but the 4 percent on which they differed covered thousands of ballots, many times the number of votes separating Bush and Gore. Professor Einer Elhauge, who served as counsel for the Florida legislature during the crisis, later wrote of the role of subconscious bias in the NORC counting:

> On ballots where at least one counter saw a potential vote for Bush or Gore, the counters disagreed 34 percent of the time, 37 percent for punch card ballots. Most worrisome, even with elaborate efforts to screen for political bias, the political affiliation of the counters affected the results. Republican counters were 4 percent more likely than Democratic counters to deny a mark was for Gore. Even more striking, Democratic counters were 25 percent more likely to deny a mark was for Bush.

If one gets this result from an unhurried, professional, nonpartisan organization whose counters were screened for bias and bound to a strict standard, imagine the inaccuracy and bias that would result from a partisan set of counters, rushing to complete a recount quickly and free to vary their standards.[55]

Republicans also suspected Democratic judges of bias during the dispute. This was most evident in one of two lawsuits coming out of Seminole and Martin Counties involving absentee ballot requests. Months before the election, Republicans had hired a firm to send out absentee ballot request forms to Republican-registered voters. This was a common practice. All the voter had to do was to fill out the absentee ballot form, mail it in, and get an absentee ballot. By lowering the cost of voting, such efforts make it more likely that supporters will actually vote.

The firm handling the ballot requests neglected to include voter identification numbers on the absentee ballot forms. Without those numbers, election officials would not send absentee ballots. In Seminole and Martin Counties, election officials let a representative from the firm into county offices, unsupervised, to fill in the missing information on the ballot request cards.

After the election, supporters of Gore (though not the Gore team itself) filed lawsuits to have all the absentee ballots from these two counties thrown out. One of the cases was assigned to Judge Lewis, who, as noted earlier, stayed pretty much above the fray during the thirty-six days of the Florida crisis. The other was assigned to Judge Nikki Clark, an African-American Democrat.

I was interviewed on Fox News while the suit was pending before Judge Clark. The conservative supporters of Bush who interviewed me were sure that Judge Clark was biased and would side with the Gore supporters. I said that there was no evidence that Judge Clark would not rule fairly, but most Republicans were unconvinced. They assumed a black Democratic judge would be biased toward Gore. The Bush lawyers tried unsuccessfully to get Judge Clark to recuse herself. It was a huge insult.[56]

After hearing the evidence, Judges Clark and Lewis each did the right thing, rejecting the argument that the absentee ballots should be thrown out. The error was not the voters' fault, and throwing out ballots because of improper ballot request cards would disenfranchise those voters and be inconsistent with the Democracy Canon rule requiring officials to read statutes when possible to favor enfranchising the voters. There was no evidence that the improper access to the absentee ballot request forms led to any illegally cast votes, and that was the end of it.

While Republicans would probably admit now that they misjudged Judge Clark, they still express less charitable opinions about the Florida Supreme Court. Indeed, that court is to Republicans what Katherine Harris is to Democrats: the personification of bias in the administration of the 2000 election.

Although the Florida legislature and governorship were controlled by Republicans, the Florida Supreme Court was dominated by Democrats. It made a number of key decisions that kept alive Gore's chances of capturing the presidency, including an order barring Harris from certifying the results of the election when she was ready to declare the counting over and an order allowing manual recounts to go forward in Palm Beach County after the county did not know whether it should keep on counting.

The court then issued a major opinion in *Palm Beach County Canvassing Board v. Harris* that required Harris to accept late returns from counties conducting recounts and allowed the recounts to go forward. The court said that the Florida election code provisions on whether counties could conduct hand recounts and whether Harris "shall" or "may" accept late returns were inconsistent and poorly written. Consistent with the right to vote enshrined in the state constitution, and consistent with the Democracy Canon, the court extended Gore's protest period and allowed the recounts to proceed before certification. This decision allowed Bush's lead to shrink to below two hundred votes.[57]

Bush appealed that decision to the U.S. Supreme Court, which essentially punted. It ruled unanimously that the Florida Supreme Court might have based its decision on the state constitution, and if so, that the decision may have improperly impinged on the right of the Florida Legislature, set out in Article II of the state's constitution, to write the rules for choosing presidential electors. The Supreme Court asked for clarification.

After Harris certified the election for Bush, including some late returns as required by the Florida Supreme Court, Gore filed his contest. A Tallahassee trial judge, a conservative Democrat named N. Sanders Sauls, held a quick trial and definitively rejected Gore's request for recounts of undervotes in the four heavily Democratic counties. He denied Gore's contest. Gore appealed to the Florida Supreme Court, which again issued a major opinion in Gore's favor, the opinion that later reached the U.S. Supreme Court as *Bush v. Gore*.[58]

The Florida Supreme Court thus became Gore's savior once again. On appeal of Judge Sauls's ruling, it said that Gore had met the standard for an election contest by demonstrating that there were legal votes cast that were not counted. Rather than give Gore the relief he requested, a recount of all the undervotes in the four handpicked counties, the court ordered a recount of undervotes in *all* of Florida's sixty-seven counties.

Republicans saw this as the ultimate affront to the rule of law, and in this they picked up an ally in Florida's chief justice Charles T. Wells, who joined two other state justices in dissenting from this second Florida Supreme Court opinion. Wells said that nothing in the Florida code authorized a statewide recount of the undervotes as part of an election contest (what about the overvotes?, he asked), and the recount timing was coming perilously close to the December 12 safe harbor deadline for Florida's electoral votes. In addition, the vote totals already included recounts that employed shifting standards, conducted selectively as Gore had requested.[59]

To Republicans, it looked as if the court was writing new rules yet again to give Gore one last shot at the presidency. Though no one knew it at the time, the NORC study later found that the only way Gore might have won the presidency was if the courts had ordered a full statewide recount in which *all* the uncounted ballots were counted, including the overvotes. There turned out to be a fair number of ballots both marked for Gore and with his name written in. So neither the relief Gore wanted nor the relief the Florida court ordered likely would have been enough. But who knows how the boards, as opposed to NORC, would have counted the votes if ordered to do so?[60]

The Florida Supreme Court ordered the statewide count on a Friday night, December 8. The counting started Saturday morning, but by the afternoon, the U.S. Supreme Court on a five-to-four vote ordered the counting stopped pending an oral argument scheduled for two days later.

The stay order ensured that time would run out for Gore's recount. To Democrats the order was unjustified. A key factor in deciding whether to stay the action of a lower court is whether the action will cause one party "irreparable harm." The harm to Gore was clear: without the ability to count now, the Bush team would have successfully run out the clock. Justice Scalia, in a rare opinion explaining the granting of the stay order, said that to allow the counting now only to reverse the result later would leave a "cloud" on the legitimacy of Bush's presidency and that this outweighed Gore's harm.[61]

Democrats were apoplectic. How could the potential for a "cloud" count as more harm than losing the chance to be the next president? But Scalia made two other points. First, it was "generally agreed" that further recounts would lead to degradation of the ballots and a less accurate count; therefore, the further counting had no guarantee of being more accurate. Here, Scalia likely relied on a statement from Bush's team in its stay request that "state and county elections officials admitted that the more the ballots are handled, the more chads fall out, and, thus, the harder it is to conduct an accurate count." The Bush team further claimed that "every time punch-card ballots are machine tabulated . . . they are degraded, causing some chads to fall out and others to become lodged in previously empty holes. Ballots with hanging chads can be counted as votes in one tabulation (because they swing open) and as non-votes in the next (because they swing shut). As a result of this machine 'sort,' it appears that Miami-Dade ended up with at least 20 precincts with *more* undervotes than it had had on the previous counts."

Like everything else, this point was contested. The Gore team later told the Supreme Court that the suggestion of ballot degradation "has scant support in the record, and there is ample evidence to the contrary." But the point seemed to have some merit. When the *Miami Herald* examined a ballot with a hanging chad after the Florida mess was over, the chad suddenly dislodged and everyone laughed.[62]

Second, Justice Scalia said that in looking at the stay order, five justices on the Court had already determined (before full briefing in the case) that Bush was likely to win. What would be the point of more drama if a majority of the Court had concluded that the Florida Supreme Court's actions were unconstitutional?

On a ridiculously abbreviated briefing schedule, the Supreme Court heard oral argument on Monday, December 11, and issued its opinion late in the evening of Tuesday, December 12, the safe harbor day. On a five-to-four vote, split on ideological lines, the Court found for Bush. Gore, out of legal options, conceded the next day. Rather than have Congress decide how to count the electoral votes, including potentially two slates of electors from Florida, the Court's decision ended the crisis. Harris declared Bush the winner in the state, Jeb Bush signed the certification, and the presidency went to Bush.

The majority's unsigned opinion, apparently written by Justices Anthony Kennedy and Sandra Day O'Connor, said that the inconsistent standards for the counting and recounting violated the equal protection clause of the Fourteenth Amendment of the U.S. Constitution. The changing recount standards, the inclusion of votes counted under varying standards, and the lack of a uniform standard going forward meant that the Florida Supreme Court was allowing one person's vote to be valued more than another.[63]

It was a bold reading of the equal protection clause, sounding more like liberal law professor Chemerinsky than conservative justices of the Supreme Court. The Court couched its decision in caveats about the "complexities" of elections, in language that many read as signaling this case was good for one day only for just one rider, George W. Bush.

Justices Stephen Breyer and David Souter, who dissented from the result, also agreed there were constitutional problems, though Justice Souter suggested that the problem was more about arbitrary standards and a violation of the constitutional guarantee of due process than equal protection. The majority opinion seized on the position of Breyer and Souter, saying that the Court was divided seven to two on finding constitutional problems with the Florida Supreme Court's order, and the "only" dispute was as to the remedy.

What an understatement! Souter and Breyer wanted a remand to the Florida Supreme Court to order a recount under a single, uniform standard for determining the intent of the voters. Such an action would ensure a constitutional recount. The majority opinion, after all, had said that the press of time was not an excuse to ignore the requirements of due process.

The majority instead had said that time was up and that there could be no recount under any new standard. It said the Florida Supreme Court—whose other views it rejected completely—understood the Florida legislature to want to take advantage of the safe harbor day, and for this reason no counting could happen after December 12.

The most conservative justices on the Court, Rehnquist, Scalia, and Thomas, issued their own opinion setting out different grounds for rejecting the Florida Supreme Court's order of a statewide recount of undervotes. They said that the Florida Supreme Court was making up new rules for the recount of votes and that this violated Article II of the Constitution, which gave sole power to set presidential election rules to the state *legislature*. (They also joined the equal protection opinion; otherwise there would have been no single basis for reversing joined by a majority on the Court.)

This, too, was a bold position. Florida's election statutes, as everyone would admit, were a huge mess. It was normally the job of the courts to interpret unclear election statutes. And Florida had a long tradition of applying the Democracy Canon—construing these statutes to enfranchise voters. Members of the legislature knew this (or should have known this) when they wrote their election provisions. But to the conservatives on the Supreme Court, the Florida Supreme Court had gone from permissible interpretation to wholesale rewriting of the statutory scheme.

Though both the equal protection and Article II arguments set out by the majority were novel, they both expressed the same Republican concern about the rule of law. The conservatives on the Court, who likely personally supported Bush, saw an out-of-control partisan state supreme court aiding partisan counting boards in changing the rules after the fact to give Gore a chance to cherry-pick counties and ballots to count in his favor.

To the liberals on the Court, who likely supported Gore, the Florida Supreme Court and canvassing boards were doing what they could to make sure that no one was disenfranchised and that technical deadlines did not get in the way of ensuring that every vote was counted. Each wrote a vigorous dissent. Justice John Paul Stevens concluded his: "Although we may never know with complete certainty the identity of the winner of this year's Presidential election, the identity of the loser is perfectly clear. It is the Nation's confidence in the judge as an impartial guardian of the rule of law."

It was a voting war between the ideals of integrity and access, between preventing fraud and assuring enfranchisement, and between Democratic officials looking to benefit Democratic candidates and Republican officials looking to benefit Republican candidates. It was a nasty dispute that stings partisans to this day, and a taste of what the nation would endure for the next decade.

2

The Fraudulent Fraud Squad

Mario Gallegos had undergone a liver transplant in Houston, and after tests showed elevated enzyme levels and the possibility of rejection, he needed a biopsy. Gallegos had complications after the biopsy, and against his doctor's advice, he went to Austin and was resting in a hospital bed installed inside the Texas capitol building.[1]

Gallegos was a Democrat representing the Houston area in the Texas Senate. In May 2007 he was the only person standing in the way of the state's adopting a strict voter identification law requiring people to show a specified form of photo ID before they could vote. Republicans outnumbered Democrats twenty to eleven in the state senate and also controlled the Texas House. Rick Perry, the governor who succeeded George W. Bush, was also a Republican. Gallegos's vote was needed for Democrats to block the law until the end of the legislative session. Under the Texas Senate's "two-thirds" rule, under which no legislation could be brought up unless two-thirds of senators present voted to do so, all eleven Democratic senators had to vote against taking up the bill, or Republicans could take it up and pass it.[2]

Republicans could have agreed to shelve the matter for the year, but they didn't. Instead, Gallegos lay in a hospital bed in the Senate sergeant's office near his senate desk waiting for the next called vote.

The Republicans could have behaved worse. Bob Duell, a Republican senator who is also a physician, arranged for the hospital bed to be sent to the capitol. The senate leaders did not call the vote the day Gallegos was actually undergoing the biopsy. But it may not have been all kindness: Republicans worried that if they passed the bill in Gallegos's absence, Democrats would retaliate by blocking other bills. With Gallegos's help, Democrats ran out the clock. "I'll be back, and if you want to fight this fight again, I'll fight it with you," Gallegos told his colleagues, who gave him a standing ovation.[3]

Texas did not adopt a voter identification bill in 2007. In the 2008 elections, Democrats gained a seat in the Texas Senate, reducing the Republican edge to nineteen to twelve and giving Democrats a one-vote cushion under the two-thirds rule. But as the first order of business in the 2009 session, Republicans passed a special rule that exempted voter identification bills—and only such bills—from the two-thirds rule. Voter ID could be taken up by a simple majority vote.

Democrats again used stalling tactics to prevent the bill from becoming law in 2009 and 2010. Senator Gallegos told the *San Antonio Current* that the voter identification law was "really targeted at suppressing minority voters. It's partisan, it's the old Karl Rove [trick] back again. . . . The Republican Party is seeing census numbers that the Latino community is voting in record numbers. . . . So I think . . . it's a last gasp to try and suppress the vote."[4]

But in 2011 Governor Perry declared the voter identification bill an "emergency item," meaning that the state legislature could debate it right away without waiting for the first sixty days of the session as normally required. Voter ID was still exempted from the two-thirds rule. Democratic stalling tactics ran out. Perry eventually signed the toughest voter identification law in the nation, tougher than the one proposed in 2009. It included a provision that made a college student's identification card invalid as ID for voting. "The right to vote is simply too important for us to take the act of voting lightly," Perry said. "Today with the signing of this bill, we take a major step forward in securing the integrity of the ballot box and protecting the most cherished right we enjoy as citizens." (As I write this, Texas was just denied approval of its law by the United States Department of Justice, which under the Voting Rights Act must approve changes in voting rules in jurisdictions with a history of racial discrimination in voting. The Obama Justice Department also denied approval of South Carolina's law on the grounds that it could have a racially discriminatory impact. The cases are now in the courts. Perry, a candidate for the 2012 Republican presidential nomination, responded at a Republican debate to a question from FOX News's Juan Williams about the preclearance requirement for states with discrimination by declaring that "the state of Texas is under assault by the federal government. . . . South Carolina is at war with this federal government and with this administration.")[5]

Texas was not alone. Between 2005 and 2007, ten state legislatures considered new voter ID legislation, and it was basically a one-party affair. In state after state with Republican-dominated legislatures, bills proposed strict new voter identification rules requiring voters to produce a photographic identification card from a list of acceptable cards or risk losing the right to vote. According to a U.S. Supreme Court brief filed by historians and other scholars in a challenge to Indiana's law, "If the house and senate votes for these ten bills are combined, *95.3 percent* of the 1,222 Republicans voting and *just 2.1 percent* of the 796 Democrats voting supported the bills."[6]

The tide of voter identification laws grew in anticipation of the 2012 elections, and this time many of them passed. Republicans promoted the measures as necessary to prevent fraud and ensure voter confidence. Democrats countered that the laws would disenfranchise many eligible voters and were a form of vote suppression of minorities, though more Democratic legislators began signing onto the legislation as the 2012 elections approached. Neither side offered much evidence. The battles often were prolonged, with much more heat than light.

How did we get to this point of having pitched battles over the technical rules for casting a ballot? Couldn't the question wait for Senator Gallegos's recovery? If they can't agree on policy, why can't Democrats and Republicans at least agree on the facts about whether voter identification laws really deter significant amounts of fraud? Enter the Fraudulent Fraud Squad.

Dick Armey, the former Republican U.S. House majority leader from Texas, was speaking at a fancy lunch in Newport Beach, California, to the Lincoln

Club, a conservative political group in Orange County, in the run-up to the 2010 midterm elections. Accusing Democrats of widespread voter fraud, Armey claimed that 3 percent of ballots cast were fraudulent Democratic ballots. "I'm tired of people being Republican all their lives and then changing parties when they die," Armey told the group. He offered no evidence to back up the statistic, nor did he apologize for the lame joke.[7]

Armey is the CEO of Freedomworks, a Tea Party group funded by the Koch brothers. He made similar claims as early voting began in 2010. Speaking to Neil Cavuto on Fox News, Armey gave his explanation for statistics showing a rise in early voting—many states allowing voting to take place at state vote centers in the days or weeks leading up to Election Day, as a convenience to voters—and the fact that Democrats seemed to be turning out in greater numbers than Republicans to vote early:[8] "I'm not surprised. This is an aberration that's borne out of the fact that in early voting there's less ballot security. The Democrats are always much more active in the areas where the ballot security is reduced. And if you start focusing on this, it is pinpointed to the major urban areas, to the inner cities."[9]

The words "urban" and "inner city" were an unmistakable reference to African-American and other minority voters, controlled by a Democratic Party–labor union urban machine. It was a fairly common theme of Republican voter fraud allegations. Armey offered no evidence to back up this assertion either.

Unsubstantiated charges of "voter fraud" have become part of the Fox News–conservative orthodoxy. Michelle Malkin wrote a syndicated column just before the 2010 Election Day entitled "The Left's Voter Fraud Whitewash": "Denial isn't just a river in Egypt. It's the Democrats' coping mechanism for midterm election voter fraud. Faced with multiple reports of early voting irregularities and election shenanigans across the country, left-wing groups are playing dumb, deaf and blind. *Voter fraud? What voter fraud?*"[10]

Of course, in November 2010 President Barack Obama and the congressional Democrats suffered a "thumping" at the polls, so either voter fraud wasn't happening on any massive scale or those Democratic fraudsters must be not only cheaters but bunglers. Neither Malkin nor Armey saw any voter fraud in the 2010 Republican resurgence. When fraud happens, it always helps Democrats. *Wall Street Journal* columnist John Fund's quick about-face in the 2011 Wisconsin Supreme Court race followed the same pattern: voter fraud happens in Democratic cities, where election victories are stolen from Republicans. When Republicans win, the cry fades away. Voter fraud? What voter fraud?

Armey and Malkin joined the Fraudulent Fraud Squad rather late in the game. They owed their tactics to the squad's pioneers, especially Thor Hearne, Kit Bond, Karl Rove, John Fund, and Hans von Spakovksy.

Mark F. "Thor" Hearne has fought the voting wars for Republicans since before *Bush v. Gore.* A promotional brochure once on the website of his former St. Louis law firm, Lathrop and Gage, shows Hearne in 2000 examining a punch card in the Broward Emergency Operating Center in Plantation, Florida. Other pictures in the brochure portray a lawyer deeply embedded in the Republican establishment. There's a picture of Hearne, who served as national counsel for the Bush-Cheney Reelection Committee in 2004, standing with President Bush in front of Air Force One. There are the personal thank-you notes from Bush and from his chief political strategist, Karl Rove. Still more pictures show Hearne with Vice President Dick Cheney and with Christopher "Kit" Bond, a Republican senator from Missouri who retired in 2010. The brochure also mentions Hearne's work as general counsel for Republican Matt Blunt's gubernatorial campaign. Hearne praised Blunt's "real leadership" as Missouri's secretary of state.[11]

Hearne's home city of St. Louis had long been a battleground in the voting wars, and when things came to a head on election night in 2000, he played a key role. Lorraine Minnite, a Rutgers professor whose study of voter fraud should be required reading for anyone interested in the subject, described what happened.[12]

According to Minnite, the St. Louis Board of Election Commissioners engaged in a major purge of the voter rolls of the city of St. Louis before the 2000 election. The National Voter Registration Act of 1993, a federal law nicknamed the "motor-voter" law because it requires states to offer voter registration materials at state motor vehicle departments and other government offices, limits how and when states can do such voter purges.[13] But the board removed large numbers of voters from the rolls in the heavily

Democratic city of St. Louis without following the procedures required by the motor-voter law. Minnite explains: "Based on these improper canvasses, the election board removed more than 50,000 names of voters who had been on the rolls in 1996 and made no effort to notify inactive voters that their registration status had changed, that their names would not appear on the voter registration lists provided to election judges in each voting precinct, and that they would face additional administrative steps on election day before they would be permitted to vote."

For example, the board removed from the rolls many eligible voters based on the faulty belief that they were registered at addresses for vacant lots. The *St. Louis Post-Dispatch* later examined more than two thousand alleged "vacant lot" addresses and "found buildings on virtually all of them." Even the city's budget director was declared an ineligible voter because the board misclassified his ten-year-old condominium as a vacant lot.[14]

Democrats yelled voter suppression before the 2000 election, and they expected that the purges would create long lines of angry voters who had been wrongfully removed from the rolls. They stood ready to ask for more time for voting on Election Day, and Republicans stood ready to oppose the request.

On Election Day, the lines were indeed long, as voters wrongly knocked off the rolls were sent from precinct workers to election judges to the board's central office and then back to polling places. Democrats got a state court judge to keep the polls open for three extra hours to accommodate voters who could not make the second trip to their polling place to vote by the 7:00 p.m. deadline. But Hearne, representing the Bush-Cheney team, joined by the St. Louis board, quickly got a Missouri appeals court to reverse the order. Only about a hundred voters likely cast their ballots after 7:00 p.m. before Hearne got the court to stop it. There's no evidence that any of them were ineligible to vote.[15]

Republicans used the dispute over the extension of polling hours to fan voter fraud flames. The rhetoric was inflammatory and hyperbolic. Senator Bond said, despite the minuscule number of people who actually voted after 7:00 p.m., that the order to keep the polls open "represents the biggest fraud on the voters in this state and nation that we have ever seen."[16]

Though George W. Bush won Missouri in 2000, Republicans lost most other statewide races that year. Perhaps not believing such a result was possible, or perhaps looking to cast doubt on the integrity of future elections, Bond blamed the Democratic machine in St. Louis for voter fraud. Speaking on the floor of the U.S. Senate and elsewhere, "Bond alleged that 'brazen,' 'shocking,' 'astonishing,' and 'stunning' voter fraud was committed, with dead people registering and voting from the grave, fake names and phony addresses proliferating across the nation's voter rolls, dogs registering, and people signing up to vote from vacant lots. In short, a 'major criminal enterprise designed to defraud voters' was underway."[17]

Bond's position on voter fraud was especially important because, in the aftermath of Florida in 2000, he became the leading Republican lawmaker on election reform. Members of Congress agreed they had to do something about the faulty voting technology evident from the Florida debacle, and the question was whether a federal election reform bill could do more than just pay for better technology.

Congress passed the Help America Vote Act (HAVA) in 2002. As a price for his support of other provisions, including those paying to phase out the horrible punch card machines, Bond demanded that the act include a provision requiring first-time voters who registered by mail to produce identification the first time they voted in person.[18]

Bond wasn't the only prominent Missouri Republican complaining loudly about voter fraud. Secretary of State Blunt issued a controversial report referring to "an unspecified conspiracy 'to create bedlam so that election fraud could be perpetrated' and to corrupt election judges put in place to manipulate the results of the election." Hearne testified before Blunt's commission. Unsurprisingly, Blunt's allegations were mostly incorrect or exaggerated.[19]

It was Hanlon's razor again—people attributing to criminality actions that could be explained by incompetence. More reliable investigations of the St. Louis controversy after 2000 revealed no significant voter fraud. Most of what Blunt called fraud turned out to be election administration incompetence. The Missouri state auditor, Claire McCaskill (who went on to become a Democratic U.S. senator from Missouri), found that even three years after the 2000 controversy, the St. Louis rolls contained numerous duplicate registrations that the board had not fixed. More than two thousand felons remained on voting rolls even though the board received regular reports of felony convictions to use for purging. As far as fraud went, the auditor found that, at most, there were twenty-eight cases in recent elections where a voter might have voted more than once. Even these cases were unconfirmed. This was hardly a wave of massive voter fraud in a state with about four million registered voters and millions voting in each election.[20]

The Department of Justice later sued the St. Louis Board of Election Commissioners, alleging their practices in handling voter registrations violated the federal motor-voter law. The board admitted wrongdoing, settled the case, and promised to fix its problems going forward. The problems were with the board, not with the voters. But neither Bond, Blunt, nor Hearne ever mentioned this.[21] Despite the falsity of the voter fraud charges, Missouri remained ground zero for voter fraud allegations throughout the 2000s. As Greg Gordon reported in 2007, "Few have endorsed the strategy of pursuing allegations of voter fraud with more enthusiasm than White House political guru Karl Rove. And nowhere has the plan been more apparent than in Missouri."[22] Thor Hearne was the Bush White House's handpicked person to bang the voter fraud drum the hardest.[23]

The problem facing the Republicans pushing the voter fraud line was that the sensational allegations of dogs voting and other malfeasance did not line up with the evidence. At most there was the occasional isolated case, but nothing remotely on a large scale. Here's where Hearne came in. In 2005, Bob Ney, an Ohio congressman who later went to jail on charges related to the Jack Abramoff lobbying scandal, scheduled a hearing of the House Judiciary Committee on allegations of problems in the 2004 election in Ohio. Republicans called Hearne to testify at the hearing about voter fraud. He did so on behalf of the "American Center for Voting Rights."[24]

Muckraking journalist Brad Friedman of The Brad Blog followed every twist of the ACVR's short life. Friedman reports that the ACVR did not have any apparent existence until just a few days before the Ney committee hearing. Hearne, on behalf of the ACVR, testified before Ney's committee and later elsewhere across the country to bolster voter fraud allegations and advocate for tougher voting laws.[25]

All it took for the American Center for Voting Rights to be taken seriously as an organization was a website and Hearne as its public face. The ACVR home page in 2005 showed a group of smiling people, most promi-

American Center for
oting Rights

HOME
ABOUT US
IN THE NEWS
IN THE NEWS

STAY
INFORMED

*Free and honest elections are the very
foundation of our republican form of
government. Hence any attempt to defile the
sanctity of the ballot cannot be viewed
with equanimity.*

-United States v. Classic, 1941

ter Email Address:

▼ IN THE NEWS

pu Have A Voice

WE MAKE SURE
YOU ARE HEARD

ACVR Refers Voter Fraud Investigation To Dept. of Justice, Congressional Oversight Panel

Report Shows Third Party Effort to Circumvent Law and Register Illegal Voters

COLUMBUS, OHIO – Today the American Center for Voting Rights (ACVR) referred a compendium of preliminary findings of registration fraud, intimidation, vote fraud and litigation to the U.S. Department of Justice. The report was previously made available to the House Administration Committee who will hold a field hearing on election fraud in Columbus today.

The Ohio report states, "Third party organizations, especially ACT, ACORN and NAACP engaged in a coordinated "Get Out the Vote" effort. A significant component of this effort appears to be registering individuals who would cast ballots for the candidate supported by these organizations. This voter registration effort was not limited to the registration of legal voters but, criminal investigations and news reports suggest, that this voter registration effort also involved the registration of thousands of fictional voters such as the now infamous Jive F. Turkey, Sr., Dick Tracy and Mary Poppins. Those individuals registering these fictional voters were reportedly paid not just money to do so but were, in at least one instance, paid in crack cocaine."
≫ FULL STORY

Mark F. (Thor) Hearne
WITNESS

Hearing Testimony
Thor Biography
Ohio Election Activities & Observations (pdf)
Exhibits* (pdf - 8MB)
Witness List
House Administration Committee

*The Exhibits PDF is a large file. To download the file efficiently, right click on the link above and save the file locally.

Screenshot of American Center for Voting Rights website home page, 2005 nently a young, athletic African-American man wearing a hoop earring, greeting visitors to the page with the slogan "You Have a Voice" above the picture and "WE MAKE SURE YOU ARE HEARD" below it.[26]

The picture had nothing to do with the organization: it was just a pleasant stock photo from Getty Images. The initial press release excerpted on the home page and titled "ACVR Refers Voter Fraud Investigation to Dept. of Justice, Congressional Oversight Panel: Report Shows Third Party Effort to Circumvent Law and Register Illegal Voters" was much more ominous:

> COLUMBUS, OHIO—Today the American Center for Voting Rights (ACVR) referred a compendium of preliminary findings of registration fraud, intimidation, vote fraud and litigation to the U.S. Department of Justice. The report was previously made available to the House Administration Committee who will hold a field hearing on election fraud in Columbus today.
>
> The Ohio report states, "Third party organizations, especially ACT, ACORN and NAACP engaged in a coordinated 'Get Out the Vote' effort. A significant component of this effort appears to be registering individuals who would cast ballots for the candidate supported by these organizations. This voter registration effort was not limited to the registration of legal voters but, criminal investigations and news reports suggest, that this voter registration effort also involved the registration of thousands of fictional voters such as the now infamous Jive F. Turkey, Sr., Dick Tracy and Mary Poppins. Those individuals registering these fictional voters were reportedly paid not just money to do so but were, in at least one instance, paid in crack cocaine."

To this day, it is not clear who covered the organization's bills—most of its expenses were legal services provided by Hearne and his firm. But it is clear that the organization was run by Hearne and a few other Republican operatives, including Jim Dyke, a former Republican National Committee communications director. Its primary mission was to support tougher voting laws that would make it harder for poor and minority voters—who tend to vote Democratic—to cast ballots that would be counted.[27]

Consisting of little more than a post office box and some staffers who wrote reports and gave helpful quotations to the press, the ACVR identified Democratic cities as "hot spots" for voter fraud, then pushed the line that preserving "election integrity" required making it harder for people to vote. The group issued reports on places of special concern, which coincidentally tended to be presidential battleground states. As we shall see, in many of these same places, the Bush White House was pressuring U.S. attorneys to bring voter-fraud prosecutions.

The ACVR's "reports" on voter fraud were submitted to Congress, state legislatures, and good-government committees examining the issue of election reform. Its job was to give a think-tank cachet to the unsubstantiated charges. The reports the organization created were just longer versions of the same type of unsubstantiated allegations made by Senator Bond, as well as reproductions and amalgamations of reports by others that were later discredited, such as the Blunt report. In 2005, Hearne was pushing allegations about voter fraud in St. Louis from 2000 that had been thoroughly debunked in 2002.

It didn't matter. Republican voters came to believe there was a vote fraud epidemic (a narrative fed by hysteria over the group ACORN [Association of Community Organizations for Reform Now]), and Republican legislators supported voter identification and other restrictive voting laws to stop the "fraud" and preserve voter confidence.

The American Center for Voting Rights, however, lived a short life. By 2007, with much of its work discredited, the organization simply disappeared.

Imagine the National Rifle Association's website suddenly disappearing, along with all the data and every report the group had ever posted on gun issues. Imagine Planned Parenthood inexplicably closing its doors without comment from its leaders. These scenarios are unthinkable, given how established these organizations are. Even if something did happen to the NRA or to Planned Parenthood, similar groups would quickly fill the vacuum and push the same ideas.

But one day in 2007 the ACVR simply disappeared as an organization, and no replacement group has arisen to take its place. With no notice and little comment, the group simply stopped appearing at government panels and conferences. Its web domain name expired, its reports are all gone (though you can still see the history of its website through the Internet Wayback Machine, www.archive.org), and Hearne, its general counsel, cleansed his résumé of affiliation with the group.

Hearne wouldn't speak to the press about the organization's demise. Someone from Lathrop and Gage went into Wikipedia to remove references to the ACVR from Hearne's page and to make changes to the ACVR's Wikipedia page. In a bit of poetic justice, Beth Kingsley, a Washington, D.C., lawyer who worked with voting rights organizations including ACORN, bought the ACVR's web addresses, and they redirected to the Brennan Center for Justice's website debunking the organization's claims, "The Truth About Fraud."[28]

Meanwhile, Hearne moved to a new law firm, Arent Fox. As I write this book, his biography at his new firm makes no reference to the American Center for Voting Rights. And when he (unsuccessfully) applied to be voting rights counsel to the California redistricting commission in 2011, his firm's proposal called him "one of the nation's preeminent civil-rights and constitutional law attorneys." But his résumé omitted his significant work for the ACVR.[29]

Karl Rove didn't put all his eggs in the ACVR basket. When people like Hearne started sounding the alarm about voter fraud in the public, Rove was also pushing the Department of Justice in Washington and U.S. attorneys across the country to investigate claims of voter fraud. At least two top government prosecutors who did not cooperate were fired.[30]

Let's consider first what the Department of Justice found in its extensive investigation of voter fraud. The department cannot possibly focus on every federal crime, and a change in administrations brings new priorities. Under George W. Bush, the Department of Justice put unprecedented emphasis on finding and prosecuting cases of voter fraud. The Fraudulent Fraud Squad had previously argued that the reason so few cases of voter fraud were discovered was that prosecutors had other priorities. The Justice Department's new focus on fraud put this contention to the test.

The result is well summarized by a *New York Times* story, headlined "In 5-Year Effort, Scant Evidence of Voter Fraud":

> Five years after the Bush administration began a crackdown on voter fraud, the Justice Department has turned up virtually no evidence of any organized effort to skew federal elections, according to court records and interviews.

Although Republican activists have repeatedly said fraud is so widespread that it has corrupted the political process and, possibly, cost the party election victories, about 120 people have been charged and 86 convicted as of last year.

Most of those charged have been Democrats, voting records show. Many of those charged by the Justice Department appear to have mistakenly filled out registration forms or misunderstood eligibility rules, a review of court records and interviews with prosecutors and defense lawyers show.

The *Times* based its data on analysis done by Minnite and others. A Department of Justice report of voting fraud prosecutions had been posted first, perhaps inadvertently, on Representative Ney's committee website, and Minnite spent weeks tracking down what happened in each of these cases.[31]

As Minnite's meticulous research revealed, federal prosecutors dug diligently, but what they found was paltry and unimpressive. Few voters were committing election crimes. Thirty-one of the seventy federal convictions for election crimes between 2002 to 2005 were not against voters at all but against party and campaign workers; ten were against government officials; and three were against election workers. That left, out of hundreds of millions of votes cast nationwide, a mere thirty-five convictions against voters. Some of those prosecutions were for inadvertent mistakes or for registration fraud that did not affecting voting. It did not appear that any of the convictions described in the *Times* report would have been stopped by a voter identification law. Not one.

In a 2010 follow-up story, the *Times* explained that of the 55 people convicted from the 95 federal prosecutions during the period covered in the article, "fewer than 20 people were convicted of casting fraudulent ballots, and only 5 were convicted of registration fraud. Most of the rest were charged with other voting violations, including a scheme meant to help Republicans by blocking the phone lines used by two voting groups that were arranging rides to get voters to the polls."[32]

The results were the same in Texas. A *Dallas Morning News* headline in 2008 read: "Texas AG Fails to Unravel Large-Scale Voter Fraud Schemes in His Two Year Campaign." Similarly, a Democratic and Republican consultant were paired up by the United States Election Assistance Commission to investigate voter fraud and suppression (in a report the EAC later tried to bury, as we'll see in chapter 4), and they reached the same conclusion. Only isolated cases of real fraud, and most of it registration fraud.[33] No systematic voter impersonation fraud.

Iglesias Story

David Iglesias was a lawyer, a naval reserve Judge Advocate General officer, and an unsuccessful Republican candidate to be New Mexico's attorney general. He was a loyal Republican. He campaigned for Heather Wilson, who became a congresswoman from New Mexico, and longtime senator Pete Domenici made a video endorsing his candidacy for attorney general. In the 2000 election, Iglesias headed a New Mexico organization called "Lawyers for Bush." After the election, President Bush appointed him U.S. attorney from New Mexico in 2001, and he received positive job evaluations by the Department of Justice.[34]

But he was sacked from his job because he would not pursue weak voter fraud allegations.

Iglesias was one of nine U.S. attorneys around the country who were fired, in a scandal that ultimately led to the resignation of Bush's attorney general and confidant, Alberto Gonzales. An investigation by the Justice Department's Office of the Inspector General found that each of the nine was fired for reasons unrelated to job performance and that Iglesias specifically was fired because of complaints from Senator Domenici about his failure to vigorously pursue voter fraud allegations.

Because Karl Rove and former White House counsel Harriet Miers would not cooperate with the investigation, some of the story is uncertain. But the Office of the Inspector General "concluded that the allegation that Iglesias was an absentee manager who had delegated too much authority to his First Assistant was an after-the-fact justification for Iglesias's termination and was not in fact a reason he was placed on the removal list." Instead, "We believe the evidence we uncovered showed that Iglesias was removed because of complaints to the Department of Justice and the White House by New Mexico Republican members of Congress and party activists about Iglesias's handling of voter fraud and public corruption cases."

The report describes the voter fraud story in great depth. The big picture is this: New Mexico is another battleground state and has been the scene of bitter fighting between Democrats and Republicans over how elections are run. There's ample evidence of incompetence in New Mexico election administration. And we know the pattern: when there's election worker incompetence, the Fraudulent Fraud Squad claims rampant voter fraud.

Republican activists in New Mexico pressed Iglesias to investigate voter fraud claims. Allen Weh, the chair of the state Republican Party, Patrick Rogers, the former general counsel to the state Republican Party, Mickey Barnett, a Republican state senator, Steve Bell, Senator Domenici's chief of staff, and Darren White, a Republican sheriff from Bernalillo, New Mexico, who chaired the state's Bush-Cheney 2004 reelection campaign, all pressured Iglesias to investigate. Representative Wilson also complained about possible fraudulent voter registrations because some mailings from her office to newly registered voters were returned as "undeliverable."

Iglesias formed an Election Fraud Task Force with prosecutors and the Federal Bureau of Investigation. He created a voter fraud hotline and announced it to the public. While these efforts drew praise within the Justice Department— Iglesias was even asked to speak on the issue of voting integrity—Republican activists wanted prosecutions. And they wanted to make more political hay out of the voter fraud allegations.

As the inspector general's report explains, Republican leaders were screaming about fraud, especially fraudulent registrations supposedly submitted by ACORN. "On September 29, 2004, Rogers sent an e-mail to Iglesias . . . and more than 20 persons associated with the New Mexico Republican Party, including Senator Domenici's press secretary Ed Hild, Domenici's Chief of Staff Bell, Representative Wilson's Chief of Staff Bryce Dustman, New Mexico Republican Party Chairman Weh, and state Republican Party Executive Director Graves." Rogers's lengthy email included the following observations:

> I believe the [voter] ID issue should be used (now) at all levels—federal, state legislative races and Heather [Wilson]'s race. . . . You are not going to find a better wedge issue. . . . I've got to believe the [voter] ID issue would do Heather more good than another ad talking about how much federal taxpayer money

she has put into the (state) education system and social security. . . . This is
the single best wedge issue, ever in NM. We will not have this opportunity
again. . . . Today, we expect to file a new Public Records lawsuit, by 3 Republican legislators, demanding the Bernalillo county clerk locate and produce
(before Oct 15) ALL of the registrations signed by the ACORN employee.

The pressure continued. Weh wanted voter fraud prosecutions filed before Election Day. As he wrote in an email to key New Mexico Republicans:
"We are still waiting for US Attorney Iglesisas [sic] to do what his office
needs to do to hold people accountable, and have informed him that doing
it after the election is too late. I have copied him on this e-mail for his info."
The task force investigated, with the help of the FBI. It found nothing.
"With respect to Representative Wilson's August 17, 2004, complaint of
voter fraud . . . the FBI ultimately determined that the correspondence from
her office to newly registered voters had been returned as undeliverable

because of incomplete addresses on voter registration cards, errors made
by Wilson's office in addressing the envelopes, or because the voters, many
of whom were college students, had changed addresses since registering."
In addition, "With respect to the allegation that an ACORN worker was
responsible for a significant number of false voter registrations, the FBI
identified and interviewed the worker in question. As a result of the investigation, the USAO and the Public Integrity Section jointly concluded that
there was insufficient evidence of criminal intent on the subject's part to
justify prosecution." Even if Iglesias could bring a case, it wasn't proper to
do so just before the election. He also knew that it violated Department of
Justice policy to bring election cases when it could affect election outcomes.
Republicans complained not only to Iglesias. They went over, under, and
around him. Rogers emailed one of Iglesias's assistant U.S. attorneys in
2006 asking for prosecutions: "The voter fraud wars continue. Any indictment of the Acorn woman would be appreciated." They went to the White
House. Senator Domenici complained to Attorney General Gonzales and to
the deputy attorney general. Activists complained to Karl Rove.
They found a receptive audience. The *Washington Post* concluded that
"Rove, in particular, was preoccupied with pressing Gonzales and his aides
about alleged voting problems in a handful of battleground states." Iglesias
was fired for his failure to prosecute nonexistent voter fraud and to success-

fully bring a public corruption case against a Democrat. He is now prosecuting alleged terrorist detainees for the government at Guantanamo.[35]

John McKay also found nothing. President Bush appointed McKay, a life-
long Seattle resident from a Republican family, as the U.S. attorney for the
Western District of Washington State in 2001. His stellar resume read a lot
like Iglesias's, including, a few years later, this detail: McKay was part of the
mass firing of U.S. attorneys by political appointees of the Justice Department. He's now teaching law in Seattle.

Because Rove, Miers, and others refused to cooperate in any way, the Office of the Inspector General could not conclude whether McKay's handling
of voter fraud allegations arising out of the contested 2004 gubernatorial
race in Washington was a reason for his firing or whether it was something
else, such as McKay's position on certain internal Justice Department procedures that put him at odds with department officials in Washington.
What is clear is that many Republicans were upset about McKay's failure to
bring voter fraud charges in connection with the 2004 election and that the
White House heard their dissatisfaction. When Miers interviewed McKay
about a possible federal judicial nomination, the first question she asked
him was about his handling of voter fraud claims.

As we'll see in chapter 5, Republicans felt burned by the 2004 governor's
race between Democrat Christine Gregoire and Republican Dino Rossi. First
Rossi was declared the winner, and then he was again declared the winner
after a machine recount. Gregoire then pulled ahead after a hand recount.
Rossi filed an election contest, which ended up going to the state supreme
court. Gregoire came out on top, served as governor, and beat Rossi in a
rematch election in 2008.

Rossi's election contest revealed numerous problems with how the election was run, especially in King County. The registration rolls were a mess. A
number of ineligible felons were registered to vote and actually did. Speaking at a conference of moderate Republicans in the state after his firing,
McKay explained: "I thought that the election smelled really, really bad, but
what I think and even what it smells like is not relevant."[36] He explained how
he "quietly convened 'an extensive inquiry' into the election at the time. Five

federal prosecutors and several FBI agents were involved, he said. . . . 'Every FBI agent and every federal prosecutor who looked into the evidence concluded it was completely insufficient to move forward in a federal investigation.'"

Why not prosecute one of the released felons who voted in the election but who had not had his voting rights restored? "The main reason was because the state sent them ballots." How are you going to prove a knowing violation of the law when the state sent them ballots urging them to vote? This wasn't voter fraud; it was official incompetence.

Though Iglesias and McKay were reluctant to bring weak voter fraud cases, especially just before the election, Bradley Schlozman was not. Schlozman, who was later investigated (but never charged) for lying to Congress about whether he used political criteria in hiring career attorneys when he was acting head of the Justice Department's Civil Rights Division in Washington, was appointed the U.S. attorney for the Western District of Missouri.[37]

Schlozman had no prosecutorial experience when he took the place of U.S. Attorney Todd Graves, another of the U.S. attorneys improperly fired by Justice. Thor Hearne had complained to the White House that Graves was not prosecuting ACORN for voter registration fraud in Missouri, although the inspector general's report concluded that Graves was let go for a different reason: Senator Bond had asked that Graves be fired because Graves would not intervene in a dispute between Bond's staff and the staff of Congressman Sam Graves, Todd Graves's brother.

While Schlozman was at the Civil Rights Division, political appointees overruled career attorneys in approving Georgia's voter identification law and a controversial and unprecedented mid-decade redrawing of congressional districts by the Texas Republican legislature to increase the number of Republicans in Congress. It is not clear what role Schlozman played in those decisions. When he became a U.S. attorney in Missouri just before the 2004 elections, he went after ACORN immediately. The group had been running a registration drive in Kansas City, and it was discovered that some workers had turned in fraudulent forms. ACORN fired the workers and reported it to authorities.

According to Charlie Savage, who investigated the prosecutions for the

Boston Globe, "Schlozman moved fast, so fast that his office got one of the names on the indictments wrong. He announced the indictments of four former ACORN workers on Nov. 1, 2006, warning that 'this national investigation is very much ongoing.' Missouri Republicans seized on the indictments to blast Democrats in the campaign endgame." There was no national investigation. And Schlozman broke Department of Justice rules against bringing charges right before an election, rules meant to prevent the "risk of chilling legitimate voting and campaign activities." Missouri Republicans used the voter fraud charges to attack Claire McCaskill in her U.S. Senate bid. She won anyway.

It should come as no surprise that all of this federal effort to prosecute voter fraud yielded virtually nothing. The lack of evidence of a massive voter fraud conspiracy is just common sense. Most people are law-abiding citizens. Even those who are tempted to commit voter fraud to affect an election outcome will likely be deterred by potential felony charges.

Most of what gets called fraud in the media turns out to be innocent error or even coincidence. The next time you hear about "voter fraud" in which someone with the same name and birthdate registered in two places, remember the "birthday problem" used in freshman statistics classes. "In its common form, a class is asked to guess the probability that two students share a birthday. For those unfamiliar with the problem, the results are surprising. There are even odds of a match in a class of only 23 students; in a class of 40, there is nearly a ninety percent chance that two students share a birthday. Legends abound of professors leveraging the problem to win bets with their classes." It turns out that the odds of two *voters* having the same name and birthdate are quite high, too, as Michael McDonald and Justin Levitt have demonstrated.[38]

But suppose you *really wanted* to commit fraud to affect the outcome of an election. It's not easy to do, especially in the ways the Fraudulent Fraud Squad suggests Democrats are doing it.

Let's start with a small local election. One possible way to influence the outcome is to bribe an election official to change the official tally. That would be dangerous to your freedom if you could not trust the election official, but if you found a crooked official, the scheme could be effective. Your chances would depend on the safeguards in place to prevent any single official from altering results. The more safeguards, the more people you would have buy off for the plan to succeed. And if people from opposite sides of the political spectrum need to supervise and sign off on the vote totals, you would be far less likely to get the cooperation necessary for fraud.

Every so often we see cases involving election crimes committed not by voters but by election officials, poll workers, or party officials supervising the vote. In fact, such cases made up a fair share of the (paltry) totals in the Department of Justice statistics of election crime prosecutions from 2002 to 2005 examined by the *New York Times.*

Another way to steal an election, if the race is small enough, is to engage in absentee ballot fraud. Often this involves outright vote-buying. My favorite example is described in the appeal from a federal prosecution in *United States v. McCranie.* Candidates in a race for county commissioner in Dodge County, Georgia (pop. 20,118), paid between twenty and forty dollars for votes via absentee ballot. As the U.S. Court of Appeals for the Eleventh Circuit described it, "Incredibly, each of the two camps . . . actually set up tables inside the courthouse at opposite ends of the hall, where supporters on both sides openly bid against each other to buy absentee votes." The fraud was somehow discovered, and a joint state-federal prosecution led to numerous convictions. When rare fraud like this happens, it is hard to keep it quiet, even in those areas, such as the Southeast, with a history of vote-buying via absentee ballot.[39]

Why were absentee ballots involved? If you pay voters twenty dollars or more to vote your way, you need a mechanism for making sure they keep their end of the deal, and absentee ballots arrive with the voters' names on them. The secret ballot makes verification of vote-buying impossible. A voter might promise to vote for your preferred candidate and then renege. In fact, the voter might take multiple payments from opposing sides and still vote for his or her preferred candidate. A clever study by the economist Jac Heckelman, published in the journal *Public Choice,* showed that as states in the United States adopted the secret ballot around the turn of the last century, turnout decreased an average of 7 percentage points, at least in part because the secret ballot discourages vote-buying.[40]

Absentee ballot fraud, which is rare, usually involves vote-buying, as in *McCranie.* There are also cases of absentee ballots being intercepted from mailboxes or otherwise filled out by someone other than the real voter. These cases do get prosecuted.

The Fraudulent Fraud Squad does not focus on election worker crime or absentee ballot fraud. It is obsessed with *impersonation* fraud, the idea that people will go to the polling place pretending to be someone else—either a voter listed on the rolls or someone who has registered with a false name—to throw the results of an election.

There are virtually no recent cases of voter impersonation fraud and no evidence in at least a generation that it has been used in an effort to steal an election. There is a simple reason for this: it is an exceedingly dumb strategy. The problem is not that "it's a type of fraud, that because it's fraud, it's hard to detect," as Chief Justice John Roberts suggested at oral argument in the case involving the constitutionality of Indiana's voter identification law. After all, the Department of Justice and Texas efforts, *McCranie,* and other cases show that *other* types of election fraud do get prosecuted. Even when there aren't prosecutions, there are credible stories of fraudulent activities. The reason voter impersonation fraud is never prosecuted is that it almost never happens.[41]

If I wanted to steal an election using voter impersonation fraud, I'd have to recruit a bunch of people to vote at the polling place using fake names. But they might not follow my directions. They might go into the polling place and not vote, they might vote under their own names, or they might vote for someone other than the candidate I paid them to vote for. This is the problem with *any* election crime scheme based on voters using a secret ballot in a polling place.

But impersonation fraud presents an even greater hurdle. There are two ways to impersonate. One way would be to have people claim to be someone else listed on the rolls. This is obviously problematic: If I send you in and direct you to claim to be Thor Hearne, who I know is registered to vote at the precinct, but Thor has already showed up to vote, you will be immediately subject to arrest.

You might be arrested even if Thor has not yet voted. In many precincts, poll workers are local individuals. One of them could well know him. "You're not Thor" could also land you in jail. Moreover, many places do a signature match. Your signature would not match Thor's.

The other way of doing impersonation fraud would be for me to get you to fill out a registration card with a false name and address. The voter registration card would be turned into election officials, who will check the name and address against existing records. These forms have to be turned in weeks before the election. I'd then need to recruit people to go to the polling place weeks later on Election Day and falsely claim to be a person on the list. And federal law already provides that first-time voters must supply a driver's license or Social Security number if they register first to vote by mail—or provide identification to election officials when they vote for the first time.

Either gambit requires assembling enough coconspirators to affect the outcome of the election. Could I do it, even in a very small election, without being caught? We don't have a single recent example of anyone even attempting it. Why try such a risky scheme when absentee ballots are so much safer and more reliable?

The chance that impersonation fraud can affect a presidential, statewide, or even large city or county election is miniscule. Missouri had about four million registered voters in the 2000s. The idea that impersonation fraud could be done on a large-enough scale to affect the outcome of any major race, without detection by government officials, is ludicrous.

How rare is such impersonation fraud? Hans von Spakovsky, a political appointee in the Bush Justice Department's Civil Rights Division and a founding member of the Fraudulent Fraud Squad, wrote in a 2008 Fox News op-ed that "one doesn't have to look far to find instances of fraudulent ballots cast in actual elections by 'voters' who were the figments of active imaginations."[42] The op-ed coincided with the release of a report, entitled *Stolen Votes*, that von Spakovsky had written for the Heritage Foundation.

"In 1984, a district attorney in Brooklyn, N.Y. (a Democrat), released the findings of a grand jury that reported extensive registration and impersonation fraud between 1968 and 1982." If we don't have to look far, why was von Spakovsky dredging up an example from the 1970s? The Fraudulent Fraud Squad desperately needed examples of significant impersonation fraud to justify voter identification laws because this is virtually the only kind of fraud that a voter identification law would prevent.

In any case, the old Brooklyn example is not even very good. Most of the

Fraud is typically at election official level — not personal level

fraud was committed by election officials or party officers, who altered voting records held at the Department of Elections. As the *New York Times* reported at the time, the grand jury found collusion among party workers and elected officials in processing falsified registrations and signatures after Election Day. Much of the problem was lax security at elections offices, not at polling places: "The grand jury said the fraud extended to the Brooklyn Board of Elections office, where intruders were able to gain access to voter registration books and cards during business hours. In at least one case, the report said, the intruders hid in a restroom-ceiling opening." The *Village Voice* confirmed that the fraud was mostly committed by insiders, and the few instances of impersonation fraud occurred with the collusion of election officials and were successfully prosecuted.[43]

Von Spakovsky must have known that his Brooklyn example was weak, because he would not share a copy of the grand jury report, even when I publicly called for him to do so on my Election Law Blog. I wrote a letter to the president of the Heritage Foundation, and the website Talking Points Memo ran a few features on von Spakovsky's failure to provide me with the report. Finally, the librarians at the University of California–Irvine law school obtained a copy from the Brooklyn district attorney's office, and I posted a copy on my website. It confirmed that most of the fraud had nothing to do with voter impersonation, and that which did involved the collusion of election workers—something a voter identification law could not stop.[44]

I wasn't surprised that von Spakovsky wouldn't make the grand jury report public, even though it is a basic principle of scholarship that one must share sources with someone who wants to verify a scholarly claim. In 2005 I noted on the Election Law Blog that I received a copy of a law review article in the mail, postmarked Washington, with no return address. I had never seen an anonymous law review article. Published under the name "Publius," the article argued in favor of voter identification laws.[45]

Fast forward to March 2006. The Bush administration moved von Spakovsky from the Justice Department to the Federal Election Commission for a recess appointment as commissioner to handle campaign finance issues. On his new website, he suddenly took credit as author of the "Publius" article. I pointed this out on my blog, and von Spakovsky got calls from the *Atlanta Journal-Constitution* and the *Washington Post* asking why he would write such an article anonymously while dealing with these issues at the same time in the Justice Department's Civil Rights Division. He removed the reference to the "Publius" article from his website, without any explanation (though he did acknowledge authorship of the "Publius" article through a spokesperson to the *Post*).

At the confirmation hearing for von Spakovsky's position on the Federal Election Commission (recess appointments expire at the end of the session of Congress following the appointment), Senator Dick Durbin of Illinois raised the issue. Von Spakovsky said he removed the reference to the article because it was a "distraction." What is not clear is why he tried to hide his identity in the first place. Did he not believe what he wrote? Did he do so because he thought it was a conflict of interest for him to publish an article dealing with the same issues he handled at the Justice Department? Perhaps he hoped that the article would later be cited in the litigation over Georgia's voter ID law. Thor Hearne cited it in testimony before the U.S. Election Assistance Commission as evidence that voter ID laws are not unconstitutional.

Aside from his mangled facts about Brooklyn in the 1980s, von Spakovsky had little else to show a serious problem with impersonation voter fraud. The other example in his op-ed was absentee ballot fraud in a 1997 mayor's race in Miami (the race that led Florida election officials to do that bad purge in 2000). But a voter identification law would have done nothing to stop absentee ballot fraud.

In 2011, von Spakovsky wrote another op-ed, syndicated in newspapers across the country, in which he stated that "a 2010 election in Kansas that ended in a one-vote margin of victory included 50 votes cast illegally by citizens of Somalia." I pointed out on my blog that the disputed election took place in Missouri, not Kansas, and that a Missouri court specifically rejected the losing candidate's claim that illegal Somali citizens had voted in the election. But the next day the op-ed appeared in more papers, now saying that the incident happened in Missouri, not Kansas, but repeating the lie about illegal votes.[46]

The Supreme Court has done no better than von Spakovsky. When the Court upheld Indiana's voter identification law against constitutional challenge in 2007, it reached back even further than von Spakovsky: to Boss Tweed's New York of 1868! A footnote in the case also pointed to perhaps a single instance of in-person voter fraud out of millions of votes cast in the disputed 2004 Washington state gubernatorial election. The bottom line is that we have no modern instances to show that voter impersonation fraud is a real problem.[47]

But what about the ACVR's revelations that the National Association for the Advancement of Colored People paid addicts with crack cocaine to register fake people like Mr. Jive F. Turkey, Sr., to vote? In 2008, journalist and *American Spectator* contributor Matthew Vadum told the *Daily Show*: "[The job of] community organizer can also lead to a very rewarding career in crack cocaine trafficking. . . . Oh yes. It is a straight line from community organizing to crack cocaine dealer. Community organizers use crack cocaine in exchange for votes."[48] (For readers unfamiliar with Vadum, I feel compelled to point out that he is an actual journalist and these comments were not a spoof.)

This is Fraudulent Fraud Squad sleight of hand: rely on incidents of voter *registration* fraud to make a claim that Democrats are stealing elections. Voter registration fraud has nothing to do with stealing elections: its purpose is to steal the money of the people paying for voter registration drives. "Jive F. Turkey" never actually shows up to vote. While it would be irrational, as I've shown, to register fake voters *to try to influence the outcome of elections*, it is not at all irrational to register fake voters to make money, especially if you have to turn in a certain number of voter registration forms to keep your job or if you are paid by the registration card.

Unlike most democracies, which use government officials to register voters, the United States relies on a private system of voter registration. It is no secret that you are more likely to be registered if you are wealthy, white, old, and haven't moved recently than if you are poor, young, a member of a minority group, or someone who moves frequently. It is also no secret that the former group includes more Republicans and the latter more Democrats. For this reason, Democrats and their allies mount major voter registration drives before national elections.

Which brings us to the case of Chad Staton, a resident of Defiance County, Ohio, who pled guilty to filling out ten fraudulent voter registration cards (of the more than one hundred he had turned in). Staton said a woman named Georgianne Pitts hired him to collect voter registration cards and agreed to pay him using crack cocaine. The Defiance County sheriff said that Pitts confirmed the story.[49]

Pitts had been recruited as a volunteer by the Ohio assistant director of the NAACP's National Voter Fund, an arm of the NAACP that was conducting voter registration. There was no evidence that the NAACP or its Voter Fund had any knowledge that Pitts, who died of a prescription medication overdose shortly after Staton was indicted, was offering drugs as payment for voter registration activity. Most important, there was no proof of any conspiracy by the NAACP or any other liberal voter registration group to use these blatantly phony identification cards to influence the outcome of any election.

But that didn't stop the fraud allegations from flying.

Hours after the news of Staton's arrest hit the media, Ohio Republican Party spokesperson Jason Mauk "cited the case in claiming that 'the effort to steal Ohio's election is under way, and it's being driven exclusively by interest groups working to register Democrat voters.'"[50]

Election officials noted that the cards Staton turned in all had the same handwriting, and many had the same address and fictitious names. Staton could have turned in one legitimate card, with his own name. But he didn't. At the time the police arrested him, he was not a registered voter in Defiance County, Ohio.

If this was the Democrats' and their labor and minority group allies' top-secret plan to steal the Ohio presidential vote in 2004, Republicans could rest easy. Dick Tracy, one of Staton's phantom voters, was not going to save Ohio for John Kerry.

Who is going to agree to walk into a voting booth claiming to be Mr. Jive F. Turkey, Sr., Ms. Mary Poppins, or Brett Favre? The allegations that such acts lead to stolen elections would be comical if there wasn't such a nefarious purpose behind it. If you Google the terms "crack cocaine" and "voter registration" together, you can read all the conspiracy theories and some racist rhetoric on conservative bulletin boards and blogs about how Democrats brought crack into the inner cities to perpetrate massive election fraud on the American people.

Journalist and veteran squad member John Fund has one-upped the reg-

istration-cards-for-drugs story by suggesting that *terrorists* could be voting
in our elections. Though the claims have been debunked by others, Fund
has suggested that at least one of the 9/11 hijackers could have registered to
vote and actually voted in a Virginia election. Minnite investigated this
claim in detail and found no evidence that any of the hijackers voted in any
U.S. election.[51]

Though the cards-for-crack episode was an isolated event, and voting by
terrorists not even that, voter registration fraud is a real problem. The problem does not affect election outcomes. But people are breaking the law by
turning in false documents. Processing the fake cards takes time away from
elections officials doing other jobs, especially in the crush of work before
Election Day. Stories about Mary Poppins or dogs registering to vote are not
going to give anyone confidence in the fairness of the election process.

What really motivates the Fraudulent Fraud Squad? Vadum, one of the
squad's newest members, inadvertently revealed what underlay his attack
on ACORN and related groups. Registering the poor to vote, he contended,
is "un-American," like giving "burglary tools to criminals." "It is profoundly
antisocial and un-American to empower the nonproductive segments of
the population to destroy the country—which is precisely why Barack
Obama zealously supports registering welfare recipients to vote."
In other words, we should once again make wealth a condition of voting.
Apparently this is no longer the kind of odious idea one should keep to
oneself.[52]

Christopher Edwards apologized. "I take responsibility for what I did. . . .
I'm sorry, I truly am." Edwards was the Nevada field director for ACORN,
and he was apologizing in a Nevada state court as he accepted probation
and a five-hundred-dollar fine for breaking Nevada law.[53]

It is a crime in Nevada to pay people by the number of cards turned
in when they register voters. The law is intended to minimize fraudulent
registrations—the theory is that people who are paid by the card are more
likely to produce phony cards than those paid by the hour. The problem
with people paid by the hour, from the point of view of their employers, is
that they may not work hard enough.

Though some facts remain unclear, it appears that Edwards designed an incentive system called—appropriately for Las Vegas—"Blackjack." Any ACORN worker who collected at least twenty-one voter registration cards per shift got a five-dollar bonus, on top of the eight-to-nine-dollar hourly salary for voter registration activities. Edwards appeared to be engaged in a rogue operation. On pleading guilty, he agreed to testify that ACORN and Amy Busefink, one of his supervisors, knew of his plans, a charge they strenuously denied. But ACORN's problems were bigger than the Edwards operation.

ACORN's policy was that workers who regularly collected a small number of cards per shift were in danger of losing their jobs. Though the organization adamantly denied that it set quotas for voter registration, here's how Michael Slater, of the ACORN affiliate Project Vote, described the requirement in a press release issued after the indictments came down:

> ACORN, in common with every other business or professional organization, needs to establish standards for performance and a reasonable basis for evaluating its employees. For canvassers, who are paid by the hour to assist members of the public in completing voter registration applications, these expectations are based on the only measurement that makes sense: the number of complete and accurate voter registration applications a canvasser collects per shift. Based on years of experience conducting community-based voter registration drives, ACORN has established 20 applications per four-hour shift as a reasonable performance standard. This performance standard does not represent a "quota," or payment per registration, but simply a baseline for job performance.[54]

Slater may not have called it a quota, but the message to workers must have been clear. If you don't regularly produce twenty cards per shift (about one every twelve minutes), you could lose your job. If you are poor and struggling, that's going to look like a quota even if it technically is not one.

Eventually, after filing for bankruptcy, ACORN pled guilty to one count of felony compensation for registration of voters. Though Busefink took a plea in exchange for probation, she continued to deny knowledge of "Blackjack," and she reserved the right to contest her plea on constitutional grounds: she argued that the law barring payment by the registration card infringes the First Amendment rights of people to associate for political causes. Her case is pending in the Nevada Supreme Court.[55]

ACORN turned out to have a flawed business model for voter registration and deep internal problems. The business model relied on giving poor people who desperately needed jobs the responsibility of registering new voters and of meeting hourly "performance standards" or risk losing their jobs. And ACORN could do little quality control once the cards were turned in: in many states, including Nevada, anyone collecting voter registration cards has a legal obligation to turn them in even if they suspect that the cards are fraudulent. (This rule prevents an organization from dumping cards of people likely to vote for candidates or a party not supported by the organization— as had been alleged in the past in Nevada by a Republican registration group.) Even flagging the suspicious cards, as ACORN and other groups sometimes did when workers turned them in, is not enough.

An alternative model is to hire people, likely at a higher hourly rate, with validated work experience demonstrating both a reputation for honesty and an ability to work in a non-commission-based setting. Or a drive could function using volunteers. The League of Women Voters, for example, has been able to conduct voter registration drives, often using volunteers, without having ACORN-type problems.

Though Project Vote and ACORN originally claimed to have registered 1.3 million new voters in 2008, Slater later told the New York Times that only about 450,000 were newly registered voters. As the Times reported, "The remainder are registered voters who were changing their address and roughly 400,000 that were rejected by election officials for a variety of reasons, including duplicate registrations, incomplete forms and fraudulent submissions from low-paid field workers trying to please their supervisors, Mr. Slater acknowledged."[56]

ACORN's problems ran deeper. The founder's brother embezzled more than a million dollars from the organization. The ties between ACORN and Project Vote were fuzzy, and an internal investigation for ACORN, done by attorney Beth Kingsley and made available to the Times, showed that the legal relationship between the organizations raised questions under the tax laws. Though the two groups claimed to be separate—Project Vote is a non-profit, tax-exempt nonpartisan voter registration organization, and ACORN engaged in some left-leaning political activity, including advocating for the rights of the poor—it was hard to draw the line between the two.[57]

ACORN was regularly blasted by Republicans during the 2008 election season. Even presidential candidate John McCain got into the act, drawing on Barack Obama's previous work as a community organizer for Project Vote. "We need to know the full extent of Senator Obama's relationship with ACORN, who is now on the verge of maybe perpetrating one of the greatest frauds in voter history in this country, maybe destroying the fabric of democracy. The same front outfit organization that your [Obama's] campaign gave $832,000 for 'lighting and site selection.' So all of these things need to be examined, of course." It was dog-whistle politics for the Republican right.[58]

The last straw for the organization was when it was caught on videotape in a sting operation by rogue conservative activist James O'Keefe. The edited tape appeared to show ACORN staffers advising O'Keefe, dressed as a pimp, how to get a mortgage and evade taxes for an underage prostitution operation.

Though the doctored tape did not appear to fairly portray what went on, this was the end of ACORN. Congress voted to cut off its funding for various projects, and the organization went bankrupt. Project Vote survived, and both it and other organizations geared up for voter registration activities in 2012.[59]

But for the Fraudulent Fraud Squad, ACORN was a gift from heaven. Its sloppy business practices, its workers who turned in ridiculously fraudulent voter registration forms, and its inability to effectively respond to charges made it the ideal target. Though there's no evidence that ACORN was the leading edge of a wave of fraudulently cast ballots (or, indeed, that any fraudulent ACORN-related registration form ever resulted in a fraudulent vote), a skeptical public, especially among Republicans hearing the anti-ACORN drumbeat, may now think that the fraud is rampant.

And this leads us to where we are today. Though we still hear concerns about voter fraud infecting our elections, the new mantra is that even if there's not enough proof of *actual* fraud, voter ID laws and strict voter registration laws are necessary to maintain the public's confidence in the fairness of the election system.

It's an idea that has the imprimatur of the Supreme Court. In 2004, Arizona voters passed an initiative aimed mostly at immigration issues. The law included a provision requiring proof of citizenship to register to vote as well as a voter identification requirement. A group opposed to the voting aspects of the initiative challenged it in federal court, and the U.S. Court of Appeals for the Ninth Circuit issued an order barring the law from being put into effect for the 2006 elections—until the trial court could make a final determination as to whether the law was constitutional.

Arizona appealed this stay to the Supreme Court, and the high court said, in a case called *Purcell v. Gonzalez*, that Arizona could enforce its law while the trial court held a full trial on whether it was unconstitutional. The law was justified, the Court said, by Arizona's compelling interest in the integrity of its electoral process: "Confidence in the integrity of our electoral processes is essential to the functioning of our participatory democracy. Voter fraud drives honest citizens out of the democratic process and breeds distrust of our government. Voters who fear their legitimate votes will be outweighed by fraudulent ones will feel disenfranchised."[60]

It was a lovely theory, but there was no evidence to back it up. There is no known instance of voter turnout going down because of a (misguided) fear that voter fraud will "dilute" real votes or of voter confidence going down because of a fear of voter fraud.

Rather than take the Supreme Court's word for it, political scientists Steve Ansolabehere and Nate Persily put these contentions to the test. In a *Harvard Law Review* article entitled "Vote Fraud in the Eye of the Beholder," they tested the Supreme Court's armchair social science with a broad national public opinion survey. "We find that perceptions of fraud have no relationship to an individual's likelihood of turning out to vote. We also find that voters who were subject to stricter identification requirements believe fraud is just as widespread as do voters subject to less restrictive identification requirements."[61] In other words, whether or not voters support voter ID requirements and whether they think fraud is a big problem or a small one have no impact on their willingness to turn out to vote or on their views about the integrity of elections. Instead, voters' views of the pervasiveness of voter fraud depend largely on partisanship: more than twice as many Republicans, compared to Democrats, thought that voter fraud was very common.

More troubling is the pervasive belief that the U.S. election system is full of voter fraud or vote theft. About a quarter of survey respondents thought that these activities were "very common," and another third thought that they happened "occasionally."

Mario Gallegos's Texas is full of people who mistakenly believe that voter fraud is common. The voting wars continue even as Texas waits to hear if its new voter identification requirement will gain approval from the Department of Justice. A new player on the Texas scene is Harris County's True the Vote, an organization that calls itself nonpartisan but whose parent organization is the King Street Patriots, a local Tea Party group. Catherine Engelbrecht is the president of both organizations.[62]

True the Vote's website explains its mission. "Election fraud attacks the heart of our political system and threatens our rights as citizens. What will you do about it? . . . If you are one of the millions of Americans outraged by the corruption of our government, help stop the corruption where it starts— at the polls. Sign up right here, right now. Let's work together to true the vote in every election across our nation!"

The organization is looking to expand to a national group combatting voter fraud. Unlike Thor Hearne's American Center for Voting Rights, True the Vote does not claim to be a research organization. Instead, it is organizing "poll watching" activities and investigations into faulty voter registrations. Where Republicans see vigilance, Democrats see voter intimidation.

Engelbrecht brought attention to True the Vote through her activities aimed at another organization, Houston Votes. Houston Votes is affiliated with Texans Together Fund, a group dedicated to minority empowerment. Fred Lewis, the founder and president of Texans Together, launched Houston Votes 2010 to register one hundred thousand voters (out of the estimated six hundred thousand unregistered voters in Harris County) by November 2010.

Like ACORN, Houston Votes has been accused of submitting many fraudulent voter registration cards. True the Vote focused on Houston Votes' activities and brought attention to faulty voter registrations such as registrations at vacant lots. Leo Vasquez, the Republican registrar of the Houston area, said that he found problems with about 5,500 of the approximately 25,000 voter registration cards Houston Votes turned in.

True the Vote defended Vasquez and stood at his side at his news conference criticizing Houston Votes. The Democrats sued Vasquez for improperly rejecting legal voter registration cards. Houston Votes and others allied with Democrats accused True the Vote of intimidating voters at the polls, in an effort to reduce turnout of poor and minority voters. The battle continues as I write this.

We could, of course, eliminate the fighting over voter registration cards if we took the job of registering voters away from private parties and made universal registration of all eligible voters a government responsibility. Unfortunately, Ansolabehere and Persily found that even if the government got into the business of registering all voters, it would not eliminate perceptions of pervasive voter fraud. Indeed, it would provide new fodder for the Fraudulent Fraud Squad.

In a pamphlet called "How the Obama Administration Undermines Our Elections," John Fund suggests that having the government register all voters would also lead to voter fraud. "Left unaddressed by [an argument for broader registration] is how stuffing voter rolls with millions of new registrants that have expressed no interest in voting won't create an automatic pool of names that vote fraudsters could mine to cast illegal ballots—either through absentee programs or in-person voting at polling places."[63]

So there's no way to win. Baseless allegations of fraud will remain with us. The list of states with Republican legislatures adopting voter identification laws in time for 2012 grows: Wisconsin, Kansas, Texas, South Carolina, and others. Florida's new voter registration rules are so tough that the League of Women Voters has given up registering voters there.[64]

So long as close elections continue, we can expect the Fraudulent Fraud Squad to be ready to roll out Mr. Jive F. Turkey, Sr., whenever he's needed.

What is the story!

Because ACORN Died FL tightens

3

¡No Votes!

Dem's used to add to motivate

"¡No *votes!*" That's what the 2010 television advertisement from Latinos for Reform urged Spanish-speaking Nevada voters. "Don't vote!" The full ad explained the logic:

It's an election year. So here come more promises about immigration reform. Last time, President Obama and the Democratic leadership made a commitment that immigration reform would be passed within a year. But two years have gone by and nothing. Not even a vote in Congress. With a Democratic president and supermajorities in both chambers of Congress, they have no excuses. Clearly, the Democratic leadership betrayed us. And now, when they need our votes, they are at it again with more empty promises. Aren't you tired of politicians playing games with your future? Do you really think it would be different this time? They had two years to do something. It was all talk, and no action.

This November, we need to send a message to all politicians. If they didn't keep their promise on immigration reform, then they can't count on our vote. Democratic leaders must pay for their broken promises and betrayals. If we just go on supporting them again this November, they will keep playing games with our future and taking our votes for granted.

Don't vote this November. This is the only way to send them a message. You can no longer take us for granted.

Don't Vote!

Paid for by Latinos for Reform.[1]

On its face, the ad sounded like an attack from the left: Democrats are not pushing hard enough for immigration reform, and they need to be pressured to get moving. So who was behind Latinos for Reform? La Raza? MALDEF? Some other, more radical Hispanic organization?

Not quite. It turns out that the largest contributor to Latinos for Reform in 2008 (the last year for which tax reports are publicly available) was John T. Finn, a prolife activist in southern California. In an obituary Finn wrote about his father, posted on his website, Prolife.com, there's no mention of any Latino heritage or concern about immigration. The obituary does, however, discuss Finn's father's work with Ronald Reagan, Young Americans for Freedom, and a slew of antiabortion groups the family was involved in for years, and it praises the five of six Finn children who have been jailed in abortion protests. The closest the website comes to discussing Latinos is the family's antiabortion outreach to Hispanics.[2]

The head of Latinos for Reform, Robert de Posada, has deep Republican ties. According to ABC News, de Posada "served as the Republican National Committee's director of Hispanic affairs . . . as one of three directors for Americans for Border and Economic Security with former GOP Rep. Dick Armey, who now runs a leading Tea Party group, FreedomWorks. De Posada also served in the Bush administration and as an advisor to former Republican Sen. George Allen of Virginia—who lost his reelection bid in 2006 after he was accused of using a racial slur against one of his opponent's aides."[3] His idea of immigration reform likely would not please many Latino Democrats: "heightened border security, and drug enforcement; employee verification; and a temporary worker program. 'No amnesty,' he said."[4]

Latinos for Reform shares a post office box with the group that produced the notorious "Swift Boat Veterans for Truth" ads accusing 2004 Democratic presidential candidate and decorated Vietnam War veteran John Kerry of being a coward in wartime. The political consultant hired by Latinos for Reform was Susan Arceneaux, a "long-time aide of Dick Armey."[5]

The far right's motivation for bankrolling the Latinos for Reform ads is not hard to understand: keeping down the number of Latino voters would help elect another Republican to the U.S. Senate. This is undoubtedly what interested Finn, given that Republican senators are more likely to support his antiabortion opinions than Democratic ones.

In Nevada in 2010, U.S. Senate majority leader Harry Reid was fighting for his political life in his reelection campaign against Sharron Angle, a Republican and Tea Party favorite. For Republicans, knocking off the majority leader would be a big deal, and in 2010 there was an outside chance that if Reid lost, control of the Senate could flip back into Republican hands.

Angle was not expected to get heavy Latino support. Her position on immigration was much like de Posada's. She told a local television station during the election season that she supported Arizona's tough immigration law. "The real question is, how do we battle Harry Reid's push for amnesty? And we have to do that by securing the borders and enforcing our laws." She ran a television ad about "illegal aliens" featuring what the *Las Vegas Sun* called "a picture of menacing-looking Mexicans." Further, she "shocked Latinos with comments during a visit to a high school near Las Vegas, where she told puzzled Hispanic students 'some of you look a little more Asian to me.'"[6]

Latinos were a key and growing constituency in Nevada. The number of registered Latino voters surged by twenty thousand in 2008 compared to 2004, and they generally support Democrats over Republicans by about a two-to-one ratio. To keep his seat, Reid needed to get out the Latino vote— preelection surveys showed Latinos less motivated than whites and African Americans to show up on Election Day. As for Republicans, though they could not get Latinos to vote for Angle, it would be almost as good to get them to stay home, reducing Reid's vote and thereby increasing Angle's chance of victory.[7]

Democrats slammed the Latinos for Reform ad and successfully pressured the Spanish-language channel Univision to pull it from the radio and keep it off its television network. In a blog posting on the Huffington Post, Democratic activist Christine Pelosi labeled it a "GOP Voter Suppression Ad." Dolores Huerta, a Latina activist and cofounder with César Chávez of the United Farm Workers union, emailed this statement to Pelosi: "We will not fall into this deceptive trap of no representation by the so called 'Latinos for Reform.' This latest Republican ploy only motivates us to work harder to make sure every eligible Latino voter will organize others to vote for the Democrats, the candidates that stand up for Latinos and Justice for our families. Our Vote is Our Voice. Sí Se Puede!"[8]

De Posada tried to backtrack a few days after Univision pulled the ad, lamely telling National Public Radio that "Don't vote!" was an editing error for which he took full responsibility. He said the ad should have ended with "Don't vote for those who betrayed you," but all those words couldn't fit in the sixty-second spot. He did not explain why "Don't Vote!" appeared twice in the ad, both times without the rest of the language he claimed he wanted included, or why "Don't Vote!" standing alone appeared as well in the English translation video made by the group and posted on YouTube, in an ad that ran a minute and a half.[9]

In the end, the ad backfired. It may even have energized Latinos and other Nevada Democrats to show up and vote. "If we do not vote, Republicans win," Huerta said. Hispanic voters in Nevada backed Reid over Angle, 69 percent to 27 percent. Reid won Nevada by more than 5 percent overall, and the Democrats retained control of the Senate (though they lost the House).[10]

Few could deny that the purpose of the "Don't Vote" ad was to depress Latino turnout in an effort to hurt the Democratic candidate Harry Reid. A harder question is whether it is fair to call it "voter suppression." A classic example of such suppression is a flyer distributed in African-American neighborhoods claiming that Democrats are allowed to vote on Wednesday, not Election Day Tuesday. The "Don't Vote" ad did not look as bad as that. Latinos for Reform was a real group, not one created just for the ad, and anyone who Googled it would see that it was Republican-oriented and without grassroots Latino support.

If the ad wasn't voter suppression, as some election law experts suggested when the controversy arose, what was it? A more charitable characterization is that it made a disingenuous argument for Latino voters to decline to exercise their right to vote. Though I believe it may have crossed the line from the rough-and-tumble political discourse we now expect in close partisan elections into voter suppression, it is hard to say where exactly that line is. Perhaps we should count the ad as a suppression effort because it discourages voter turnout. Telling people not to exercise a right that American soldiers have died defending seems beyond the pale of accepted political discourse. Perhaps the ad's disingenuousness alone should put it over the line: it advocates abstention from voting on grounds that Democrats have not done enough to help undocumented immigrants gain legal status, when in fact Latinos for Reform leaders believe that *less* should be done to help these immigrants. But whether it deserves to be called "voter suppression" is a close call.

Democrats have learned to yell "voter suppression" almost as often as Republicans yell "voter fraud." In 2000, Democrats alleged that the Florida felon purge was racially motivated against African Americans or politically motivated against Democrats, but there was no proof of anything more than gross incompetence at work. Democrats also alleged in 2000 that Republican law enforcement officials in Florida put up physical roadblocks to prevent African Americans from getting to the polls on Election Day. But even the Democratic-leaning report from the U.S. Commission on Civil Rights investigating Florida in 2000, in a chapter giving "First Hand Accounts of Voter Disenfranchisement," did not include any testimony substantiating this claim. It appears to an urban myth accepted by some Democrats as fact.[11]

When Florida passed its tough new voting restrictions in 2011, making it harder to register new voters and for black churches to organize early voting caravans after services on the Sunday before Election Day, Democrats made similar claims of disenfranchisement. Debbie Wasserman Schultz, a Democratic member of Congress from Florida and head of the Democratic National Committee, called the Florida changes a new "Jim Crow" law.[12]

Jim Crow laws in the South from the nineteenth century to the passage of the Voting Rights Act in the 1960s made it almost impossible for African Americans to vote. They also mandated racial segregation of schools, restaurants, bathrooms, drinking fountains, public transportation, housing, and jobs. Jim Crow was a system of legally recognized apartheid touching every facet of life. As bad as Florida's new law might be, it was a far cry from Jim Crow's literacy tests, poll taxes, and other devices that effectively shut down the African-American vote. The fact-checking organization Politifact rated Wasserman Schultz's charge "False," and she quickly retracted it.

But many others on the left used the "Jim Crow" language, including the editorial board of the *New York Times*. Former president Bill Clinton, with more subtlety than Wasserman Schultz, told a college crowd in 2011 that "there has never been in my lifetime, since we got rid of the poll tax and all the Jim Crow burdens on voting, the determined effort to limit the franchise that we see today." Not Jim Crow, the president suggested, but the worst since Jim Crow. Democrats now regularly bemoan the "G.O.P's war on voting."[13]

The bottom line on (mostly Democratic) charges of voter suppression since 2000 is mixed. Some charges are justified, others are arguable, and others are no more legitimate than Republican cries of voter fraud based on the registration of Mary Poppins. Sometimes there is intent to suppress the Democratic vote, but it is not effective. Sometimes, as with century-old felon disenfranchisement laws (passed for their own partisan reasons after Reconstruction), there is a partisan effect (because racial minorities are disproportionately represented in the criminal justice system and minorities generally support Democratic candidates). Sometimes there is both intent and effect. And sometimes, it is very difficult to know.

The "Don't Vote!" ad, apparently intended to squelch the Latino vote, does not seem to have worked. As we'll see, exaggeration of voter suppression is not only a Democratic disease; recent Republican efforts to make a huge-deal out of a single incident involving two militant members of the "New Black Panthers" at a Philadelphia polling place in 2008 also qualify. It would be shocking if more than a handful of voters were deterred by either tactic.

Just as Republicans like Pat Rogers of New Mexico want to use voter fraud as a "wedge issue" to motivate Republican voters—even to the point of urging U.S. Attorney David Iglesias to bring charges against ACORN workers before the 2004 elections—Democrats sometimes use claims of voter suppression in their fundraisers and get-out-the-vote efforts. Remember Herera's line in response to the Latinos for Reform ad: "If we don't vote, Republicans win."

In a June 2011 email message to supporters of the Democratic Governors Association, party activist Donna Brazile began her fundraising pitch with this statement, "When my sister tried to vote in Florida, in the 2000 election, she was a victim of voter suppression." Memories of *Bush v. Gore* still haunt Democratic activists. After telling readers that her sister was illegally asked for multiple forms of identification in 2000, Brazile turned to the restrictive voter identification and registration laws being passed in advance of the 2012 election: "In Florida, Pennsylvania, Ohio, Wisconsin, and Texas, extremist governors or legislators are willing to violate people's civil rights in order to win elections."[14]

Whether or not there's a lot of voter suppression, fear of it and Democratic efforts at "election protection" seem to help bring in Democratic money and bring out Democratic voters.

"Let's not beat around the bush: The Indiana voter photo ID law is a not-too-thinly-veiled attempt to discourage election-day turnout by certain folks believed to skew Democratic." Those words came not from Donna Brazile but from the late judge Terence Evans of the U.S. Court of Appeals for the Seventh Circuit. They are the opening of his opinion reviewing the constitutionality of Indiana's strict new photo ID law for voting.[15]

It was hard not to credit Judge Evans's view of the Indiana legislature's intent: Why would Indiana Republicans unanimously support what was then the toughest photo identification law in the country—and Indiana Democrats uniformly oppose it—if not for partisan reasons? Especially given the scant evidence of actual voter fraud, it seems reasonable to attribute the Indiana vote to partisan motives rather than to sound principles of election administration. Judge Evans thought the law was unconstitutional because of its partisan motive and lack of evidence to support it.

But Judge Evans wrote his words in dissent. The case, known as *Crawford v. Marion County Election Board,* eventually reached the U.S. Supreme Court. A federal district court judge had rejected a constitutional challenge to the law, in which the Democratic Party, the League of Women Voters, and the American Civil Liberties Union argued that it violated the Constitution's equal protection guarantees by discriminating against poor, elderly, and minority voters, who are less likely to have valid government-issued identification. They appealed the decision, losing before a panel of three Seventh Circuit judges, including Judge Evans, then before the entire Seventh Circuit, and then, on a six-to-three vote, in the Supreme Court.

Along the way, as with most other challenges to voter identification laws, the judges reviewing the law's constitutionality mostly divided along party lines. Judges appointed by Republicans generally vote to uphold voter identification laws, and judges appointed by Democrats generally oppose them. These judges, like everyone else, had preconceived notions about the extent of voter fraud and voter suppression problems that colored their constitutional analysis.

Given that the fraud such a voter identification requirement would prevent seems to be almost nonexistent, you might think that proof of bad partisan intent would be enough to get laws like these struck down. But a majority of the judges found a more fundamental problem with the challengers' claims: lack of proof that people would be injured by these laws. There wasn't enough evidence of an unconstitutional effect. And without proof of such an effect, even if the challengers had technical legal "standing" to bring their claim, the laws appeared to impose only a minor burden. Therefore the courts did not require the states to come up with evidence to justify the laws.

In the Indiana case, the challengers' briefs did a great job explaining how the law *might* injure voters. Some could be so old that they could not track down a certified copy of a birth certificate, which they would need to get a government-issued voter identification card. Others might be unable to pay for a copy of their birth certificate. Under the Indiana law, if you were too poor to get the documents needed for an identification card, you could file a "provisional ballot," which election officials would put aside rather than count. If you wanted your vote actually counted, you would have to make a trip, at your own expense, to a county office (which could be thirty or more miles away) to fill out a "Declaration of Indigency." And it wouldn't be enough to do this just once—you'd have to do the same thing in *every election* in which you lacked the identification. If you were poor enough that you couldn't pay for a birth certificate, it did not seem likely that you could afford the expense of getting to the county seat to have your vote counted.

The problem for the law's challengers was that they did not find voters who actually could testify about their difficulties in obtaining an identification card. Instead, the challengers brought a "facial" challenge to the law, saying that it was unconstitutional for everybody—and for this reason that they did not need to produce any actual disenfranchised voters to win their case.

Whether that technical point was correct as a matter of law (the courts eventually said no), it made for terrible public relations. Often when a public interest law firm sues the government, the firm brings out to the public those hurt by government action. The tactic puts a human face on an abstract legal issue. Without those faces humanizing the case, the general public and the courts were going to be skeptical that the Indiana law would affect real voters.

Federal district judge Sarah Barker, noting that the challengers to the law said it could disenfranchise up to one million Hoosier voters without driver's licenses or other acceptable forms of identification, was dismissive of the challengers' skimpy evidence of the law's burden. Some of the plaintiffs in the case actually had identification cards that would allow them to vote; others could easily get them; others were exempt from the law because they were over sixty-five and could vote using an absentee ballot without an excuse and without identification. (This assumes that absentee balloting is just as good as voting in person, which is not always true. In some places, absentee ballots are less likely to be accepted as valid votes because of technical problems with how they are filled out or mailed.) The judge expressed contempt for what she saw as the plaintiffs' evidentiary failings.

"Despite apocalyptic assertions of wholesale voter disenfranchisement, Plaintiffs have produced not a single piece of evidence of any identifiable registered voter who would be prevented from voting pursuant to [the law] because of his or her inability to obtain the necessary photo identification. Similarly, Plaintiffs have failed to produce any evidence of any individual, registered or unregistered, who would have to obtain photo identification in order to vote, let alone anyone who would undergo any appreciable hardship to obtain photo identification in order to be qualified to vote." She rejected the constitutional challenge.

When the case got before the Seventh Circuit on appeal, Judge Richard A. Posner was even more dismissive of the challengers' claims. Judge Posner is a brilliant but controversial judge, a former University of Chicago law professor, and one of the founders of the "law and economics" movement. "Law and economics" is a field of legal studies bringing insights from economics to legal problems, and those who use this type of analysis often argue that judges should decide cases so that the law promotes economic efficiency—not necessarily justice or fairness.

Judge Posner's opinion in the Indiana case, which provoked Judge Evans's dissent, focused less on the lack of evidence put forth by the challengers and more on what he saw as the low stakes of the case:

> A great many people who are eligible to vote don't bother to do so. Many do not register, and many who do register still don't vote, or vote infrequently. The benefits of voting to the individual voter are elusive (a vote in a political election rarely has any *instrumental* value, since elections for political office at the state or federal level are never decided by just one vote), and even very slight costs in time or bother or out-of-pocket expense deter many people from voting, or at least from voting in elections they're not much interested in. So some people who have not bothered to obtain a photo ID will not bother to do so just to be allowed to vote, and a few who have a photo ID but forget to bring it to the polling place will say what the hell and not vote, rather than go home and get the ID and return to the polling place.

What the hell, indeed!

Under Judge Posner's view, it didn't matter if Republicans were trying to suppress the Democratic vote because, for any individual voter, the vote wasn't worth much anyway. It was an odd analysis from a judge whose job is to make sure that people do not face unconstitutional discrimination in exercising their legal rights.

I was so incensed by Judge Posner's opinion belittling the right to vote that I took to the pages of the *Washington Post,* begging the Supreme Court to agree to hear the *Crawford* case and set things straight: the right to vote was more important and more worthy of protection than Judge Posner recognized.[16] I quickly learned, however, that the Roberts Court was the last place to look for protection of voting rights. The Court agreed to hear the

Crawford case (though my op-ed probably had nothing to do with it). While the Court did not endorse Judge Posner's clinical description of the right to vote, it agreed with Judge Barker of the district court that there was not enough proof of injury to justify striking down the Indiana law.

Three of the most conservative justices—Alito, Scalia, and Thomas—said it would not matter even if there were evidence of some people disenfranchised by the law, so long as *most people* would not face a serious burden. But the controlling opinion, written by Justice Stevens and joined by Chief Justice Roberts and Justice Kennedy, was narrower.

The usually moderate-to-liberal Justice Stevens wrote that the "facial" challenge failed because the law was not very burdensome for most people (who have ID) and was justified to prevent fraud and preserve voter confidence. But he left the door open for a follow-on lawsuit brought by Indiana voters who could show that the voter identification law imposed a big burden *as applied to them.* When the three votes for the Stevens opinion were put together with the votes of the three dissenters (Justices Breyer, Ginsburg, and Souter), there was a Court majority ready to hear another case if evidence of a significant burden could be established for identified groups of voters.

Why was it so hard for the Indiana challengers to find actual voters hurt by the Indiana voter identification law? One possibility, and the most likely one, is that there are actually few voters, even poor and elderly ones or those on Indian reservations, who actually lack (and cannot afford to obtain) some form of government-issued identification or a birth certificate, which could be used to get a free identification card and who want to cast a ballot. As Judge Posner noted, people use an identification card to do just about everything these days, from flying to cashing a check, and many poor people would do what they could to get a valid identification card. (Strictly speaking, it is possible to fly and cash a check without an ID, but most of the new voter identification laws don't allow you a way around the requirement unless you qualify for a religious exemption or meet an old age requirement.)

Another possibility is that these voters are out there but that it was too hard to identify them as the law was being rolled out. Soon after the new law went into effect, the Associated Press reported on twelve nuns in their eighties and nineties who were turned away from voting by a fellow sister serving as a poll worker:

Sister Julie McGuire said she was forced to turn away her fellow sisters at Saint Mary's Convent in South Bend across the street from the University of Notre Dame because they had been told earlier that they would need [a photo] ID to vote.

The nuns, all in their 80s or 90s, didn't get one but came to the precinct anyway.

"One came down this morning, and she was 98, and she said, 'I don't want to go do that,'" Sister McGuire said. Some showed up with outdated passports. None of them drives.

They weren't given provisional ballots because it would be impossible to get them to a motor vehicle branch and back in the 10-day time frame allotted by the law, Sister McGuire said. "You have to remember that some of these ladies don't walk well. They're in wheelchairs or on walkers or electric carts."[17]

This incident made great PR for the anti–voter identification forces—it is hard to imagine these octogenarian nuns serving as the front for an ACORN-inspired voter fraud scheme—but how many others in Indiana would be similarly disenfranchised? In fact, the nuns did not need to get an ID from the motor vehicle bureau or file a Declaration of Indigency with the county: because they were over sixty-five, they could have voted from the convent without proof of excuse, using absentee ballots.

Beyond anecdotes, evidence developed after *Crawford* showed at most a moderate problem with Indiana's new law. Professor Mike Pitts, of Indiana University's law school, and one of his students looked at all the people who filed provisional ballots in the 2008 elections in Indiana. Though the authors faced serious problems in collecting accurate data, they found that of the 2.8 million Indiana voters casting ballots in that election, 1,039 showed up at the polls without valid identification and cast provisional ballots, and of those, 137 ultimately had their ballots counted. (Note how the number of potentially disenfranchised, even if very small, swamps by many times the number of cases of proven voter impersonation fraud!)[18]

It wasn't clear how many of those 1,039 just forgot their identification, said "what the hell," and didn't bother to go back home for their ID before showing up at the county board of elections. And it wasn't clear how many lacked valid identification but did not want to or could not spend the resources to get to the county board within ten days of the election to file a Declaration of Indigency. We also don't know how many of those voters produced identification after the fact but failed to persuade authorities to count their ballots.

Pitts's numbers were limited in another important way, as he readily acknowledged. They measure only those people who actually bothered to show up to vote without identification and do not include would-be voters without identification who were deterred by the law's requirements and didn't come to the polls. If you don't have the necessary identification, and you know you won't go to the county board to fill out a Declaration of Indigency—or are unaware that this is an option—why bother to show up?

It is easy to make sloppy empirical arguments about the effect of voter ID laws on voter turnout. Indiana secretary of state Todd Rokita, a driving force behind Indiana's law, used the overall increase in voter turnout since the adoption of the requirement to argue that the law actually increased turnout. But such thinking confuses correlation with causation. No valid study I've ever seen shows that voter identification laws increase turnout.[19]

On the other side, a number of empirical studies, using data from public opinion surveys, show a modest depression of turnout, perhaps 1 to 2 percentage points, in states with tough voter identification requirements. But political scientists Robert Erikson and Lori Minnite (both of whom oppose voter ID laws) argue that there are simply not enough data to know if and how voter identification laws affect turnout. They conclude that we should be wary of empirical claims from all sides.[20]

We know even less about the new wave of voter identification laws coming before the 2012 elections, such as Texas's law, which does not allow students to use their student IDs as proof of identity to vote. Many students move to Texas for college, establish state residency, and intend to live there indefinitely—making them constitutionally entitled to vote—but do not drive and therefore do not have a Texas driver's license. If the state makes it hard for students to obtain identification cards other than drivers' licenses, the law could make a serious dent in voting by students, a group that voted heavily for Democrats in 2008.

voter ID laws not a big deal in voting   *then: surf*

When it comes to voter identification laws, then, it seems reasonable to conclude that at least some Republicans favor them because they believe they will suppress the Democratic vote, and some Democrats oppose them for the same reason. The Democratic concern is not just with people who can't get identification but also with those "what the hell" voters who will forget their ID and not go back to vote. Mario Gallegos is not a saint; he is worried that Texas's voter ID law will cost Democratic seats.

Other supporters of voter identification laws push the issue out of a genuine concern about voter fraud or because it is a "wedge issue" in elections, sometimes with racial overtones. But regardless of intent, we do not know how such laws will actually affect voter turnout.

The best argument against voter identification laws is not that they will have a large effect—they most likely won't—but that such laws are unnecessary to prevent voter fraud, and in a razor-thin election, we cannot dismiss the partisan ramifications of disenfranchising even a small number of voters for no good reason. This is especially true because election administrators may administer voter ID laws in a discriminatory manner. Further, even if the laws had no partisan effect, they still disenfranchise voters for no good reason. And the constant refrain about the need for an ID to combat fraud may undermine confidence in our elections.[21]

Chuck McGee was a retired marine who was the executive director of the New Hampshire Republican Party. His job was helping Republicans win office, and he approached it like a military campaign.

In October 2002, McGee received a flyer in the mail from the state Democratic Party with phone numbers for voters to call for a ride to the polls on Election Day. The flyer listed six phone numbers from around the state, including five Democratic Party offices and the firefighters union in the town of Manchester. McGee later testified that after reading the flyer, "I paused and thought to myself . . . I might think of an idea of disrupting those operations. . . . Eventually the idea coalesced into disrupting their phone lines. . . . [It's] military common sense that if you can't communicate, you can't plan and organize."[22]

McGee talked with Jim Tobin, the New England regional director for the

Republican National Committee, about jamming the six phone lines to make it harder for Democrats to get to the polls. As the U.S. Court of Appeals for the First Circuit later explained, "During this conversation McGee asked for the name of someone who might be able to assist in a plan of this sort. Tobin provided the name of Allen Raymond, a longtime acquaintance, who owned a business that coordinated and designed telephone services for candidates and campaigns. Tobin and McGee did not speak again, but Tobin made a telephone call to Raymond to alert Raymond to expect Mc-Gee's call."[23]

Raymond said that after the calls from Tobin and McGee, he consulted an election lawyer, Ken Gross, to find out if the proposed operation was illegal. Raymond said that Gross told him "while I don't necessarily recommend that you do the program, I don't see anything illegal about it."[24]

Gross is a well-respected member of the election law bar, a former associate general counsel to the Federal Election Commission, and the winner of an ethics award. I asked him whether he gave such advice. "I was never his lawyer and he never asked for legal advice. I don't think I even knew he had a telemarketing business. I have no recollection of telling him anything." There is nothing to substantiate Raymond's claim aside from his word. And it is hard to take the word of a person who later wrote a book called *How to Rig an Election: Confessions of a Republican Operative.*[25]

Whether or not Raymond actually got any legal advice, he agreed to arrange the phone jamming for the New Hampshire Republicans. He determined that he had to use live callers to make calls to the six numbers and have the callers hang up the phone after a few seconds; using automated calls would have been too expensive. He said he contacted a number of companies that made political calls, and a couple of operators said, "I'm not touching that." But Shaun Hansen at a call center in Idaho agreed to make the calls. Hansen charged Raymond $2,500 for the phone-jamming operation, and Raymond in turn charged the state Republican Party $15,600, a nice markup.[26]

Early on Election Day in 2002, calls and hang-ups started overwhelming the Democratic Party offices in New Hampshire and at the Manchester firefighters' union. The *Washington Post* noted that the blocked calls occurred between the "crucial morning hours" of 7:00 and 9:00 a.m., when people may have wanted to vote before going to work. The *Post* quoted Manchester firefighter Jeffery S. Duval, who was volunteering at the phone lines. "The phones were starting to ring, and as I would pick up one phone, it automatically bumped over to another line. . . . There was nobody on any of the phones. The phone lines were dead once we went to pick them up. . . . We gave the police department a call."

After about eighty-five minutes, John Dowd, chair of the New Hampshire Republican Party, pulled the plug, fearing that the operation was illegal. It doesn't appear that Dowd knew anything of the phone-jamming plan before it unfolded; McGee had apparently had forged Dowd's name on the check to Raymond to pay for it.[27]

The phone-jamming operation was a colossally bone-headed scheme. Putting aside the legality and ethics of the effort, what did the conspirators think would happen? That Democrats wouldn't alert the media to the calls? That the calls couldn't be traced back to Hansen's call center, and eventually to Raymond, and then to the state Republican Party? And what about the optics of blocking the calls to Democrats and firefighters? Democrats have been making political hay out of this episode ever since it happened.

Moreover, it is hard to know how effective the eighty-five minutes of call-blocking were in stopping Democrats who needed rides to the polls. The marquee race in New Hampshire that day pitted Republican John Sununu against Democrat Jean Shaheen for a U.S. Senate seat. Sununu won by more than nineteen thousand votes, a 51 percent to 47 percent margin. The phone-jamming could not have affected the outcome. Still, as Raymond later admitted, it could have affected races further on down the ballot, where some Democratic candidates lost by fewer than two hundred votes. Even that is iffy.[28]

The FBI investigated, and the U.S attorneys prosecuted. Raymond and McGee each pled guilty to a federal statute making it a crime to harass people over telephone lines. McGee served seven months. A judge initially sentenced Raymond to five months but then reduced the sentence to three months based on Raymond's cooperation with authorities in the prosecution of Tobin.

While Raymond paid for his own defense, the Republican National Committee defended Tobin, eventually paying the white-shoe law firm of Williams and Connolly three million dollars for the effort. Tobin was convicted of conspiracy to violate a federal statute making it a crime to make or cause "the telephone of another repeatedly or continuously to ring, with intent to harass any person at the called number." He was sentenced to ten months in jail.

Tobin appealed, and the First Circuit reversed his conviction. The appeals court did not express any doubt that Tobin put McGee and Raymond together to undertake the phone-jamming scheme. But the court said that the trial judge had incorrectly interpreted the statute for the jury by failing to require the jury to find that Tobin had the purpose to "harass" those who received the calls. Even worse for the prosecution, the appeals court said that "despite the unattractive conduct, this statute is not a close fit for what Tobin did. If the government thinks this a recurring problem, it better seek an amendment."

When the case went back to the trial court, the trial judge entered a judgment of acquittal for Tobin without letting the case go to a jury, ruling that the statute required proof that Tobin intended to emotionally upset those people who received the phone calls, and the government had no such proof to offer at trial. The First Circuit affirmed the acquittal, and Tobin stayed out of jail. The government then dropped its case against Shaun Hansen, the operator of the Idaho center. The criminal cases ended.[29]

While Tobin's criminal case was bouncing across the federal courts, the New Hampshire Democratic Party brought a civil case against the New Hampshire GOP, and liberals kept the issue alive in the press and blogosphere. Documents produced during litigation showed that in the days before the election there were numerous phone calls between Tobin and Ken Mehlman, who directed the White House political office for George W. Bush. Democrats alleged that the White House was part of the phone-jamming conspiracy, pointing to the phone calls and claiming that the decision to pay Tobin's very large legal bills was a way to keep him quiet. Mehlman denied involvement with any phone-jamming decisions and said he had lots of legitimate RNC business to discuss with Tobin in the days before the election.[30]

Democrats leading the House Judiciary Committee held a hearing on phone-jamming, alleging that that the Department of Justice dragged its feet on the investigation for political reasons. The issue fit well into the Democrats' charges of voter suppression, and there was no disputing that this was a bona fide, modern (though spectacularly failed) voter suppression effort.[31]

The New Hampshire Democrats asked for $4 million in damages in the civil suit and the Republicans said they should pay only $4,000 (the cost of renting phones for the get-out-the-vote effort on Election Day 2002). The case was settled for $135,000, less than one-twentieth of the cost of Tobin's criminal defense. But the publicity and emotional boost the case gave to Democrats was worth far more.[32]

What lessons should we draw from the 2002 phone-jamming incident? First, it validates the Democrats' point that some Republicans are willing to cross ethical and legal lines to suppress Democratic votes. But there's no persuasive evidence, despite Democratic charges, that this was a mainstream Republican operation directed by the Bush White House. There's also no evidence that the dirty trick had an impact on any statewide election, but it's hard to say whether it could have affected some very close smaller races. So unlike Republican claims of voter fraud, Democratic claims of voter suppression are sometimes real, although the extent of the problem is often exaggerated.

The good news for those who don't like voter suppression is that it was easy to catch the perpetrators and to stop the scheme. Even better news is that not everyone who engages in dirty tricks is a genius. But the bad news is that our laws are not necessarily up to the task of stopping such dirty tricks in the future. It is not clear, for example, that certain Internet-based voter suppression activities that will likely proliferate in upcoming elections (and which I will not describe here) are any better covered by existing federal statutes than the phone-jamming activities were.

There are also lower-tech dirty tricks that federal law doesn't yet cover. For example, as Professor Gilda Daniels recounted, "In 2006, on Election Day in Prince George's County, Maryland, which is predominately African American, voters arriving at the polls received a voting guide announcing that prominent African Americans had endorsed the Republican candidates, including an African American U.S. Senate candidate. The voting guide falsely suggested that prominent Maryland Democrats were endorsing Re-

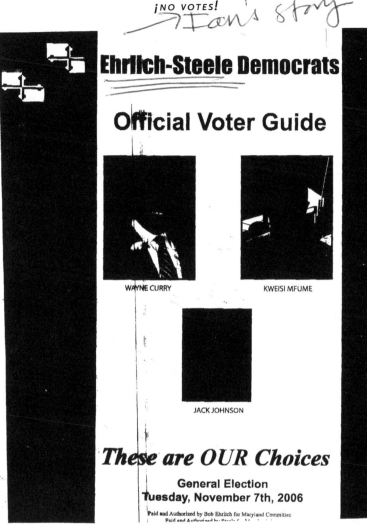

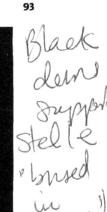

¡*NO VOTES!* 7 Ian's story

Ehrlich-Steele Democrats

Official Voter Guide

Black dem support Stelle - based in poops?

WAYNE CURRY   KWEISI MFUME

JACK JOHNSON

These are OUR Choices

General Election
Tuesday, November 7th, 2006

Paid and Authorized by Bob Ehrlich for Maryland Committee
Paid and Authorized by Steele f...

Election flyer, Prince George's County, Maryland, 2006 (Courtesy The Lawyers'
Committee for Civil Rights under Law)

publican candidates in the hotly contested gubernatorial and U.S. Senate election." Once again the practices are troubling, but it was unclear how widely
distributed the flyer was or whether anyone was fooled by it. And again, Democrats made political hay of the ham-handed attempt to fool the voters.[33]

Or consider the flyer distributed by a Republican congressional candidate's
committee and the College Republicans at the University of Wisconsin–

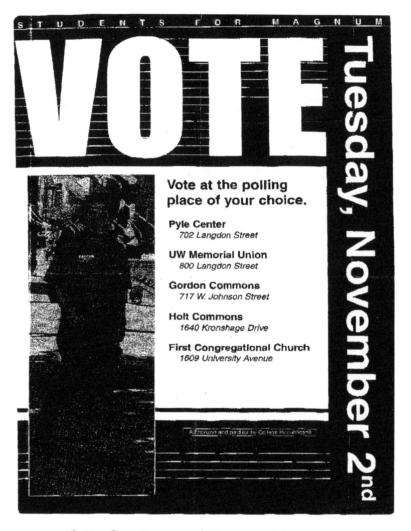

Election flyer, University of Wisconsin–Madison, 2004

Madison a few days before Election Day 2004. It invited voters to "Vote at the polling place of your choice," with a list of five possible voting centers.[34]

The flyer had a devilish appeal: *you* choose your polling place. What could be more American? The problem: if you cast your ballot at the wrong polling place, your vote could not be counted.

College Republicans eventually apologized for the flyer, calling it an "honest mistake." Congresswoman Tammy Baldwin, a Democrat, told a local newspaper that "this is either a case of utter incompetence or a purposeful effort to mislead voters on campus." In response to the incident, the university distributed information about voting at the proper polling place, and Democrats organized for the same purpose. Again, it is hard to know how many, if any, students were misled by the flyer into trying to cast a vote in the wrong polling place or gave up on voting after being sent elsewhere. Maybe the corrective measures actually boosted turnout.[35]

The chance that Congress will pass a federal law to deal with misleading materials seems slim. When he was a senator, President Obama introduced a bill in the U.S. Senate along with Senator Charles Schumer, a Democrat from New York, to make it a crime to engage in certain deceptive election practices, including providing false information about voter eligibility, polling places, or the date of the election.[36]

The bill went nowhere. Republicans were not interested in the Democrats' concerns about suppression, and there were questions about whether the law might deter legitimate campaign activity and violate the First Amendment's guarantees of freedom of speech and association. Who is to say what's "deceptive" when a flyer contains something aside from an outright lie about a clear statement of fact? Is the Latinos for Reform ad "deceptive"? Is "Vote at the polling place of your choice" actually a lie?

Whether or not the Obama approach to deceptive election practices makes sense, there's little First Amendment danger to banning the jamming of phone lines or denial-of-service attacks (computer attacks that prevent people with legitimate reasons from reaching a website) on election- or candidate-related websites with an intent to interfere with election-related activities. But there's also little reason to believe that Republicans in Congress would be interested in a bill targeted even at a narrow class of obviously dirty tricks. Not in the middle of the Voting Wars.

As things stand, not only are the outright lies (like the false endorsement in the Maryland ad) not barred by federal law, but it remains unclear after the First Circuit decision whether the New Hampshire phone jamming is illegal. *That* is a crime.

Democrats were on more solid ground in claiming voter suppression in the phone-jamming case, compared to the ineffective Latinos for Reform ad. But not all Democratic claims of voter suppression are valid. Some are exaggerated, like Congresswoman Wasserman Schultz's charge that the 2011 Florida election laws were the new Jim Crow. At most they will cause a slight depression in turnout because churches can no longer mobilize African Americans to engage in early voting on the Sunday before Election Day. This is worth fighting over, but it's not Jim Crow.[37]

Some voter suppression claims (often from the far left) are completely unsubstantiated conspiracy theory. These run the gamut from charges that Diebold voting machines contained hidden software code that flips votes for Republicans to claims that Ohio election officials in 2004 deliberately sent too few voting machines to Democratic-leaning districts to cause long lines and frustrate voting and to claims of election official fraud based on vote totals that do not match the exit polls.[38]

The group Election Defense Alliance, for example, believes that the voting machine companies have been part of a vast right-wing conspiracy to shift election results to favor Republicans, beginning in the 2004 election with John Kerry in Ohio and continuing with Tea Party victories and Republican Scott Brown's victory over Martha Coakley in the special race to replace the late Senator Edward Kennedy of Massachusetts. Almost all the voters in the Brown-Coakley race voted with number 2 pencils and optically scanned ballots, but officials ran the marked ballots through computerized equipment to tally the votes—equipment the alliance says is rigged to favor Republicans. "We cannot say with 100% certainty that the 97% of votes counted on optical scanners were subject to manipulation. But we can fairly ask: *'What evidence exists that they were not?'*"[39]

The group's leader, Jonathan Simon, promoted similar suspicions about voting equipment in the following letter posted on the group's website and submitted as a Letter to the Editor of the *New York Review of Books* (although it does not appear to have been published):

> The advent and proliferation of computerized voting has created, over the past decade, opportunities for outcome-determinative electoral manipulation on a mass scale. The vulnerabilities have been documented by top-line researchers from Princeton to Johns Hopkins to the Congressional GAO. The far right-wing pedigree of the major voting equipment vendors and servicers is no secret. And the "red shift" (vote counts to the right of exit polls, tracking polls, and hand-counts) has been consistent and pervasive in

competitive elections since 2002—including the Democratic victories of 2006 and 2008, where 11th-hour political developments turned close elections into manipulation-masking blowouts.[40]

The Election Defense Alliance is not alone. Robert F. Kennedy, Jr., in a widely read *Rolling Stone* article (which has since been removed from the magazine's website), claimed that Republicans stole the 2004 elections from Democrats in Ohio. Farhad Manjoo and others have thoroughly debunked the claims, point by point. But the conspiracy theories continue to have their adherents.[41]

On inspection, most outlandish claims of voter suppression, stolen elections, and trickery easily fall apart. Reports of flipped votes often are the result of a failure to calibrate voting machine touch screens properly (a very common problem with touch-screen technology, and one I often suffer when I use a "smart board" in a lecture hall to illustrate something to my students). Investigations of the 2004 election in Ohio by the Democrats themselves showed that long lines in Democratic areas were the result of poor planning by election officials in predicting turnout and a need to allocate scarce voting machines in times of economic austerity.[42]

As for those exit polls showing a Kerry win in Ohio, the problem was with the exit polls, not the election results. Pollsters failed to get a random sample of voters: Republicans were less likely than Democrats to answer questions and were therefore undersampled in the survey. Following 2004, news organizations revamped their approach to exit polling to make it more accurate.

We cannot say with certainty that the people advancing these outlandish conspiracy theories are simply paranoid. But we can fairly ask: "What evidence exists that they are not?"

The shaky camera phone video showed two black men standing in front of an assisted living center, which was serving as a polling place in a heavily African-American Philadelphia neighborhood. Both were dressed in paramilitary gear and berets. The shorter, bearded one was holding a nightstick. It was Election Day 2008, and Pennsylvania was a key state in the presidential battle between Barack Obama and John McCain.[43]

After local Republican Party received a call about the two men, Chris Hill, a party poll watcher, went with two lawyers to investigate. He spoke with an African-American poll watcher inside, a Democrat who was hired for the day to work for the Republican Party. According to Hill, the poll watcher did not feel safe going outside (though he later told the U.S. Commission on Civil Rights he did not feel threatened), and Hill called the police. The police filed a one-page police report about the incident and did nothing further.

Stephen Morse, a Republican party volunteer and recent University of Pennsylvania graduate, shot the video as he walked up to the entrance of the building. Morse confronted the two men, Samir Shabazz (also known by other names, including Maruse Heath) and Jerry Jackson, who were members of a fringe antiwhite and anti-Jewish group, the New Black Panthers Party.

"Hi, I'm here at 1221 Fairmont in Philadelphia, and there's a guy with a billy club right here. So, do we have any problems here? What's going on? Everything ok? I'm just making sure," Morse said as he walked up the driveway. After some cross talk, Morse and Shabbaz got into a heated discussion.

"Why y'all taking pictures?" Shabbaz asked.

"I'm here, I'm just a media guy, and that's all I'm doing."

"Who are you with?"

"I'm with the University of Pennsylvania."

"You have identification for that?"

"No, who are you with, sorry?"

"Security."

"Ok, I . . . have a poll watcher certificate, so I can go inside."

"I'm wondering why you come up taking pictures." . . .

"Ok, I mean, I think you might be a little bit intimidating that you have a stick in your hand, that's why."

"Who are you to decide?"

"I mean that's a weapon, so that's why I'm a little worried."

"Who are you to decide?"

"I mean I am a concerned citizen and I'm just worried that you might be . . ."

"So are we. That's why we are here."

New Black Panther
w/ Billy
clubs

"Ok, but you have a nightstick in your hand."

"You have a camera phone."

"I have a camera phone, which is not a weapon."

At this point, the video ends. It was the beginning of a controversy that has now lasted years. The Morse video was posted on Electionjournal.com, a website run by Mike Roman, a former director of Election Day operations at the Republican National Committee. Election Journal is "dedicated to raising public awareness of vote fraud and election irregularities," but it seems to focus only on incidents favoring Republicans' claims against Democrats.[44]

From there, the video quickly went viral (by the summer of 2011 it had over seventeen million hits on YouTube): the controversy became an obsession of the right. In one two-week period in the summer of 2010, Fox News made ninety-five references to the incident and spent more than eight hours discussing it.[45]

How did a single incident of intimidation gain such national prominence? It is not as though the New Black Panthers (no relation to the original Black Panthers Party of the 1960s) had been deploying men with clubs and sticks throughout Philadelphia, or elsewhere. There isn't a shred of evidence of systematic intimidation of voters at the polls anywhere in 2008. Shabbaz's actions were deplorable, and voters could have felt intimidated by a man with a club dressed in military gear in front of a polling place. But did the story deserve sustained national attention? If the intention was to discourage white Republican voters, standing in front of a polling place in a heavily African-American, Democratic precinct seems like the wrong approach.

dumb

The New Black Panthers story took on a life of its own because of the drumbeat about the issue from the right and the Obama Department of Justice's handling of the incident. The right tried to use the story to sully the Obama administration and Attorney General Eric Holder, the first African American to hold that position. The Justice Department made things worse by failing to effectively explain its controversial handling of the case.[46]

The Voting Section of department's Civil Rights Division plays a crucial federal role in ensuring that there is no discrimination in the conduct of elections across the United States. The Voting Rights Act of 1965 gives the Voting Section a key role in reviewing voting changes made in parts of the country with a history of discrimination, as well as bringing suits to enforce other parts of the act and other voting laws, such as the motor-voter law. Though most of the lawyers at the Department of Justice and in the Voting Section are career attorneys, the section's leadership changes with each change in presidential administration, and naturally the priorities of a Republican administration will differ from those of a Democratic administration. We saw in chapter 2 that under the George W. Bush administration, the Justice Department spent considerable effort looking for and prosecuting voter fraud, and there was great controversy over its enforcement decisions in those years. For example, Democrats criticized the department's approval of Georgia's voter identification law and the Texas decision to redraw its congressional districts in the middle of the 2000s.

Another controversy during the George W. Bush years came from the department's decision to bring suit against Ike Brown, an African-American Democratic Party leader from Noxubee County, Mississippi. The department sued Brown for violating section 2 of the Voting Rights Act, which bars certain acts of racial discrimination in voting. Among other things, the government proved that Brown manipulated an absentee ballot drive to make sure that African-American voters were targeted to turn in their ballots and that only African-American poll workers processed and counted the ballots and judged disputes.[47] The federal district court reviewing the evidence against Brown and the local Democratic Party concluded that they

> administered and manipulated the political process in ways specifically intended and designed to impair and impede participation of white voters and to dilute their votes. [Defendants] engaged in improper, and in some instances fraudulent conduct, and committed blatant violations of state election laws, for the purpose of diluting white voting strength. Although the extent of the abuses of the absentee ballot processes in Noxubee County by Brown and the NDEC is not known, the court is convinced there have been such abuses, that these abuses have been racially motivated, and that the result of these practices has been an infringement of the rights of white voters.

The Ike Brown case was controversial within the Voting Section. Some career attorneys in the department ostracized those who worked on the case, believing that the Voting Rights Act should be used primarily to help minority voters. They defended themselves during a later investigation by the department's Office of Professional Responsibility by saying that their "hostility to the *Brown* case stemmed from the fact that after five years in which no section 2 cases were brought to remedy discrimination against racial minority voters, the first one approved by the Bush administration was to benefit white voters."[48]

The New Black Panthers case thus arose in an atmosphere of division over how the department should use its prosecutorial resources. The case caught the attention of J. Christian Adams, an attorney in working the Voting Section. A former volunteer for the National Republican Lawyers Association, Adams had been hired by Bradley Schlozman, the controversial U.S. attorney who later brought the ACORN prosecutions in Missouri described in the last chapter. Unlike most career attorneys in the Voting Section, many of whom were liberal Democrats heavily committed to protecting minority voting rights, Adams was a conservative Republican.[49] He later told the *Washington Post* that he saw Morse's video of the New Black Panthers confrontation and knew he needed to act: "I thought, 'This is wrong, this is not supposed to happen in this country. . . . There are armed men in front of a polling place, and I need to find out if they violated the law, because in my mind there's a good chance that they did.'"[50]

Adams worked under section chief Christopher Coates, who had a more liberal pedigree, having worked for the ACLU before coming to the Department of Justice during the Clinton administration. But Coates faced controversy within the department for bringing the Ike Brown case. The Panthers would bring much more.

The problem for Department of Justice attorneys looking into the Panthers was that no voters were complaining of intimidation. The local district attorney's office in Philadelphia received numerous calls after the Morse video was broadcast on Fox, "but staff members realized they were from cable news viewers as far away as Florida." It was hard to make an intimidation case without intimidated voters. The state took no further action.

Without evidence to support a criminal prosecution but believing that the New Black Panthers had acted improperly, Coates and his team decided to file a civil suit under section 11(b) of the Voting Rights Act, a rarely used provision barring voter intimidation. The *Ike Brown* court, which found other voting rights violations, rejected an 11(b) charge against Brown.

In 2006, the Bush administration had declined to bring an 11(b) suit in similar circumstances. As Thomas Perez of the department testified before the U.S. Commission on Civil Rights, "The Civil Rights Division received a complaint from a national civil rights organization regarding a matter in Pima, Arizona alleging that during the 2006 election, three well-known anti-immigration advocates–one of whom was wearing a gun–allegedly intimidated Latino voters at a polling place by approaching several persons, filming them, and advocating against printing voting materials in Spanish."[51]

But the department filed an 11(b) suit against Shabbaz, Jackson, the national head of the New Black Panthers, and the organization itself. None of the defendants showed up to contest the charges; it was up to the department to then seek a default judgment. The department initially sought a nationwide injunction barring the defendants from engaging in certain intimidating activities near polling places.

At this point the Panther case became the most controversial. Coates and Adams contend that the Department of Justice, now taken over by Obama administration political appointees following the 2008 elections, pressured them to drop most of the suit against the advice of other career attorneys. They saw this pressure as evidence of a racial double standard in the new Obama department; once again, the question was whether the Voting Rights Act should be used to protect white Americans' voting rights.

Others within the department saw problems with seeking a broad injunction against the four Panther defendants, especially against the head of the organization, who disavowed the two agitators' activities. The First Amendment rights of speech and association would be implicated by an injunction barring electoral activity, and courts have rejected nationwide injunctions when there is no adequate evidence of a nationwide violation of law. Even though the Panther defendants did not fight and the department would automatically get a default judgment, the federal district judge would require the department to explain and justify the extent of the relief sought against the defendants.

Coates's bosses did not think that the court would approve a nationwide injunction, given the lack of proof of a nationwide problem and the fact that the group had posted on its website a message disavowing Shabbaz's actions. (Coates and his team did not bring this disavowal message to the attention of his superiors, which caused even more tension in the office.) Despite the default judgment, department leaders above Coates decided to drop the case against all but Shabbaz—the only defendant who had shown a weapon. The department also put a shorter time limit on the injunction against Shabbaz, to bar his poll-related activities only through 2013, and sought to limit his activities only within one hundred feet of the polls (rather than the two hundred feet originally proposed).

This was a small case—a handful of defendants involved in a minor incident at a single polling place—but by all accounts the dispute was exceedingly bitter, with thrown memos and swearing within the normally staid Department of Justice.

Coates transferred to South Carolina, and according to a *Washington Post* report, he "vented his frustration" at a good-bye lunch in Washington, D.C., "criticizing the department for failing to enforce the law 'on a non-racial basis.'" He later agreed to represent South Carolina in its suit against the department over approval of the state's voter ID law. Adams quit and became a leading opponent of the Obama Justice Department, starting his own blog on election-related issues and representing right-wing voting groups, including True the Vote. Against Department of Justice instructions, both Coates and Adams testified at hearings about the incident at the U.S. Commission on Civil Rights. [52]

The Department of Justice bungled the public-relations end of the controversy. It issued no detailed public explanation for its decisions to drop the case after a default judgment against three of the four defendants and to reduce the scope of the injunction against Shabbaz. Its refusal to let Coates and Adams testify before the commission was meant to protect internal communications, but it looked like stonewalling. (Many internal communications had been made public anyway, thanks to a Freedom of Information Act request brought by the conservative public interest group Justice Watch.) The department took no actions against Adams or Coates after they testified.

The full story came to light three years after the controversy, when Democrats on the House Judiciary Committee posted a slightly redacted version of an Office of Professional Responsibility report. The office conducted a detailed and by all appearances fair-minded investigation and released a seventy-nine-page report. It concluded that all the attorneys—both those who favored a broader injunction and those who did not—"made good faith, reasonable assessments of the facts and law, but reached different conclusions." The Department of Justice leadership, according to the report, neither engaged in professional misconduct nor exercised poor judgment, and the White House had not influenced the prosecutors' decisions. There was "no evidence that partisan politics was a motivating factor in authorizing the suit against the four defendants" and "no evidence to support allegations that decision makers were influenced by the race of the defendants, or any other improper considerations."

In contrast to the Office of Professional Responsibility's even-handed conclusions, the U.S. Commission on Civil Rights—which also released a partisan report on Florida 2000—issued 220 pages of charges and countercharges in separate opinions by the conservative and liberal commissioners. Full of invective and accusations, the opinions read as though the fate of the Republic depended on answering burning questions about who knew what when at the Department of Justice.

One commissioner, conservative Abigail Thernstrom, did not go along with the other conservative commissioners in excoriating the Justice Department under Obama (she had also dissented from the partisan Democratic report from Florida 2000). She described the whole New Black Panthers controversy as "small potatoes." The other conservative commissioners seemed to have lost perspective.[53]

Christian Adams, Hans von Spakovsky, and others continue to hawk the New Black Panther controversy, peddling the story of a Justice Department that is intent on allowing discrimination against white voters to go unpunished. They are a good match for the left-wing conspiracy theorists who think that malicious code running the machines counting optically scanned ballots is flipping votes for Republicans.

The Voting Wars continue.

4

Who Counts?

A s in 2004, the 2008 presidential election in Ohio was nasty and contentious. The race there could determine the next president. Democrats and Republicans were engaged in an all-out war over election rules, from registration to early voting to cleaning up the voter rolls. Jennifer Brunner, the Ohio secretary of state, was at the center of the storm.

Secretaries of state serve as chief elections officers in most states, and in thirty-three of them, including Ohio, the position is an elected partisan one. Ohioans elected Brunner, a Democrat, in 2006 following the controversial tenure of her Republican predecessor, Kenneth Blackwell. Democrats viewed Blackwell as evil incarnate, comparable to Florida's 2000 secretary of state, Katherine Harris. He was a conservative Republican who, like Harris in 2000, had served in 2004 as a state chair of George W. Bush's reelection committee. As secretary of state, Blackwell made several controversial decisions that many viewed as helping President Bush win Ohio in 2004. One of the most notorious, later reversed, involved a directive to reject voter registration forms that were not printed on heavy-enough paper.[1]

Brunner promised in 2006, "I will work day and night for you to restore your trust to elections so that when you are dealing with the presidential election in 2008, perhaps no one will know my name like Ken Blackwell or Katherine Harris, because the Secretary of State is doing her job."[2] But during the 2008 campaign, everyone in Ohio knew Brunner's name, as Republicans loudly accused her of being "the most partisan chief elections officer in the history of the state." The state Republican Party ran a television advertisement showing a video clip of Fox News commentator John Gibson offering a "heads up" to the people of Ohio that "someone's trying to steal your election: Jennifer Brunner." The party and Brunner eventually fought all the way to the U.S. Supreme Court over the state's election rules.

Brunner came into office with significant support from the Secretary of State Project, a nationwide political organization formed to elect Democratic secretaries of state and "to protect our election from dirty Republican tricks." The project spent at least $167,000 to support Brunner, then a significant amount for a low-profile race, making the group one of Brunner's top supporters. If a national partisan group dedicated to the election of supposedly neutral state chief elections officers appears unseemly, it is a natural consequence of having partisan officials run our elections. After *Bush v. Gore,* no one would ignore the power a secretary of state could have over a close election.[3]

Republicans lambasted the Secretary of State Project as a venture funded by liberal billionaire George Soros, even though Soros had given the group just ten thousand dollars. In June 2011, the conservative *Washington Times* ran an article about the organization called "Soros and Liberal Groups Seeking Top Election Posts in Battleground States." The only problem with the article, aside from the lack of a major role for Soros, was that the project apparently went out of business more than a year earlier. But it was a way to bash Soros and his allies, in the same way that some conservatives continued to attack ACORN even after it disbanded.[4]

The Secretary of State Project disappeared without explanation in 2010, its website evaporating like that of the American Center for Voting Rights. When Brunner decided not to run for reelection and to try (unsuccessfully) for the U.S. Senate seat being vacated by Republican George Voinovich, the project appeared to raise no money for Maryellen O'Shaughnessy, the Democrat in the 2010 secretary of state race. O'Shaughnessy was crushed by Republican Jon Husted, 53 percent to 41 percent, ensuring that a Republican would be Ohio's secretary of state during the 2012 election. Husted outraised O'Shaughnessy by a five-to-one margin, raising over five million dollars for his campaign, an astonishing amount for an Ohio secretary of state race.[5]

While the Secretary of State Project is not likely to have any influence in 2012, it seemed to have had great influence in 2006, and it apparently put more money and effort into electing Brunner in Ohio than on any other secretary of state's race. The project certainly took some credit for Brunner's victory.

Democrats defended the Secretary of State Project as a way to restore fairness after years of what they saw as Republican excesses in running elections. The Democratic candidates, the group argued, would make decisions not to help Democrats but to ensure every voter's right to a fair and impartial process.

Brunner's fairness was put to the test in 2008, when Republicans and the McCain-Palin presidential campaign launched an absentee voter drive. Absentee ballot drives are a crucial strategy for Republicans, who are more likely than Democrats to vote absentee. An Ohio elections statute sets out the rules for a voter to request an absentee ballot by mail. It says that no particular form is required to request an absentee ballot, but any request must include a statement from the voter indicating that he or she is a "qualified elector." The McCain campaign mailed out about one million forms to registered Republican voters in Ohio, which they could fill out and mail to local election officials in order to receive an absentee ballot.

As Ohio law required, the McCain campaign included on each form the statement: "I am a qualified elector and would like to receive an Absentee Ballot for the November 4, 2008 General Election." But the campaign made a minor error: it placed a check box next to the statement on the ballot, which was not required by Ohio law. Brunner took the position that if a McCain form came in without the box checked, election officials could not send out the absentee ballot because the person filling out the form was not attesting to being a "qualified elector." Republicans disagreed, and local election officials waited for Brunner to provide directions for treating requests lacking the check mark.

like
car

Brunner had to make a choice. In terms of conducting a fair election, there was no good reason for her to order counties to reject unchecked absentee ballot request cards. Did anyone really believe that a voter who did not check that box was in fact *not* a qualified elector but was willing to commit a felony by requesting an absentee ballot to which he or she was not entitled? Yet as a loyal Democrat, Brunner had a good *political* reason not to accept those ballot application forms: it could mean fewer Republican votes on Election Day, as voters who requested but never received absentee ballots might decide to stay home, perhaps worrying that they would not be permitted to vote at a precinct on Election Day after having requested an absentee ballot.

Brunner made the choice that could help her party, instructing county boards of elections to reject applications with unchecked boxes. Republicans sued. The case went to the Ohio Supreme Court, with all Republican justices, which unanimously ruled against Brunner.[6]

The court slapped down the secretary's argument against accepting those ballot applications. "No vital public purpose or public interest is served by rejecting electors' applications for absentee ballots because of an unmarked check box next to a qualified-elector statement. There is also no evidence of fraud. As [the Republicans] persuasively assert, the 'only reason to complete the form was to obtain an absentee ballot for the November 4, 2008 election,' and signing it necessarily indicated that the applicant represented, 'I am a qualified elector and would like to receive an Absentee Ballot for the November 4, 2008 General Election,' regardless of whether the box next to the statement was marked."

The court also said that it had a responsibility to "liberally construe" election statutes consistent with the right to vote. As we saw in chapter 1, this Democracy Canon rule for interpreting election statutes had existed for more than a century and had been relied on by scores of state courts in hundreds of cases. It is a sensible principle: there is often more than one way to read technical legal language in an election statute. When such a statute has two reasonable interpretations, one that disenfranchises voters and one that gives them an effective vote, the enfranchising interpretation must be preferred.

As a matter of good policy, Brunner should have chosen the enfranchis-

[handwritten annotations in margins: "Demo better Brunner partisan", "no better than Republican election officials", "DH", "5 DAY"]

ing interpretation of the Ohio absentee ballot request statute, but she didn't. We don't know for certain what motivated her. She could well have put her party allegiance ahead of her responsibility to help voters exercise the franchise. If so, that's troubling.

To be charitable, we could say that her party allegiance unconsciously colored her view of the dispute. We saw this phenomenon in Florida, too: had the candidates' positions been reversed, people wonder how the U.S. Supreme Court would have decided *Gore v. Bush*, and it is a good question. When there are multiple ways to decide a close legal question, even people striving hard for objectivity may be subtly affected by their political views.

Legal scholar Cass Sunstein noticed a correlation, even in academic writing, about the legal issues in *Bush v. Gore*, between the writer's political beliefs and his or her views of the election law: liberals analyzing the case tended to attack the decision and conservatives tended to support it. Sunstein attributed this not to conscious bias but to psychological factors that lead us to reach conclusions in line with our preexisting beliefs.[7]

Objectivity is a point I constantly struggle with as I analyze disputes in the Voting Wars. Readers of this book need to be self-reflective, too. I suspect that many who read this chapter come in as either skeptical of Brunner's motives (because she's a Democrat) or skeptical of Blackwell's motives (because he's a Republican). And I suspect that this skepticism correlates very nicely with the reader's own politics. I hope that by the time you finish this chapter, you will be more suspicious of the motives of *both* Democratic *and* Republican election officials.

All of Brunner's other decisions placed her on the side of enfranchising voters. None of the other controversies over her decisions, however, put her in the same position as she was concerning the McCain absentee ballot applications: having to choose between the interests of party and the interests of enfranchising voters. On that crucial test, she failed.

During the 2008 presidential election, Brunner tangled with Ohio Republicans in two other major disputes. One involved new voters and voters who had moved. Ohio required these voters to register thirty days before an election if they wanted to vote in that election. The state also had an "early voting" program allowing voters to cast their votes up to thirty-five days before Election Day. Putting these two laws together potentially created a five-day window of time in which someone could register to vote and cast an early ballot simultaneously.[8]

Ohio Democrats saw this as a great opportunity. It is tough to get new voters registered and then to get them to show up on Election Day. Get-out-the-vote efforts are expensive and difficult, especially with new voters. Letting them register and vote at the same time could help put Obama over the top in Ohio. (In the end, Obama won the state by about two hundred thousand votes, with a little over thirteen thousand new voters taking advantage of registering and voting in the five-day window.)[9]

Republicans opposed allowing the new voters to use the five-day window, calling it an opportunity for fraud. They said the window could allow unqualified electors, including the homeless and college students, to show up and cast fraudulent ballots. As a matter of interpreting Ohio election statutes, Republicans argued that the five-day window violated Ohio law because it would allow someone to vote before they had been registered for a full thirty days before voting.

Brunner issued a directive to county boards of elections throughout Ohio that they were required to accept registrations and votes cast in the five-day window. Three Republican counties received legal advice that they should not follow Brunner's directive, and the case ended up before the Ohio Supreme Court.

On a five-to-two vote, the Ohio Supreme Court sided with Brunner. The court said that Brunner's interpretation to allow voting during the five-day window was reasonable and supported by the Democracy Canon. As to the requirement that voters be registered thirty days before the election, the court said that a ballot submitted early was not actually counted until Election Day, so the thirty-day requirement was not violated. Last, the court noted flatly that "neither college students nor homeless people are per se ineligible to vote." The court might have added that the early voting period left time for elections boards to investigate any early voter they suspected of registering or voting illegally.

Brunner's other major dispute with Republicans made it to the U.S. Supreme Court. *Ohio Republican Party v. Brunner* started off as a federal court challenge to the Ohio five-day window dispute but quickly morphed into

BRUNNER 5DAY → voter roll DMV

something else entirely: whether Brunner was handling the state's list of voters in a way consistent with federal law. The story is complicated, but it lays bare the convoluted, contradictory, partisan, decentralized mess our election systems have become and illustrates how the courts keep getting dragged into the morass.[10]

Though Brunner, as Ohio's secretary of state, was also the state's chief elections officer, that title is misleading. In federal elections, the secretary shares power with local elections boards and the federal government. We do not have a single entity that is in charge of our federal elections from start to finish, even within each state.

The federal role in federal elections is limited but important. Congress added to that role in significant ways in 2002 when it passed the Help America Vote Act. The act was a compromise between Democrats concerned about voter access and Republicans concerned about voter fraud, and as in many such compromises, much of what the sides could not agree to was simply fudged through omissions or unclear language.

Ohio Republican Party v. Brunner concerned a technical provision in the Help America Vote Act that says that the "chief state election official and the official responsible for the State motor vehicle authority of a State shall enter into an agreement to match information in the database of the statewide voter registration system with information in the database of the motor vehicle authority to the extent required to enable each such official to verify the accuracy of the information provided on applications for voter registration." Despite this requirement, Brunner resisted sharing mismatch information with county officials, because she trusted neither the information nor the officials.

Blackwell had produced lists of mismatched names by cross-referencing the motor vehicle and voter registration records and had sent lists of such mismatches to county election officials; Brunner stopped this program. She continued, as required by the act, to share information with the Ohio Bureau of Motor Vehicles, and the statewide voter registration database did contain information about whether each name in the voter database matched a name in the motor vehicle records. But she did not provide the information in an easy-to-use list for county officials, and there was no way to query the database about the status of particular voters.

Her reason for not producing a mismatch list for counties was simple:

the matching system was likely to lead to many "false positives"—valid voters being mislabeled as a mismatch because of errors in the database (such
as not matching a "James" Smith with a "Jim" Smith or input errors by
state workers). A Brennan Center amicus brief filed in the case explained
that "when the database match is conducted, anywhere from 15 to 30 percent of registered voters will fail to match." The ACLU submitted an amicus brief offering evidence that mismatch data "bar non-white voters more
frequently than white voters." Both the voter database and motor vehicle
database were riddled with errors, and putting the two together was not
likely to lead to a better result.

Brunner feared that some county boards of election would use the faulty
mismatch information to purge legitimate voters from the list. She had no
power to require county election officials to double-check information on
the list, to listen to her advice not to rely on the list, or to attempt to make
sure that legitimate voters were not disenfranchised.

Those defending the production of the mismatch list said that false positives were no big deal, because any voter mistakenly removed from the
voter rolls could simply cast a "provisional ballot." Under the Help America
Vote Act, voters who show up at the polls but whose names do not appear
on a valid voter list have the right to one of these ballots. But the act does
not direct state or local election officials to conduct any particular investigation to determine whether the provisional ballot should be counted. The
question of voter eligibility is left to individual boards. Anyone who wants
his or her vote to count should avoid casting a provisional ballot; you don't
know how election officials will handle them.

The Ohio Republican Party sued to require Brunner to make the mismatch list available to county election officials. They said that her interpretation of the statute would make the HAVA matching requirement mean-
ingless, because she was just sitting on the information produced by the
matching process, not using it "to verify the accuracy of the information
provided on applications for voter registration."

In a lawsuit filed in late September 2008—a crunch time for the secretary's office—the party demanded that Brunner restart the computer matching program. She told the court that it would be a burden to reprogram the
computers to produce the mismatch list, but apparently her staff testified

Brunner OH Mismatch

motor-voter law

that the reprogramming could be done in two or three days. Brunner's real concern appeared to be not the administrative burden of reprogramming the computer but the quality of the data that would be generated.

Reprogramming raised another legal complication. Under the federal motor-voter law, in a provision incorporated into the Help America Vote Act, "any program the purpose of which is to systematically remove the names of ineligible voters from the official list of eligible voters" must be completed at least ninety days before an election. So if Brunner, so close to the election, provided mismatch data that county election officials then used to purge voters, she could have been violating the motor-voter law.

A federal district court judge, George C. Smith, an appointee of Ronald Reagan, issued a temporary restraining order requiring Brunner to reprogram her department's computers to provide the mismatch lists to the counties. Sweeping away her objections that Congress did not give entities such as the Ohio Republican Party a right to sue for violation of the mismatch provision of the act, Smith wrote that it was "clear" that Brunner was in violation of the HAVA requirement. Further, relying on two newspaper articles from Ohio focusing on alleged voter registration fraud by ACORN, the court said that the potential for fraud made reprogramming an urgent need.

Brunner immediately sought to overturn Judge Smith's order. A panel of three judges from the U.S. Court of Appeals for the Sixth Circuit, on a two-to-one vote, reversed the order. The court majority, made up of two Democrats (one a visiting judge from the Eighth Circuit), expressed doubt that the party was even allowed to seek federal court relief for this type of HAVA violation but said that even if the party could seek such relief, there was no violation.

In her majority opinion, Judge Karen Nelson Moore wrote that a plain reading of the statute required only that the secretary and head of the motor vehicle bureau agree to match data between their databases: the statute did not require that anything be done with the data. Further, she concluded, the remedy demanded by the Ohio Republican Party—producing a mismatch list for the counties—would violate the motor-voter law.

Finally, the majority dismissed the district court's concerns about ACORN-related voter fraud: "What is striking about the district court's decision is the complete lack of factfinding. The district court stressed that the public, as well as ORP [Ohio Republican Party], would be injured by voter fraud if a TRO [temporary restraining order] were not granted. This kind of inquiry demands that extensive factfinding. However, rather than undertake such factfinding, the district court, citing two newspaper articles, merely assumed that there will be wide-spread voter fraud absent the issuing of a TRO."

Judge Richard Allen Griffin, a George W. Bush appointee, dissented in a strong opinion that began: "Defendant Ohio Secretary of State Jennifer Bruner's lack of concern for the integrity of the election process is astounding and deeply disturbing." In a dissent that mostly consisted of appending and endorsing the district court judge's initial opinion granting the temporary restraining order, Judge Griffin wrote that the panel should not have even issued a decision, because the Republicans had filed a petition for consideration of the case before all of the judges of the Sixth Circuit.

The acrimony continued when the entire Sixth Circuit heard the appeal of the case en banc—that is, in a rehearing before all the judges on the court. The Sixth Circuit divided almost perfectly along party lines, with judges appointed by a Republican president voting to reinstate the temporary restraining order and the Democratic-appointed judges voting against the order. The Republican side won.[11]

The deep and bitter dispute about the merits of the case sometimes gave way to personal sniping. Some of the judges in the en banc majority criticized the original three-judge panel for overturning the temporary restraining order while the en banc petition was already pending. One of the Democratic-appointed judges in turn criticized a Republican-appointed judge for not recusing herself while her husband ran for reelection as a Republican candidate for the Ohio House of Representatives.

On the merits, the judges disagreed strongly over the need for the temporary restraining order and over whether Brunner's conduct deserved praise or condemnation. Judge Jeffrey Sutton, a leading conservative judge and a George W. Bush appointee, wrote the lead opinion supporting the district court's grant of the temporary restraining order. He stressed the anti-fraud purposes of the act, held that Congress granted entities such as the Ohio Republican Party the right to sue to enforce the mismatch provision, and interpreted the provision to require Brunner to reprogram the database computers to create a mismatch list that would have to be sent to the counties.

Judge Moore, who had written the majority opinion for the original three-judge panel, also wrote the leading dissent for the en banc court. She disagreed with just about every point made by Judge Sutton. This was not an appropriate case, she wrote, for en banc review under the Sixth Circuit's standards; the Ohio Republican Party did not have a right to sue for a HAVA violation (the statute allowed only the Department of Justice to do so); the plain text of the act did not require a state's chief elections officer to prepare a list of mismatches for use by the county officials; and any alleged harm from voter fraud was unsupported speculation that did not justify producing inaccurate voting lists.

The debate on the Sixth Circuit mirrored the public debate on these issues. The Republican judges were worried about voter fraud and ruled in a way that would minimize that danger even if it meant disenfranchising some voters. The Democratic judges were skeptical of the voter fraud claims and voted against ordering Brunner to take steps that could disenfranchise voters, even if it raised the potential for fraud by new voters.

So strong were these countervailing instincts that judges seemed to abandon their usual jurisprudential philosophies. Generally speaking, conservative judges are much more hesitant than liberal judges to read federal statutes expansively so as to give individuals a right to sue for their violation—what lawyers call "a private right of action." (In 2001, as a private lawyer, Judge Sutton had argued in the United States Supreme Court against an expansive reading of the "private right of action" doctrine.) Liberals are much more willing to interpret statutes expansively, consistent with their overall purposes; conservatives tend to favor narrower more "textual" readings that adhere to what they perceive to be the "plain meaning" of the statute.[12]

In *Ohio Republican Party v. Brunner,* however, the Republican judges read the Help America Vote Act broadly to create a private right of action and interpreted its matching provision well beyond the plain meaning of the text, which on its face required no more than that the chief elections officer engage in a matching exercise. The Democratic judges read the act narrowly, contending that Republicans had no right to sue, and they read the statute in a narrow, textual way. The subtle psychological forces that Cass Sunstein identified in *Bush v. Gore* seemed to be at work once again.

After the loss before the entire Sixth Circuit, Brunner sought emergency relief from Justice Stevens of the Supreme Court (the justice who handled emergency appeals from the Sixth Circuit), and Justice Stevens sent the question to the entire Supreme Court. In a short, unsigned opinion, the Court unanimously reversed the Sixth Circuit, saying it was very unlikely that Congress had authorized entities such as the Ohio Republican Party to sue for violation of HAVA's matching requirement. On that refreshing note of unanimity—the Supreme Court somehow managed to avoid the partisan divide of the Sixth Circuit—the case went away as an issue in the 2008 election. Obama's huge margin of victory in Ohio in 2008 eliminated any chance for the Republicans to make an issue out of Brunner's refusal to share the mismatch data.

Bob Bennett, the head of the Ohio Republican Party, had clashed with Brunner well before the 2008 controversy. In addition to sitting as chair of the state party, Bennett was one of four members—two Republicans, two Democrats—of the Cuyahoga County Board of Elections.

Cuyahoga is the most populous county in Ohio, and it includes the Democratic stronghold of Cleveland. The decentralized nature of our election system meant that the Cuyahoga board had more power over who could vote and how votes would be counted than either the Ohio secretary of state or the federal government. The county chose the voting machines, distributed registration materials, administered the counting, organized and trained the poll workers, resolved disputes over provisional ballots, and took all the other steps necessary to allow the area's voters to cast their ballots and to produce final results. Federal law and the secretary of state's office constrained some of its actions, but on a day-to-day level, the board and its staff ran the show.

For decades, Cuyahoga conducted its elections incompetently.

A remarkable 2007 commentary by Edward B. Foley, director of the indispensable Election Law @ Moritz program at the Ohio State University, supported Brunner's unusual decision to seek the removal of all four members of the Cuyahoga board, including Bennett. Foley is one of the most fair-minded, even-tempered people you could ever meet. Cautious, lawyerly, and strictly nonpartisan on election law issues—he was recently appointed reporter for the prestigious American Law Institute's new project on election law—he would not lightly call for an entire elections board to resign.[13]

Foley traced the Cuyahoga board's incompetence back to at least 1972, when sixteen polling places did not open on Election Day for the presidential primaries and a court had to order an additional day of voting. He then fast-forwarded to 2004, when two Cuyahoga employees rigged a recount of the presidential election ballots cast in the county because they didn't want to bother conducting it. "The fact that their motive apparently was laziness, rather than partisanship, does not sufficiently allay concerns about the integrity of vote counting in that county." The workers each went to jail for eighteen months.

Things got even worse in 2006.

The severe problems of the May 2006 primary are too numerous to detail here, but among the most serious are the loss of memory cards electronically recording vote totals from fourteen percent of the county's precincts and spoiled paper records for ten percent of the county's electronic votes. Even after all the attention devoted to fixing problems of this sort before the November 2006 general election, major problems persisted. According to a Plain Dealer report, almost 12,000 ballots were cast in Cuyahoga County on November 7 by individuals who did not sign the poll books and whose eligibility to vote apparently was never properly verified by precinct officials, despite the requirements of state law that mandate these procedures. The most likely explanation for this breach of the rules is that substantial confusion occurred at these polling places, and poll workers allowed the individuals in question to bypass the check-in line and go straight to voting machines. Just imagine the nightmare, however, if one of the prominent statewide races last year—for example, the one between Mark Dann and Betty Montgomery for Attorney General—had turned out close enough that these 12,000 ballots provided a basis for contesting the result.

The 2006 fiasco led the board to appoint a set of independent commissioners, including election law professor Candice Hoke, to examine the problems and propose solutions. The commission produced a detailed (and in some respects scathing) 398-page report. The introduction was understated: "Unquestionably, the County's elections must improve and improve quickly."[14]

Brunner vs Bennett

But things did not improve quickly, and in 2007 Brunner called for the Cuyahoga elections board members to step down. Three of the four resigned, but not Bennett, who accused Brunner of a power grab. (Brunner would maintain authority over the county's elections until a new board could be appointed, and some feared she would keep that authority through the 2008 elections.) Brunner suspended Bennett, accusing him of pressuring election staff to hire a public relations firm to support the board.

When Brunner attempted to bring Bennett before an administrative hearing to assess whether he should be removed for cause, he sued in state court to block the hearing. Unfortunately for Bennett, his case got assigned to Judge John Connor in Franklin County, a Democratic judge whom Bennett had earlier criticized for being too lenient in sentencing a child molester. Connor was a frequent target of the far right: in 2006 he had been ambushed by a Fox producer for the Bill O'Reilly show asking questions about the supposed leniency of Connor's criminal sentences.[15]

Connor denied the motion to block the administrative hearing, saying that he could not interfere with Brunner's duty to make sure that elections were being run properly. "I can almost take judicial notice of the mess in Cuyahoga County. . . . I'm not saying Mr. Bennett is responsible for that."

After a few postponements of the hearing, Bennett agreed to resign, and both parties dropped their complaints. He told a local newspaper: "I recognize that continuing to serve on the board with the current adverse relationship with the Secretary of State was not in the public interest. . . . And she came to understand that, while there had been problems in the past, there was no wrongdoing by the board. The Secretary of State wants to create the board in her own image, and she will have that opportunity."[16]

Democrats and Republicans each picked two members for the board, with the secretary of state serving as the tie-breaker, if necessary. It was a bipartisan model of election administration, a step above the one-party rule prevalent in Florida county election boards but nothing like the nonpartisan election administration in most other mature democracies.

The new board came in just a week before primary elections. A press release from Brunner's office noted the tall order facing the board: "Top items on the new board's agenda include managing a successful primary election Tuesday, hiring a permanent director and deputy director and reviewing the county's voting systems for changes needed for the voter turn-out expected in next year's presidential election."[17]

Problems persisted even under the new board, as it moved to phase in optical scan voting machines. This was the third major voting system in three election cycles: first punch cards, then electronic voting equipment (which Brunner successfully fought to have replaced), and now optical scan systems.[18] Voters record their choices on a paper ballot using a pencil on a card, which is then fed into the optical scan machines. Just days before the 2010 elections, 10 percent of these machines failed an important test. Cuyahoga still had a long way to go.[19]

Cuyahoga's problems were far from unique. As Heather Gerken explained in her proposal to rank states by their ability to fairly administer elections, there is a wide variation in competence, fairness, resources, and accuracy across the country in how we run our elections. Decentralization and partisanship, as well as budget cutbacks, complicate reform efforts.[20]

Many local election administrators do a good job, especially in tight budget times. But we should not think of Cuyahoga as some kind of crazy outlier. Remember from this book's introduction Kathy Nickolaus, the Waukesha County, Wisconsin, election official who kept Election Day vote totals on her personal laptop and forgot to include an entire city's vote totals in a nationally watched race for state supreme court justice. When she figured out that she had omitted the city's results, her amended returns swung the race from the Democrat to the Republican. Consider, too, the testimony of a pollworker in a recent Hamilton County, Ohio, dispute who sent voters to the wrong voting precinct because he could not understand that "798" was an even, not an odd, number.

What an odd way to run our elections. In the end, so much of how elections are handled is just out of the control of the federal government or even each state's "chief" elections officer. In Ohio, as elsewhere, the secretary of state is hardly the elections czar: he or she has limited control over how counties run the election or even what equipment they use. The secretary has to follow unclear federal and state statutes, some of which contradict one another. This role is supervised by state and federal courts, which can impose shifting rules as elections approach and cases work their way through the appeals process. And because the secretary is chosen in a partisan election, the other side views his or her every step with suspicion, despite ef-

How loose fed'l state guidelines are

forts to do the best possible job of administering the election. Party pressures will at least tempt the secretary to act for his or her party, and not necessarily for the voters.

Ken Blackwell, who held the secretary of state job in Ohio before Brunner, was an even more controversial figure than Brunner turned out to be. Blackwell made a series of decisions about how to run the 2004 Ohio election, all of which seemed to benefit Republicans. Again, we can question whether he acted out of partisan motives, but the trend of his decisions is unmistakable: they made it harder for new voters to register and cast a ballot that would be counted.

In 2005, Ohio State University law professor Dan Tokaji, one of the country's leading experts on the Help America Vote Act and election law, summarized the most important of Blackwell's controversial decisions in the lead-up to the George W. Bush–John Kerry contest.

Foremost among the secretary of state's decisions that provoked criticism were: (1) forbidding individuals from even receiving a provisional ballot unless their eligibility to vote within the precinct could be confirmed; (2) the refusal to provide provisional ballots to voters who had requested but claimed not to have received absentee ballots; (3) declining to count provisional ballots by voters subject to HAVA's ID requirement, unless they provided their identifying number or acceptable documentation by the time the polls closed; (4) the initial decision to allow both pre-election challenges and election day challenges; (5) the requirement that voter registration forms be rejected if certain information was omitted; and (6) the rejection of registration forms on less than eighty-pound paper weight.[21]

Tokaji called Blackwell's initial refusal to accept photocopied registration forms because of the weight of the paper "one of the oddest controversies to emerge anywhere in the country in the weeks leading up to Election 2004." Facing public controversy, Blackwell backed down. Besides lacking any plausible reason (the lighter paper was not going to disintegrate before the information could be entered into Ohio's voter registration database), Blackwell's decision was a terrible public relations move. It confirmed Democrats' worst fears about him.

Each of the six decisions flagged by Tokaji has its own fascinating story, but I will focus on just one of them, another arcane but important fill-out-the-forms story.

Ohio's voter registration form included a "Box 10," in which voters had to write in either their state driver's license number or the last four digits of their Social Security number. Election officials needed this information so that they could enter it in the statewide database of voters that the HAVA law required each state to create.

The Help America Vote Act says that if a voter does not have a driver's license or a Social Security number, the state must create a unique voter identification number to be used in the state voter registration database. But state officials can refuse a registration form if the voter *has* a license or Social Security information but does not provide it. Further, the act says that first-time voters who registered by mail but do not have a driver's license or Social Security number must show identification before they can vote. This requirement does not apply to first-time voters who registered in person. So the act treats first-time voters who registered by mail tougher than in-person registrants.

The problem arose over how to treat voters who turned in registration forms with Box 10 left blank. Was the box left blank because the voter did not have a driver's license or Social Security number? Or because the voter refused or forgot to fill it in? Remember, state officials could reject the registration form only if the voter had one of the two identification numbers but would not share it.

Even though HAVA treats voters who register by mail worse than those who register in person (the mail-in registrants must show identification the first time they vote in person), Blackwell issued rules that reversed these priorities: he instructed county boards to accept registrations from mail-in voters who left Box 10 blank, and these voters were simply asked to provide the information, if they had it, when they showed up to vote. But he instructed boards to reject forms from voters whose registration forms were hand delivered (coming from a third party registration group or from a public library or motor vehicle office) with the Box 10 information left blank. Voters had to write "None" on these handed-in registration forms to have them accepted, but as Tokaji explained, there was "no guarantee that those accepting registration forms at public libraries, motor vehicle offices, or even boards of election [would] instruct voters lacking a Social Security or driver's license number to write in 'None.'" Blackwell likely did this because this interpretation of the Box 10 rule could limit county boards in accepting registration forms from groups such as ACORN and the League of Women Voters.

Democrats sued to get Blackwell to reverse his decision on Box 10 for handed-in registration forms, but the suit came too late: a federal district court said that it was so close to the election that there was nothing a court could do even if it agreed that Blackwell's directive was unlawful. It is hard to know how many voters' registration forms were dumped because the voters failed to fill in Box 10.[22]

Issues like this are completely arcane, and for this reason they often escape the attention of journalists and the public—and sometimes even of party insiders (think of the Republicans in 2008 who missed Brunner's change in the procedures for flagging database mismatches until late in the campaign). But the Box 10 controversy shows how technical rules can be manipulated for partisan gain, or if not purposefully manipulated, then inadvertently changed with surprising consequences. If someone like Blackwell *wanted* to manipulate election rules for partisan gain, there were ample opportunities.

Jon Husted became the Ohio secretary of state in 2010, following Blackwell's and Brunner's terms. We do not know yet if he will be the lightning rod for criticism that his predecessors turned out to be, but an early sign was hopeful.

Ohio, with a Republican legislature and Republican governor, adopted new election legislation in 2011. The legislation made a number of changes to the state's election rules, including shortening the early voting period for the 2012 election to remove the last Sunday before Election Day and to eliminate that five-day window for same-day registration and voting. Critics saw this as a move to prevent Democrats from organizing early voting caravans and buses from African-American churches that Sunday.[23]

Ohio legislators also considered a new voter identification requirement,

and the debate over the provision saw the usual divide between Republicans who favored the law and Democrats who opposed it. But the newly elected Republican Husted deviated from the script. He opposed the measure, issuing a statement one would have expected from a Democrat: "I want to be perfectly clear, when I began working with the General Assembly to improve Ohio's elections system it was never my intent to reject valid votes. I would rather have no bill than one with a rigid photo identification provision that does little to protect against fraud and excludes legally registered voters' ballots from counting." Husted's opposition scuttled the identification provision, at least temporarily.[24]

A few days later, the Ohio House of Representatives amended Ohio's new voting law to eliminate a provision Husted strongly favored, allowing for online voter registration. It was unclear if the decision was revenge for Husted's heresy on voter identification.[25]

Legislative supporters of the bill threatened to reintroduce the voter identification law as a stand-alone bill, and Democrats, led by former secretary Brunner, circulated referendum petitions to repeal parts of the new law, which they said would make it harder for people to register and vote. Meanwhile some Democrats saw Husted's actions on voter identification as a cynical ploy to play to the middle, and they saw a Republican bias in other actions of his, such as his decision to bar counties such as Cuyahoga from sending absentee ballot request forms to all county voters at the board's expense. Husted said this was necessary to ensure equal protection—that voters in all counties had the same chance to vote using absentee ballots. Some Democrats called it voter suppression. The issue was settled when the state agreed to send the applications to all voters in the state.[26]

The Voting Wars in Ohio will continue, regardless of whether Husted can remain above the partisan fray.

✔

Ray Martinez and Buster Soaries had little in common. Martinez was born in the south Texas town of Alice, famous in the election law world for Lyndon Johnson's notorious ballot-box stuffing in 1948. Johnson squeaked by in a U.S. Senate runoff thanks to two hundred late-arriving extra votes cast in Alice in the infamous ballot box 13. "The votes for Johnson," according to an article in *Texas Monthly,* "were written in the same handwriting, signed in the same ink, and cast in alphabetical order."[27]

Martinez has spent his life working in public policy circles on the Democratic side. A lawyer by training, he has served as a staffer in the Clinton White House, the Texas House of Representatives, the Texas Senate, and the Texas attorney general's office. Soft-spoken, thoughtful, and cautious, he was one of the first four commissioners appointed to serve on the United States Election Assistance Commission, created by Congress as part of the Help America Vote Act to dole out money for voting machine upgrades, serve as a clearinghouse for information on running elections, and recommend best practices for state and local election officials.

The Reverend DeForest "Buster" Soaries is a Baptist minister and a motivational speaker. Born in New York and raised in New Jersey, Soaries was the secretary of state for New Jersey appointed by Republican governor Christine Todd Whitman, and he ran unsuccessfully as a Republican candidate for Congress. A New Jersey political blog called him "the state's most visible Republican African-American clergyman," and he is anything but quiet: in a 1995 *New York Times* profile, he did not disagree with local papers' description of him as "an unabashed self-promoter whose ego matches his desire to help people." He was another of the first four election assistance commissioners.[28]

Martinez and Soaries eventually shared something else: despair over the commission and the promise of federal election reform.

Soaries told *Rolling Stone* why he resigned from the commission before his term expired: "It was probably the worst experience of my life. I found that there is very little interest in Washington for true election reform. That neither the White House nor either house of the Congress seems to be as committed to guaranteeing democratic participation in this country as we seem to be in other countries. It's an embarrassment that we don't have a broad enough consensus among political leaders that true reform should take place. I could count the members of Congress on one hand that took these issues seriously."[29]

Martinez, more circumspect, described his first year at the commission as "what it must feel like to be piloting an airplane, deep in a thick fog of clouds, in zero visibility, with no instrument panel to guide your direction

ming to kill the commission before the start

and no fuel gauge to tell you how much time you have left in the air." He said the "lowest point" of his tenure was when the National Associations of Secretaries of State called on Congress to disband the Election Assistance Commission—before the agency even had a chance to do anything. A survey of local election officials revealed similarly dismal views of the commission.[30]

Shortly before he followed Soaries in resigning from the commission—for family reasons—Martinez issued a statement forecasting its politicized future. He feared the emergence of "an overly partisan federal agency that is more prone to deadlock than to fulfilling its ultimate and, in my view, most important promise of serving as a national clearinghouse and creating the 'gold standard' in national voting system standards and certification."[31]

Ask anyone on the street what he or she thinks about the job the EAC is doing and you are bound to get one answer: Who?

And that's the way Congress designed it. When legislators were writing the HAVA legislation in the wake of the Florida 2000 fiasco, one key battle was over whether there should be a federal agency to oversee federal elections and what role it should have. State and local officials opposed a major federal role, and they won the battle against good government groups who wanted significant federal oversight.

Leonard Shambon, one of the key staffers behind the drafting of HAVA, explained that "the EAC was designed to have as little regulatory power as possible. It has an even number of Members (four), any Commission action requires the approval of three Members (not a majority of sitting Members) . . . , and for the most part it cannot 'issue any rule, promulgate any regulation, or take any other action' imposing a requirement on any state or unit of local government."[32] The commission was meant to do little more than fund voting machine upgrades and provide guidance and a public forum for advocating good election reform practices. It was not designed to threaten state and local officials' power to run elections. Yet they viewed it as a major bureaucratic competitor.

If the main divide we've seen so far in the Voting Wars has been between Democrats and Republicans, there's another deep divide, more hidden from public view: between state and local elected officials over who controls

Commission's fate undecided

the election process. We have already seen this in Cuyahoga County, Ohio, and state-local election administration battles are fairly common across the country, especially now that the Help America Vote Act strengthened states with rules such as the one mandating a single state database of registered voters.

Yet these rivals had a common enemy in the Election Assistance Commission. The National Associations of Secretaries of State called on Congress to disband the commission in 2005, and it has periodically repeated this demand, with support from both Republican and Democratic secretaries of state. The divide has now hit Congress. In 2011, the House voted to abolish the commission. The bill, which also would have eliminated voluntary public funding for presidential elections, passed with no Democratic votes and only one Republican vote opposed. Although the bill was not expected to be taken up by the Senate, the commission's future is uncertain.[33]

The Election Assistance Commission was hobbled from the start. Besides giving it anemic authority, Congress did not provide adequate funding, and for a while the commission had to borrow office space from the Federal Election Commission. With two Democratic commissioners and two Republicans, each political party had an incentive to nominate candidates who would toe the party line—lest a rogue commissioner take some action that could give the other party a future advantage. Somehow, Martinez and Soaries made it through the vetting, giving the the commission two fair-minded, independent commissioners for a time. Before they left, it looked as if the commission could take at least some baby steps toward improving our elections.

Soon enough, though, the commission got caught in the Voting Wars. You would not think that its milquetoast function as a "clearinghouse" for information could get it into trouble, but that's exactly what happened. It hired two researchers, Tova Wang, a liberal who had written extensively on election issues, and Job Serebrov, a Republican election lawyer from Arkansas, to coauthor a report on voter fraud and intimidation and to suggest topics for future research.

Wang and Serebrov worked with an advisory group for a year and produced a draft report. The commission sat on the report for six months. Then it issued its own report—which it said was based on the Wang-Serebrov study—but was not the Wang-Serebrov draft and reached different conclusions.

Someone leaked the draft report to the *New York Times*, which ran a front-page story, "U.S. Panel Is Said to Alter Finding on Voter Fraud." The *Times* explained one of the key alterations, "Though the original report said that among experts 'there is widespread but not unanimous agreement that there is little polling place fraud,' the final version of the report released to the public concluded in its executive summary that 'there is a great deal of debate on the pervasiveness of fraud.'" The Election Assistance Commission report excluded most of the Wang-Serebrov draft discussion of intimidation issues.[34]

They say the cover-up often is worse than the crime, and in the EAC's case, it was. Not only did the story land on the front page of the *Times*, but the commission's contract with Wang and Serebrov contained a confidentiality agreement that prevented Wang from speaking to the press about the report and her dealings with the commission. Her supporters called this a gag order and kept the issue alive. (As one of them, I often posted "Free Tova Wang!" messages on my Election Law Blog.)

To make matters worse, the commission's decision to not release the draft report came on the heels of its releasing another report while publicly distancing itself from it. That report, written by a different set of researchers, concluded that voter identification laws could cause a decrease in turnout, especially among minorities. The commission's note accompanying that report questioned its methodology.

Martinez, who left the EAC before it decided to issue its own report on voter fraud, opposed efforts to keep the Wang-Serebrov draft private: "Methodology concerns aside, we commissioned the reports with taxpayer funds, and I argued that they should be released. . . . My view was that the public and the academics could determine whether it is rigorous and if it wasn't then the egg was on our face for having commissioned it in the first place." The commission eventually relented on the gag order, and Wang took to the op-ed pages of the *Washington Post* to explain the key differences between her study with Serebrov and the report the commission released:

> We said that our preliminary research found widespread agreement among administrators, academics and election experts from all points on the political spectrum that allegations of fraud through voter impersonation at polling places were greatly exaggerated. We noted that this position was supported by existing research and an analysis of several years of news articles. The

commission chose instead to state that the issue was a matter of considerable debate. And while we found that problems of voter intimidation were still prevalent in a variety of forms, the commission excluded much of the discussion of voter intimidation.

We also raised questions about the way the Justice Department was handling complaints of fraud and intimidation. The commission excised all references to the department that might be construed as critical—or that Justice officials later took issue with. And all of the suggestions we received from political scientists and other scholars regarding methodologies for a more scientifically rigorous look at these problems were omitted.[35]

Congress investigated, and the Election Assistance Commission released forty thousand pages of related documents and emails. (I ordered a copy of the materials, which came on four DVDs, and I was surprised to discover that emails I sent privately to Martinez—suggesting people he should consult on various election law questions—were part of the document dump. It taught me a valuable lesson: never send anything to a government email address that you don't want to turn up in some future investigation.)

Wang suggested in her op-ed that the released documents showed that Department of Justice interference—especially from Fraudulent Fraud Squad member Hans von Spakovsky—was responsible for the commission's spiking of the draft report and the changed conclusions in the report it did issue. The EAC inspector general investigated and only partially vindicated Wang's claims.[36]

The inspector general found that there was "confusion" over the scope of the original project and that commission officials believed that the Wang-Serebrov report was "poorly written" and "contained unsupported conclusions and, therefore, required substantial editing." It found no evidence that the commissioners deliberately changed the final report for political reasons.

Yet there was evidence of some political pressure put on Republican commissioners to kill the Wang-Serebrov study. Martinez said that a Republican commissioner, Donetta Davidson, came into his office complaining that she was getting pressure not to release the Wang-Serebrov report. It was unclear whether that pressure came from the Bush White House. Martinez said he did not ask Davidson who was pressuring her, but others within and outside the commission recalled that Martinez had said it was the White House. Davidson denied being pressured and claimed that when she spoke with Martinez she was actually upset about the *other* controversial report, the one on voter identification laws and turnout.

The inspector general's report also confirmed that Hans von Spakovsky, then at the Department of Justice, was complaining to the other Republican commissioner at the time, Paul DeGregorio, about the Wang-Serebrov draft. Von Spakovsky expressed concern to DeGregorio that "Serebrov might not be an adequate Republican foil to Wang's liberalism and aggressive personality." More generally, according to DeGregorio, von Spakovsky "thought DeGregorio should use his position (on the EAC commission) to advance the Republican Party's agenda."

This report hardly ended the controversy. Former Department of Justice civil rights attorney Gerry Hebert criticized the report for not saying whether the White House had pressured Davidson. Hebert found Martinez's testimony on this question not credible. In an interview, DeGregorio suggested that von Spakovsky may have blocked his reappointment to the commission, presumably because DeGregorio was not enough of a Republican team player. DeGregorio's replacement, Caroline Hunter, was a loyal Republican foot soldier whom von Spakovsky offered up as a resource to controversial conservative economist John Lott, whom von Spakovsky was trying to persuade to do a counterstudy on voter identification laws and turnout.[37]

Wang issued a statement responding to the charges that the report was poorly drafted:

> The "draft report" that we submitted to the EAC staff and then was released to the press was just that—a "draft report." I NEVER expected that version to be a final report or that it would be released to the public. It clearly required editing and revision, a process I expected would be undertaken through a collaborative effort with myself, Job Serebrov, EAC staff and Commissioners, as I believe was the process followed with respect to other EAC consultant reports. That never happened. Instead, the EAC took the report, refused to let us have any further involvement, and edited and revised it into what they released as the final report.[38]

After this controversy, with all the original commissioners gone, the promise of a meaningful federal role in improving elections evaporated. Subsequent commissioners have sometimes acted as hacks, voting along party lines on disputed issues. A few have taken brave stances. But no one pays attention. Even the fact that the commission had *all four* commission seats vacant during the 2012 election season escaped the media's notice. Yet the National Association of Secretaries of State and local election officials still want to kill off the commission for fear that it might usurp some of their own power over elections.[39]

Speaking at a 2006 conference, Soaries revealed that within one week of starting his job at the Election Assistance Commission, he went to the Bush White House to tender his resignation, saying, "You people aren't serious, and I told you if you weren't, there'd be a problem."[40]

He did not resign that day but stayed in his job for a year, fearful that leaving the commission in the period before the crucial 2004 elections would have been a mistake for the country. Lamenting the Voting Wars between Democrats and Republicans over voter suppression and voter fraud allegations, Soaries said that politicians were focused on the minutiae when there were big problems to solve:

> What do we do about 40 percent voter turnout? What do we do about polling places that are not accessible for people that are physically challenged? What do we do . . . about the fact that the average person on Election Day has as their chief problem just finding out about where to vote? What do we do about the fact that there are parts of this country where the elections administrators are so underfunded that they keep voter registration applications in a shoebox under their desk? What do we do about the fact that there's no formal training for elections administration, so that if you want to be an airplane pilot, you go to school; if you want to be a barber, you go to school; but if you want to be an elections administrator, you just have the right political contact in the right place?

They were good questions in 2006, and they remain good ones today.

5

Margin of Litigation

The morning after Election Day in 2008, Norm Coleman faced a tough question from reporter Curt Brown of the Minneapolis news paper the *Star Tribune*. "If you were down by 725 [votes], would you say forget it and save the taxpayers' money?"[1]

It is a question no candidate slightly ahead of a competitor wants to answer. Although the public accepts election totals as they come in on election night as an accurate representation of the truth, such numbers are usually wrong and almost always incomplete. In the rush to get everything done on Election Night, election officials sometimes misreport numbers or, as we saw in the Wisconsin Supreme Court race, even forget to report totals from entire towns. It takes days for officials to verify and recheck the numbers. Many states also have absentee ballots to process and count, and now, in part thanks to the Help America Vote Act, there are often piles of provisional ballots to consider.

When the apparent winner is ahead by thousands of votes in a statewide race, and Election Day comes and goes with no reports of widespread problems or irregularities, it is usually safe for candidates to expect that the outcome will not change. Election officials then certify the results weeks later. But when the margin is closer, candidates concede or declare victory at their peril.

Remember Al Gore calling George W. Bush to retract his concession in November 2000, moments before Gore was to give his concession speech? Democrats were not going to make the same mistake twice. In 2004, John Kerry conceded in Ohio to George W. Bush only after Kerry's lawyers satisfied themselves that the election was beyond "the margin of litigation": the vote gap between the leading candidates was large enough that there was no point in contesting or litigating to a potentially better result.

Norm Coleman, the incumbent U.S. senator from Minnesota, didn't declare victory in his race for reelection against Democratic challenger Al Franken and independent candidate Dean Barkley that morning, but he came close. Ahead by 725 votes over Franken, and much more over Barkley, Coleman expressed a confidence in the vote margin that would later come back to bite him: "Curt, to be honest, I'd step back. . . . I just think the need for a healing process is so important, the possibility of any change of this magnitude in the voting system we have is so remote, but that would be my judgment. I'm not . . . again, Mr. Franken will decide what Mr. Franken will do. But do I think under these circumstances it is important to come together? I do."

Months later, after Franken took the lead following a recount and election contest, Coleman saw less need for "healing." He contested and litigated all the way to the Minnesota Supreme Court, which ultimately voted unanimously to reject his challenge to Franken's lead. Although the election was in November and the winner was supposed to be seated in January, the protracted legal battle meant that Minnesota was missing one of its two senators until July 2009, when Franken was at last sworn into office.[2]

Coleman did not have a monopoly on flip-flopping. When Franken was behind in the polls, his mantra echoed Al Gore's: count every vote. But by the time the dispute made it to the Minnesota Supreme Court, Franken, now in the lead, had changed his tune. The court had to decide the standard for including in the count absentee ballots that may not have perfectly conformed to the technical requirements of Minnesota law, and Franken urged "strict compliance": no excusing those minor errors. What happened to "count every vote"?[3]

Franken "celebs" factor

Coleman, meanwhile, argued for a more forgiving "substantial compliance" standard that would have excused minor errors. By this point, his
attorneys were channeling Al Gore's lawyer, David Boies. The Republican-
majority Minnesota Supreme Court, citing a history of using "strict compliance" for evaluating the validity of absentee ballots, unanimously sided with
Franken. Coleman conceded the race rather than seek review in the U.S.
Supreme Court.

The flip-flopping by both sides was neither surprising nor new. Never
mind that outside of the recount-contest arena, Democrats line up more
with broad enfranchisement arguments and Republicans urge sticking to
the rules as written. It is elementary that if you are behind in the count you
need to mine for votes, calling for the counting of as many uncounted ballots as possible (ideally, cherry-picked from supporters' districts, though
sometimes it makes sense to cast a wider net). If you are ahead, you need
to make it clear that "the people have spoken" and it is time to move on.

Here's James Baker on November 11, 2000, with the classic "closure" statement after the completion of the mandatory machine recount of ballots
required in razor-thin elections under Florida law: "As I said yesterday, the
vote in Florida has been counted and then recounted. Governor George W.
Bush was the winner of the vote. He was also the winner of the recount.
Based on these results, we urged the Gore campaign to accept the finality
of the election, subject only to the counting of the overseas absentee ballots
in accordance with law."[4]

Franken was much more in favor of counting every vote when he was
behind than when he was ahead. Coleman, at the exact opposite times, was
the same.

The idea of a recount is not a post–*Bush v. Gore* invention. Professor Ned
Foley, for example, has written of a particularly bitter postelection dispute
in 1792 between George Clinton and John Jay (then the first chief justice of
the United States) over the governorship of New York, which drew in as
litigants or commentators many of the Founding Fathers.[5] There have been
other important recounts in U.S. history, along with election-related litigation that has changed the outcome of elections. In 1997, an appellate court
threw out all the absentee ballots in the Miami mayor's race because of
rampant absentee-ballot related fraud, changing the outcome of the election.

It was a stronger remedy than the trial court would have opted for, which was to hold a new election. The Florida Supreme Court and U.S. Supreme Court, unlike their action in *Bush v. Gore* a few years later, refused to second-guess the appellate court's decision to change the election results.[6]

interest graph?

So what's changed since 2000 about election-related litigation?

To start with, there's much, much more of it. When I first started teaching election law in the 1990s, the off-season for election disputes was all the time except for the fall in even-numbered years. These days, it is hard to keep up with all the litigation filed every year (though it peaks in presidential election years). I track the court action on the Election Law Blog, and I've posted more than thirty thousand items since 2003.[7]

In the period just before *Bush v. Gore,* courts in the United States collectively decided on average fewer than 100 election-related cases per year. Since 2000, that figure has more than doubled, to more than 230 such cases nationally each year.[8] Candidates are litigating early and often.

Early especially: much of the litigation tries to set the rules that will be used on Election Day and in postelection litigation. Although this push toward preelection litigation might increase the number of cases, it makes a lot of sense. It is far better for judges to decide such cases when the issues are more abstract and it is not always clear which candidate might benefit from the judge's decision. This helps the courts preserve legitimacy and stay out of the political thicket.

As a corollary, some courts have become skeptical of lawsuits brought after the election when the issue could have been litigated before. This, too, makes sense: a candidate who sits on a problem until after the election essentially retains an "option" over whether to sue. If ahead, the candidate doesn't sue. If behind, he or she does. So if you don't sue early if you have the chance to do so, you might lose your chance to sue later. Think of a candidate who knew about the butterfly ballot and the kind of havoc it could cause days before the election in Florida but decided to "wait and see" rather than go to court to enjoin the use of the terrible ballot layout for voting.

We do not know exactly why there has been an explosion in election litigation since 2000, but here are some possibilities. First is the emergence of election law as political strategy. The resistance to challenging election rules in court seems to have evaporated. Although the matter is somewhat in dispute, Nixon supposedly accepted Kennedy's very close victory in the presidential election of 1960 rather than dispute the results because conceding defeat was in the national interest. Today, candidates have apparently become more emboldened (or simply learned that courts may grant relief) in the face of a close election and inevitable election problems. These problems became clear to everyone in 2000, and the possibility of "another Florida" gives candidates more hope of prevailing even if they are behind.[9]

It worked for Franken. He didn't take Coleman's self-serving advice on election night to throw in the towel. Although Coleman ended up losing the later court battle, can anyone really blame Coleman for doing what Franken did when he was behind—fight until the fighting was futile? We can't expect candidates to do anything but fight in such an environment.

Two other factors—both indirectly a result of Florida 2000—also may have made litigation more attractive. First, there's a lot of new election law and technology since 2000. Provisions of the Help America Vote Act kicked in nationwide beginning in 2003, and some of those rules have provoked bitter and nasty court fights over "wrong precinct" voters, database "mismatches," and other questions. States changed their rules, too (think of the new voter identification laws and changes to voter registration rules), or changed their voting machines. Each change offers lawyers room to argue over gaps and ambiguities in applying the new law to new technology or the old law to new technology or even the new law to old technology—this is how election lawyers earn their money. In a close election, those gaps give the lawyer a foot in the courthouse door.

Second, concern about the partisan biases of election administrators, which came to light in the Florida controversy, has energized the opposition. If you are a Republican and Jennifer Brunner is secretary of state, you are likely to believe that every step she takes is calculated to help Democrats. If you are a Democrat and Ken Blackwell is secretary of state, you have the converse inclination. As we will see in chapter 7, the Internet magnifies these partisan feelings and encourages more litigation, not just by candidates but by parties, interest groups, and voters. The Voting Wars are the most elaborate and protracted when they take place in court.

Some candidates or parties may want to undertake postelection litigation even if they don't expect it to overturn the election results: a suit can sometimes delay the seating of the winning candidate (as happened with Franken) or weaken the announced winner by calling his or her legitimacy into question. This may have been the real reason Coleman did not concede after he lost decisively in his election contest before a three-judge trial court, prior to the state supreme court deciding his appeal.

Bush v. Gore as legal precedent, ironically, does not appear to be the cause of much of the rise in litigation. Although the Supreme Court in that case created a new equal protection right to some kind of rudimentary fairness in the nuts and bolts of elections, few of the lawsuits since 2000 actually have led to successful *Bush v. Gore* claims, and most lower courts have read the case narrowly when it has come up. This has been a sore spot for Democrats, who believe that the Court's equal protection holding was disingenuous, creating a one-day-only ticket good just for George W. Bush to claim the presidency.

The *Bush v. Gore* majority's unsigned opinion said that the inconsistent standards for counting and recounting established by the Florida canvassing boards and the Florida Supreme Court's orders violated the equal protection clause of the fourteenth amendment of the U.S. Constitution. The changing recount standards, the inclusion of votes counted under varying standards, and the lack of a uniform standard going forward meant that the Florida Supreme Court was allowing one person's vote "to be valued more" than another. Two other justices, Breyer and Souter, agreed that the Florida standards created either an equal protection problem or a "due process" problem, because the shifting vote-counting rules seemed arbitrary. (These two justices wanted to send the case back to the Florida Supreme Court to order a statewide recount under uniform standards.)

The majority opinion contained two sentences in which the Court tried to limit the reach of its holding. "Our consideration is limited to the present circumstances, for the problem of equal protection in election processes generally presents many complexities." And: "The question before the Court is not whether local entities, in the exercise of their expertise, may develop different systems for implementing elections." As Professor Chad Flanders has explained, the Court's "limiting" language in *Bush v. Gore* was unprec-

edented. Although the Court sometimes limits the reach of an earlier decision when deciding a *later* case, *Bush v. Gore* is the only case so far in which
the Court sought to limit its holding to the facts in *the very same case*.[10]

Another unusual thing: as of the end of 2011, more than a decade after
the decision, no Supreme Court opinion—not even a dissent—mentioned
Bush v. Gore for *any* reason. Usually the Court cites its own earlier opinions
for all sorts of uncontroversial propositions. But not for *Bush v. Gore*. The
closest the Court came was in a concurring opinion of Chief Justice Roberts
in the controversial 2010 campaign finance case, *Citizens United v. FEC*.
The Chief Justice cited my 2003 book, which has the case name in the title
(*The Supreme Court and Election Law: Judging Equality from* Baker v. Carr *to*
Bush v. Gore), for a point unrelated to *Bush v. Gore*. That's it. This silence
has left lower courts and commentators debating whether the *Bush v. Gore*
decision has any precedential value and if so, what it means.[11]

Soon after the case came down, some optimistic election law scholars
told a "lemonade from lemons" story. Although there was much to criticize
about the Court's handling of the case, this argument went, perhaps it
could usher in a new era of court-mandated election reform based on the
Court's statement that it was unconstitutional "to value" one person's vote
more than another.[12]

It was not to be. No lemonade; only lemons.

One of the earliest questions about the case's reach concerned whether
people who lived in counties using punch card machines could sue election
officials to have those machines removed, on grounds that the use of unreliable voting machines with high error rates in some parts of a state but not
in others would "value" one person's vote more than that of another, in violation of *Bush v. Gore*'s equal protection holding. (These suits came before
the Help America Vote Act provided a pot of federal money to phase out
these machines.) In a law review article written soon after the Florida debacle, I said that if we took *Bush v. Gore* seriously, these suits should be
successful: of course it values one person's vote over another's if one person, thanks to the voting technology used, has a much greater chance of
casting a ballot that will actually count.[13]

Still, given the controversy over the case's meaning and the scope of the
new equal protection rights, I expected that lower courts would divide on

the question, with some reading the case broadly and others narrowly. Ultimately, I thought, the conservative Supreme Court would suck any precedential life out of the opinion, but maybe not before the case had been useful in lower courts to spur election reform.

One of the first punch card suits came in my own state, California. Common Cause sued Bill Jones, then the secretary of state, to get him to decertify the use of punch card machines throughout the state. Jones settled the suit and agreed to phase out the cards by the 2004 election. When the parties settled, in 2002, no one expected that a statewide election would again take place in California using punch card ballots; the next scheduled election was March 2004, by which time the machines would be decertified.

But then opponents of California governor Gray Davis collected enough signatures to put him up for a recall vote in 2003. It was a media circus. A questionable interpretation of California election law by the new secretary of state, Kevin Shelley (who later resigned in an unrelated scandal concerning misappropriated HAVA money), made it very easy for replacement candidates to qualify for the ballot. Our recall circus had 135 candidates, including a porn star, the former child actor Gary Coleman, and the watermelon-smashing comedian Gallagher.

Once the unprecedented effort to recall Gray Davis qualified for the ballot in a special October 2003 election, the American Civil Liberties Union, on behalf of a coalition of voting rights organizations, filed suit to delay the election until the bad punch card machines could be replaced. I filed an amicus brief in the case supporting the ACLU's *Bush v. Gore* equal protection argument, but it didn't help. The district court judge, Reagan appointee Stephen Wilson, denied the ACLU's request for a preliminary injunction. He said that *Bush v. Gore* mandated only minimal "rational basis review" of challenges to the use of different voting machines across the state and that punch cards passed such review because it would be expensive to replace the machines.

Less than a month before the election, a panel of the Ninth Circuit made up of three liberal judges reversed the district court. The court described the equal protection issue as a "classic voting rights equal protection claim": "The weight given to votes in non-punchcard counties is greater than the weight given to votes in punchcard counties because a higher proportion of the votes from punchcard counties are thrown out. . . . The effect . . . is to discriminate on the basis of geographic residence." The court continued: "Like the Supreme Court in *Bush*, 'The question before [us] is not whether local entities, in the exercise of their expertise, may develop different systems for implementing elections.' Rather, like the Supreme Court in *Bush*, we face a situation in which the United States Constitution requires 'some assurance that the rudimentary requirements of equal treatment and fundamental fairness are satisfied.'"

The ruling didn't last long. The entire Ninth Circuit quickly voted to hear the case en banc, and an eleven-judge court—including some liberal judges— unanimously reinstated the trial court's decision: no delay of the recall election. Mostly ducking the question of how to interpret *Bush v. Gore*, the Ninth Circuit said that enjoining the election so close to Election Day would create a hardship for California voters. The court left open the possibility of postelection litigation if the punch cards proved to be a problem.

It's a good thing that the election was a blowout, with a strong majority of Californians voting to recall Governor Davis. Otherwise there would have been a very tough issue in postelection litigation. As I noted in the Introduction, 9 percent of Los Angeles voters who voted in the election were not recorded as having included a valid "yes" or "no" vote on the recall question. The hanging chad strikes again.

But in Alameda County, a county similar to Los Angeles except that it used electronic voting machines, the undervote on that "yes" or "no" question was less than 1 percent. It had to be the machines that caused the problem, and there would have been an ugly legal dispute if the vote had been close.

Punch card litigation in Ohio followed a pattern much like California's. A federal district court judge, Reagan appointee David Dowd, rejected the argument that the disparity between punch card systems and other voting systems violated equal protection principles. The case went to the Sixth Circuit, where a bitterly divided court reversed the trial court by a two-to-one vote.

Drawing on my 2001 article arguing that the Supreme Court would eventually limit *Bush v. Gore*'s holding to its facts, the dissent took the position that *Bush v. Gore* should not be applied as valid precedent to require the elimination of punch card machines. "Since Professor Hasen's article, the Supreme Court has had ample opportunity to prove him wrong [that the case would ultimately have no precedential value] by explaining, or even citing to, its decision in *Bush v. Gore*. But despite taking a steady load of election-related cases, the Court has not cited *Bush v. Gore* even once."

The Sixth Circuit majority, however, "reject[ing] the dissent's claim that Professor Hasen's article has overruled the Supreme Court's decision in *Bush v. Gore*," held that its equal protection holding was binding precedent: "Murky, transparent, illegitimate, right, wrong, big, tall, short or small; regardless of the adjective one might use to describe the decision, the proper noun that precedes it—'Supreme Court'—carries more weight with us. Whatever else *Bush v. Gore* may be, it is first and foremost a decision of the Supreme Court of the United States and we are bound to adhere to it." The majority read *Bush v. Gore* as requiring application of strict scrutiny (the most demanding standard of review) to the question before it, holding that because of the lesser chance that a vote cast on a punch card machine will be accurately counted, the equal protection clause is violated.

But the victory for punch card opponents was also short-lived. As in the California recall case, the entire Sixth Circuit voted to hear the case en banc—with the effect of wiping out the two-to-one opinion as precedent. The state had argued that the case should be dismissed as moot because it had already decided to abandon punch card voting. The two of three judges on the original Sixth Circuit panel had rejected that argument, but plaintiffs filed a letter with the en banc court conceding mootness—no doubt fearing that the entire Sixth Circuit, with more conservative than liberal judges, would agree with the dissenting panel judge. It was also apparent that Ohio was unlikely to hold another election using the punch card machines. The en banc court, seeing no remaining controversy given plaintiffs' concession, remanded the case to be dismissed as moot.

Bush v. Gore seems to have failed so far as a vehicle for election reform advocates to force remedies to problems with voting machinery *directly*, although many of those problems were later solved when Congress funded new machines through the Help America Vote Act. A harder question is whether its equal protection holding *indirectly* caused state and local election officials to impose greater uniformity on election procedures.

Coleman v. Franken raised this uniformity issue in an unusual way. The dispute was legally complex and took nine months to resolve. Professor Ned Foley needed two long law review articles and a fifteen-page unpublished appendix to lay out all the legal details of what he termed the "Lake Wobegone" recount: above average, pretty good, but way too long. I might add that, like *A Prairie Home Companion,* parts of the Minnesota recount process were also dreadfully boring, even for an avid NPR listener and election law junkie.

Journalist Jay Weiner's excellent account of the controversy, *This Is Not Florida,* gave an inside picture of the litigation strategies of both sides. Both Weiner and Foley agree that the Franken legal team outlawyered Coleman's. Coleman's eventual reliance on *Bush v. Gore* was a Hail Mary pass.

Although Coleman led by 725 votes on election night, as the additional numbers and corrections trickled in from around Minnesota, his lead fell to just over 200 votes, leading many of his supporters to question the veracity of the numbers. Though such fluctuations occur in every election, as Professor Foley explained, "even after the entire saga was over, the editorial page of the *Wall Street Journal* complained that suspicious changes in precinct totals during the canvass cast doubt over the integrity of the final result." The *Journal's* editorial page and parts of the conservative blogosphere irresponsibly screamed of a "stolen" election, and it is an allegation that Franken's opponents make to this day.[14]

Nothing could be further from the truth. Foley called the Minnesota process the "Lake Wobegone" recount for good reason: because of the transparency and fairness with which it was conducted and, for the most part, the bipartisan cooperation among the decision makers. As in Florida 2000, the closeness of the official total (in this case, Coleman's 215-vote lead) led to an automatic recount of the results. The first phase of recounting, at 107 different sites in Minnesota, lasted from mid-November to January 5. At the end of this phase, there were over 6,600 challenged ballots out of about 3 million recounted, aside from rejected absentee ballots that had not been opened. The candidates withdrew some challenges, leading to 1,337 contested ballots to be considered by the state canvassing board, and a Franken lead of 49 votes.

The 1,337 ballots went before a five-person commission, composed of the Democratic secretary of state Mark Ritchie (who, like Jennifer Brunner in Ohio, was a favorite of those on the left and the Secretary of State Project), two Republican state supreme court justices, a judge who had been appointed years earlier by then-governor Jesse Ventura, and a judge who had been elected to office without partisan affiliation. The board conducted its review openly—all the ballots could be viewed on line in real time, and newspapers and radio stations allowed voters to determine the intent on questioned ballots—and, mostly unanimously, agreed on whether to accept or reject nearly 96 percent of the challenged ballots. The review had its moments of levity, such as the ballot in which Al Franken's bubble was filled in, and apparently crossed out, with a write-in vote for "Lizard People." After the ballot drew national attention, even from Chris Matthews on MSNBC's *Hardball,* a twenty-five-year-old named Lucas Davenport came forward to Minnesota Public Radio claiming (credibly, based on his handwriting) to be the "Lizard People" voter.

"I don't know if you've heard the conspiracy theory about the Lizard Men," Davenport said. "A friend of mine, we didn't like the candidates, so we were at first going to write in revolution, because we thought that was good and to the point. And then, we thought the Lizard People would be even funnier, and there was kind of a running inside gag between some friends and I." As MPR explained, "Lizard People refers to the conspiracy theory [that] there's a race of shape shifting lizards masquerading as humans who rule the world, but Davenport doesn't consider himself a believer."[15] Franken was not awarded his vote.[16]

Although the Lizard People and the challenged ballots got the initial attention—the latter reminded people of the fight over hanging chads in *Bush v. Gore*—the real action soon shifted to the uncounted absentee ballots.

Minnesota, like many other states, has seen a broad increase in the use of absentee ballots as a convenience for voters who don't want to make it to the polls on Election Day. Under Minnesota law in place in 2008 (the state legislature later made some changes), such ballots had to meet four re-

RALPH NADER AND
MATT GONZALEZ
Independent

amendment, completel
word "YES" for that qu
proposed constitutiona
fill in the oval next to t
question.

BOB BARR AND
WAYNE A. ROOT
Libertarian

40
41
42
44

CLEAN W/
CULTURAI
NATU

CHUCK BALDWIN AND
DARRELL CASTLE
Constitution

Shall the Minnesota
dedicate funding to
sources; to protect
wetlands, prairies,
wildlife habitat; to
heritage; to suppo
protect, enhance,
streams, and gro
sales and use ta
three-eighths of
until the year 20:

Lizard People

write-in, if any

U.S. SENATOR
VOTE FOR ONE

YE!

DEAN BARKLEY
Independence

N(

NORM COLEMAN
Republican

CO

AL FRANKEN
Democratic-Farmer-Labor

SOIL ANI
DIS

CHARLES ALDRICH
Libertarian

JAMES NIEMACKL
Constitution

Lizard People

write-in, if any

U.S. REPRESENTATIVE
DISTRICT 7
VOTE FOR ONE

SOIL A

51

GLEN MENZE

SOIL A

"Lizard People" ballot, Minnesota, 2008 (Copyright © 2008 Minnesota Public
Radio; Photo by Tom Robertson, Minnesota Public Radio.org)

quirements to be counted: the voter's name and address on the return envelope must be the same as on the absentee ballot application; the signature on the outside of the absentee ballot must match the voter's signature
on file; the voter has to be eligible to vote; and the voter cannot have voted
in person or cast another absentee ballot. Minnesota election officials were
required to reject absentee ballots that didn't meet all four requirements
but were not permitted to reject them for other reasons.

Although the parties fought over other issues, too—including 132 missing ballots from a lost envelope in Minneapolis and allegations of double
voting—in the end the dispute came down to absentee ballots. Of 12,000
rejected absentee ballots statewide, the parties estimated that about 1,600
had been wrongly rejected.

When Franken was behind, he successfully sued to get counties that
would not voluntarily comply to supply the campaign with a list of voters
whose absentee ballots had been rejected. Armed with this information,
and believing he would do well to have more absentee ballots counted,
Franken asked the board to require local officials to reexamine rejected absentee ballots to see if they had been wrongfully rejected. He also argued
that the local officials should use a "substantial compliance" test: if the excluded absentee ballot came reasonably close to following the rules, it
should be opened and counted.

Coleman, then still ahead, argued that counties should not go back over
rejected absentee ballots during the recount period, and went all the way to
the state supreme court to block their inclusion in the recounted totals. His
argument was that the only ballots that could be "recounted" were those
that had already been counted: any fight over excluded absentee ballots
should await an election contest after the recount ended.

The Minnesota Supreme Court issued an order, on a three-to-two vote
(the two justices serving on the canvassing board recused themselves), allowing local election officials to count absentee ballots that the officials believed were wrongly rejected, but only if both candidates' legal teams agreed
for the ballot to be counted. It was an odd order, giving the candidates a veto
over the counting of ballots, and in echoes of *Bush v. Gore*, the court's decision broke on partisan, or at least ideological, lines. Justice (and former
National Football League player) Alan Page began his pungent dissent with:

[handwritten margin notes: "Min fight over absentee - What should be counted - What shouldn't"]

"Josef Stalin is alleged to have once said, 'I consider it completely unimportant who . . . will vote, or how; but what is extraordinarily important is this—who will count the votes, and how.'"[17]

The divide was a low point in the Minnesota controversy, but the odd order actually may have sped up the slow recount process. The court majority reminded the parties that they could be subject to sanctions for frivolous challenges to absentee ballots, leading the Coleman team to agree to count a number of absentee ballots they might otherwise have challenged.

When the board finished counting and recounting, it certified Franken as the winner by 225 votes. It was now Coleman's turn to contest and to demand that more absentee ballots be counted. He struck out before a three-judge court and the Minnesota Supreme Court, both of which unanimously rejected his challenges. The three-judge court was composed of a Democrat, a Republican, and an independent-appointed judge. The trial proceedings added more months to the dispute without advancing Coleman's case. The state supreme court case took even more time.

Coleman's lawyers dropped the ball. It started with problems like trying to introduce photocopies of disputed ballot envelopes—photocopies with markings on them of unknown origin and that contained missing information, rather than the ballot envelopes themselves—and went downhill from there. Rather than attempting to prove that *particular* absentee ballots that should have been counted were not—or that particular counted ballots should not have been—the Coleman legal team painted in broad strokes, attempting to show inconsistencies across counties in the treatment of absentee ballots. It was not the kind of detailed proof that the trial court, or the state supreme court, needed if it was going to overturn the results of an election, a ruling that would surely bring intense scrutiny and controversy.

Here is where Coleman's *Bush v. Gore* argument came in. His basic claim, at least by the time he got to the Minnesota Supreme Court, was that if one county had wrongfully accepted a class of absentee ballots that did not comply fully with the state's statutes, *Bush v. Gore*'s equal protection principles required the counting of *all* wrongfully rejected ballots throughout the state. Unsurprisingly, the court said *Bush v. Gore* did not require the counting of such ballots. It was a bold theory, one that would have compounded errors in counting by making those errors apply statewide.[18]

The state supreme court brushed the argument aside.

> Variations in local practices for implementing absentee voting procedures are, at least in part, the question at issue here. . . . The trial court here found that the disparities in application of the statutory standards on which Coleman relies are the product of local jurisdictions' use of different methods to ensure compliance with the same statutory standards; that jurisdictions adopted policies they deemed necessary to ensure that absentee voting procedures would be available to their residents, in accordance with statutory requirements, given the resources available to them; and that differences in available resources, personnel, procedures, and technology necessarily affected the procedures used by local election officials in reviewing absentee ballots.

The Minnesota court also rejected Coleman's argument that under state law, the court should order the counting of absentee ballots that "substantially complied" with state law. This was the argument Franken had made before, but now, doing his best James Baker imitation, he opposed it. The court pointed to its history of requiring strict compliance with absentee ballot laws (the state had no Democracy Canon for such ballots), relying on the anachronistic notion that absentee voting is not a right but a privilege. Ironically, had the court agreed with Coleman on this point, it would have given *Franken* a new legal issue to take to federal court in the event that counting more absentee ballots swung the election back to Coleman. Another line of cases says that you cannot change the rules for counting votes in the middle of an election contest, and if you do, this change would violate the right to "due process" also protected in the Constitution. The Minnesota courts had so consistently (in my view wrongfully) said that strict compliance applied to the counting of absentee ballots that to change the rules for Coleman raised the serious possibility of constitutional error. Maybe the court or the legislature will change that rule at some point when it is not in the middle of a postelection contest.

Foley believes that Coleman would have had a better chance if he had made a narrow *Bush v. Gore* argument: count those absentee ballots that were excluded because of errors by election officials, not by voters. Whether that narrower argument would have succeeded is anyone's guess, but it is fair to say that the case did not advance the use of *Bush v. Gore*'s principles of uniformity in election administration.

Was Minnesota's handling of *Coleman v. Franken* better than Florida's handling of the 2000 controversy? Certainly. Minnesota had, from the beginning and throughout the long recount and contest, more bipartisanship and transparency. Its laws were more cleanly written than Florida's, and its culture of niceness contributed to the relative calm of the proceedings, although this was not reflected in the intemperate comments of many in the blogosphere about conspiracies and stolen elections.[19]

But the interminably long time Minnesota took to resolve its dispute deprived the state of a senator for half a year. Its timeline would have been intolerable in a dispute between presidential candidates. And it would be hard to replicate Minnesota conditions, especially the niceness factor, across the country in the next election meltdown.

The Sixth Circuit, which has seen more than its share of election litigation since 2000, may have had the last word on the meaning of *Bush v. Gore* before the 2012 elections. Mercifully, the dispute came in a low-stakes case, *Hunter v. Hamilton County Board of Elections.*[20]

The case involves a contested 2010 election for Hamilton County juvenile court judge. The Hamilton County elections board declared Republican John Williams the winner over Democrat Tracie Hunter by twenty-three votes. Hunter complained about what she claimed was the board's unconstitutional, inconsistent treatment of provisional ballots cast in the "wrong precinct." The board accepted for counting twenty-seven provisional ballots cast at the board's offices in downtown Cincinnati before Election Day but for which voters, because of pollworker errors, received ballots from the "wrong precinct." What kind of errors? As we saw in the last chapter, one pollworker couldn't tell odd-numbered addresses from even ones.

This wrong precinct issue had become a major one after the passage of the Help America Vote Act. The act tells states they must offer a provisional ballot to any voter who wants to cast one, but it doesn't require states to count ballots cast by voters in a different precinct from the one in which they are lawfully registered. Of course, wrong precinct ballots should not be counted when a voter votes in a race where he or she has no right to vote, as for the adjoining city council district. But what about wrong precinct votes for *statewide* races and other races that go across more than one precinct? Should they be counted?

The Hamilton board accepted those twenty-seven ballots because it determined that voters received the wrong precinct ballots because of "clear pollworker error" at the central election offices. But it refused to investigate whether hundreds of other provisional ballots cast on Election Day in the wrong precinct also should be counted because of clear poll worker error. A fair number of those ballots apparently were cast in the right physical polling place, because a number of Hamilton County polling places consisted of numerous "precincts" at different tables within the same polling place. If the election worker did not direct the voter to the right table, should the voter be disenfranchised?

Hunter sued and Republicans countersued, leading to cases in federal district court, the Sixth Circuit, the Ohio Supreme Court, and even briefly in the U.S. Supreme Court. Along the way, Democratic secretary of state Jennifer Brunner issued directives that would cause the board to count some of these provisional ballots, the Ohio Supreme Court issued an order compelling Brunner to rescind her orders and ruling that it was against Ohio law to count ballots cast in the wrong precinct, and Jon Husted, the Republican secretary of state who replaced Brunner when she ran for U.S. Senate, filed briefs opposing the federal courts' intervention in the cases. Husted also broke a partisan tie vote on the board over whether to seek an emergency stay of the Sixth Circuit's decision from the U.S. Supreme Court. At the time I write this, the case is ongoing.

Unlike those in the Minnesota dispute, the decision makers in *Hunter* generally seemed to act in accordance with their partisan affiliations. This is the more familiar pattern in these cases.

What's especially notable about *Hunter* is the Sixth Circuit majority opinion and what it said about *Bush v. Gore.* (Judge Karen Nelson Moore, who wrote the opinion, is the Clinton appointee who was in the middle of the Sixth Circuit blowup, described in the last chapter, in the *Ohio Republican Party v. Brunner* case over Brunner's decision not to release mismatch data in 2008.) Relying on *Bush v. Gore,* Judge Moore wrote that the federal district court had been right to order the Hamilton board to count similarly situated provisional ballots cast in the wrong precinct. "Constitutional concerns regarding the review of provisional ballots by local boards of elections are especially great. As in a recount, the review of provisional ballots occurs after the initial count of regular ballots is known. This particular post-election feature makes 'specific standards to ensure . . . equal application,' particularly 'necessary to protect the fundamental right of each voter' to have his or her vote count on equal terms." She further explained that the "lack of specific standards for reviewing provisional ballots can otherwise result in 'unequal evaluation of ballots.' In contrast to more general administrative decisions, the cause for constitutional concern is much greater when the Board is exercising its discretion in areas 'relevant to the casting and counting of ballots,' like evaluating evidence of poll-worker error. To satisfy both equal-protection and due-process rights, such a discretionary review must apply similar treatment to equivalent ballots."

Under the Sixth Circuit's ruling, the Hamilton County board's initial mistake in counting wrong precinct ballots because of poll worker error meant that it had to compound the problem by counting *more* wrong precinct ballots, in violation of Ohio law, in order to satisfy the Constitution. Think of it as Revenge of the Lizard People: this was exactly the kind of remedy the Coleman team requested from the Minnesota Supreme Court as required by *Bush v. Gore* and got rebuffed. Fix the initial error of counting improper ballots by counting more improper ballots. A novel theory, to be sure.

Judge John Rogers, a George W. Bush appointee who was on the other side of Judge Moore in the *Brunner* case, expressed great reservations about the *Hunter* majority's approach to *Bush v. Gore*. And it is far from clear that other courts will follow Judge Moore's broad reading. If Judge Moore was trying to make lemonade from lemons, more than a decade after *Bush v. Gore,* Judge Rogers was having no part of it.

Dino Rossi threw in the towel. On June 6, 2005, more than seven months after he had been declared the apparent winner by 261 votes in the 2004 Washington state gubernatorial election, a trial judge rejected the Republican's challenge to the results that, after two controversial recounts, eventually put his competitor, Democrat Christine Gregoire, on top.

"With today's decision," he declared, "and because of the political makeup of the Washington State Supreme Court, which makes it almost impossible to overturn this ruling, I am ending the election contest. Now I'd like to wish Christine Gregoire and her family all the best over the next three years."[21]

Rossi had good reason to be frustrated with how Washington conducted its 2004 election, although Chief Justice Gary Alexander of the Washington Supreme Court strongly disputed Rossi's claim that he wouldn't get a fair shake in front of the majority-Democratic high court: "I've been on the court for ten years and the court simply does not have a partisan bias. In the ten years I've been here, I don't think the court has ever said anything or written anything that could lead someone to that conclusion."

Even if the state Supreme Court was not to blame for Rossi's problems, and if Chelan County trial court judge John Bridges had correctly ruled against Rossi in his election contest, there was plenty of blame to go around and myriad reasons for Republicans to lose confidence in the fairness in the state's election process.

If Minnesota's 2008 controversy led to the "Lake Wobegone" recount, Washington state's controversy in 2004 was more like the Three Stooges recount. First an automatic machine recount, then a hand recount, and finally an election contest revealed problems throughout the state, especially in King County, a Democratic stronghold with one-third of the state's voters that includes the state's most populous city, Seattle. Judge Bridges commented on the "deep and significant problems during the 2004 general election and the tabulation that followed" in the county.

In the end, Judge Bridges declared Gregoire the winner by 133 votes, but he recognized that at least 1,678 illegal votes had been cast by felons, ineligible voters, and a handful of people who voted twice.

From the beginning, the parties focused on King County, out of the belief that Democrats would look there for additional votes to make up Gregoire's deficit. With Rossi in the lead, Democrats initially sued King County to get the names of people whose provisional ballots had been rejected because of problems like a missing or mismatched signature. After winning rights to the names, Democrats tracked down Democratic voters (but apparently not Republican ones) and offered assistance to help correct their ballots in time to have them counted under the county's rules. State law allowed some corrections before certification of the results.

Republicans were the next to sue, challenging the "ballot enhancement" and "ballot duplication" procedures used in King County. If a ballot came in with voter intent apparently clear but with the ballot marked in the wrong way—for example, if the bubble next to Rossi's name was circled rather

than bubbled in—state law gave King County election officials the authority
to fill in the ballot's bubble correctly or to create a duplicate ballot. Republicans unsuccessfully argued that this procedure gave too much discretion to
election officials and would put illegal ballots into the mix.

A federal court denied the Republicans' attempt to stop the enhancement, even as Republicans yet again tried to invoke *Bush v. Gore:* "Applying
counting standards in selected counties different from those in others vio-
lates the equal protection and due process protections of the U.S. and
Washington constitutions and ultimately will deny Washington voters . . .
their fundamental right to vote."

After the automatic recount, Rossi's lead had fallen to 42 votes. Democrats decided to go ahead with a hand recount, at a cost of $730,000 (to be
refunded if there was a change in the election result), and the conservative
blogosphere erupted with claims of Democrats trying to steal the election
from Rossi. Conservatives also attacked Republican secretary of state Sam
Reed and even started recall proceedings against him.

In the midst of the hand recount, King County election officials discovered 573 mailed ballots that had been wrongly rejected. The county had put
the ballots aside because the computer could not match the signatures on
the mail-in ballots with the registration signatures on file (this problem was
partly due to a botched software change shortly before the 2004 election).
The parties fought over whether those 573 ballots could be counted in a recount. The state supreme court ruled that there could be no inclusion of
ballots that had not been counted before, but it also said that election official error could be corrected, leaving the issue somewhat open.

The King County board then voted along party lines to include the 573
votes in the total—the two Democrats on the board, including the elections
director, Dean Logan, voted for inclusion; the Republican, the county's prosecuting attorney, opposed the motion.

Then election officials found more ballots: first 22 and then 162 more.
The found ballots kept on coming, and as their number rose, Republican
confidence in the fairness of the election plummeted. Republicans persuaded a state court judge to exclude the 573 votes from the county count,
and the county appealed. The state supreme court sided with the county,
allowing the ballots. No doubt this ruling diminished Rossi's confidence

FOUND Ballots

that the state supreme court would side with him in any appeal of the election contest. Democrats lost, though, in an attempt to get the courts to allow the counting of new ballots as part of the recount.[22]

At the end of the hand recount, Gregoire had taken the lead, thanks in great part to those King County found votes, with a margin of 129 votes. Rossi then brought an election contest, which revealed even more problems with the conduct of the election.

King County election officials admitted they had allowed up to 300 voters to feed provisional ballots into the vote counting machines without first verifying that the ballots came from eligible voters. Evidence also emerged of alleged voting by dead voters, voting by many felons whose voting rights had not been restored, and other problems.

Still more problems surfaced. It turned out to be 660 provisional ballots, not just 300, fed into the machines without confirming eligibility. County officials found another 94 absentee ballots that had never been counted. Then absentee ballot supervisor Nicole Way admitted under oath that she falsified a report stating that all the absentee ballots had been accounted for. Hanlon's razor was at work again: not fraud intended to swing the election to Gregoire but great incompetence.

After a trial on all these issues, Judge Bridges found no intentional election fraud but painted a picture that was not pretty: "Based on the findings, the Court concludes that 1,678 illegal votes were cast in the 2004 general election. This includes felons established by petitioners totaling 754, felons established by intervenors totaling 647, deceased voters totaling 19, double voters totaling 6, provisional ballots in King County totaling 96, provisional ballots in Pierce County totaling 79 and additional votes in Pierce County for which there could not be found a registered voter through crediting, at least, totaling 77. And, therefore, the total is 1,678."

An illegal vote did not mean that the voters intended to commit criminal fraud. Many of the felon voters, including former felons on probation, thought they had the right to vote, especially when they were sent registration materials by Washington state election officials. This was why John McKay, the fired U.S. attorney in Seattle discussed in chapter 2, refused to bring federal prosecutions in these cases.

Rossi and his supporters argued that because the number of illegal votes greatly exceeded the margin between the two candidates, the court should call for a revote or declare him the winner. The court rejected the revote as not a permissible remedy under Washington law. By the time of trial, Rossi faced the harder burden of trying to get the court to declare him the winner on the basis of illegal votes.

Rossi put on the testimony from two political scientists, Anthony Gill and Jonathan Katz, arguing for "proportionate reduction" of illegal votes. Under this theory, the court would deduct illegal votes from Gregoire and Rossi based on each candidate's percentage of votes in the precincts containing the illegal votes. Rossi's experts said this statistical method should lead the court to declare Rossi the winner.

The trial judge rejected this argument. An election could be overturned only if Rossi could prove not only that illegal votes were cast but that they were cast *for Gregoire* in large enough numbers to overturn the results. Gregoire had put in evidence of four illegal voters voting for Rossi, moving her total margin from 129 to 133. Rossi put in no evidence of illegal votes being cast for Gregoire.

As to "proportionate reduction," the judge viewed the statistical method as not credible. It focused only on votes in Gregoire counties, and it committed what statisticians call the "ecological fallacy": mistakenly inferring individual behavior from aggregate statistics. That 70 percent of voters in an area voted for Gregoire was not proof that 70 percent of the voters *who cast an illegal ballot* voted for her as well.

> The ecological fallacy leads to erroneous and misleading results. Election results vary significantly from one similar precinct to another, from one election to another in the same precinct and among different candidates of the same party in the same precinct. Felons and others who vote illegally are not necessarily the same as others in the precinct. . . . The Court finds that the statistical methods used in the reports of Professors Gill and Katz ignore other significant factors in determining how a person is likely to vote. In this case, in light of the candidates, gender may be as significant or a more significant factor than others.

The judge even concluded, based on the rebuttal witnesses of the Democrats, that if the "proportionate reduction" method was correctly applied to all the illegal votes cast in the election, Gregoire deserved to be the winner.

MARGIN of ERROR Exceeded
Winners ma...

In the end, Republicans could not win because they could not prove enough illegal votes that were cast for Gregoire. But the contest painted an ugly picture of Washington's elections. Once again, the margin of error vastly exceeded the winner's margin of victory. No wonder the public's confidence over vote counting was low.

It was especially low among the state's Republicans. In a January 2005 Elway Poll of Washington voters, in the midst of the controversy after Gregoire had taken the lead, 68 percent of Republicans thought the state election process was unfair, compared to 27 percent of Democrats and 46 percent of Independents.[23] These results were the mirror image of national voter confidence numbers after *Bush v. Gore.* In 1996, four years before the Florida controversy, about 10 percent of the public (8 percent of Democrats and 12 percent of Republicans) thought that the manner of conducting the most recent presidential election was "somewhat unfair" or "very unfair." The number skyrocketed to 37 percent of the public (44 percent of Democrats and 25 percent of Republicans) in 2000 following the Florida debacle. By 2004, the number had fallen to a still worrisome 14 percent of the public holding strongly negative views of American election administration. The gap between Democrats (22 percent) and Republicans (3 percent) in 2004 remained quite large. It is hard to avoid the conclusion that views of the process's fairness are driven, at least in part, by recent outcomes. If my candidate won, it must have been fair; if the other one won, the election must have been stolen.

Much of the blame for the lack of confidence in Washington State must go to the abysmal performance of King County election officials. At the beginning of reading his oral opinion in the Rossi election contest, Judge Bridges said he was declining the parties' invitations to use his decision to "send a message," but he sent one anyway.

> Mr. Logan in his testimony in court and, more particularly, in his deposition testimony referred to the culture he found when he assumed the responsibilities of the Director of Elections in King County. Almost anyone who works in state or local government knows exactly what this culture is. It's inertia. It's selfishness. It's taking our paycheck but not doing the work. It's not caring about either our fellow workers or the public we are supposed to serve. It's not taking responsibility. It's refusing to be held accountable. And so it is the voters who should send the message.

Public faith in elections

v i[r]s election officals

Unlike Al Gore, Rossi got another turn, running against Gregoire for governor again in 2008. This time Gregoire defeated him soundly. The state switched to all-mail balloting for its elections, and although the procedure had its critics, including those who worried about the potential for fraud and abuse, the state seemed to have taken major steps to improve its elections, especially in King County. Dean Logan, the King County elections director who walked into a mess in Seattle shortly before Rossi-Gregoire hit, has now moved to be the chief election official in Los Angeles County, the largest election jurisdiction in the nation.

✔   *2010 Tea Party "write-in"*

Lisa Murkowski faced her election law difficulties in 2010, stemming from her difficult-to-spell last name. The incumbent Republican U.S. senator from Alaska faced an unexpectedly strong Tea Party challenge from Joe Miller and ended up losing the Republican primary.[24]

So she decided to run as a write-in candidate, and this is where the spelling issue arose: how to handle the "Leeza Markovsky" vote. "Murkowski" is not easy to spell, and Miller and Murkowski ended up litigating, both before and after the election, over whether misspelled write-in votes for Murkowski should be counted. Election officials said they would count misspellings where voter intent was clear, though they sent conflicting signals on whether a "Lisa M." ballot would count for Murkowski. The dispute led another "Lisa M." to enter the race as a write-in, presumably to help Miller.

The litigation between the candidates ended when it was clear that even without misspelled ballots, Murkowski had enough votes to beat Miller. Still, it is useful to review the controversy to show how even a decade after *Bush v. Gore,* fundamental questions about resolving election disputes remain up in the air and would have been grist for more contentious court decisions had the election been within the margin of litigation.

To begin with, the fight illustrated a tension we saw in *Bush v. Gore* and *Coleman v. Franken* between deferring to the voters' apparent intent and sticking to clear rules—established ahead of time—so that election officials or judges can't manipulate the process of judging voter intent to favor a particular candidate. Miller's argument against counting misspellings depended upon the Alaska statute providing that write-in votes "shall be counted if the oval is filled in for that candidate and if the name, as it appears on the write-in declaration of candidacy, of the candidate or the last name of the candidate is written in the space provided." The statute further says that the rules are "mandatory and there are no exceptions to them. A ballot may not be counted unless marked in compliance with these rules."

Miller read the rules to require perfect spelling, but Alaska election officials went with a looser standard of "voter intent," which allows for misspellings. That decision followed the Alaska Supreme Court's long-standing use of the Democracy Canon to construe unclear statutes and to follow an intent-of-the-voter standard. Ultimately, the Alaska Supreme Court affirmed, yet again, that election officials could count misspelled ballots when the voters' intent was clear.

Miller raised three other arguments, all related to *Bush v. Gore*. First, he argued that the plan for counting the Murkowski write-ins amounted to a new rule established for this election, and so it must come from the Alaska legislature, not election officials. The elections clause of the Constitution gives each state *legislature* the power to choose the rules for picking members of Congress (unless Congress overrides a state's choice). This argument is just like the Republican contention that the Florida Supreme Court had usurped the power of the Florida legislature when it set the rules for counting the votes in the 2000 presidential election. In *Bush v. Gore*, only three justices (Rehnquist, Scalia, and Thomas) bought that argument. If it was accepted in the Alaska case, this idea would have profound implications. It would mean that election officials could never come up with regulations to implement the legislature's rules for congressional elections.

Miller's other *Bush v. Gore* argument was the familiar one about equal protection. He said that counting misspelled ballots based on voter intent would violate the Constitution's equal protection clause by treating similarly situated ballots differently. But in Alaska, it appears that one person, the director of elections, would judge all the contested ballots, which minimizes the risk of inconsistency.

In his federal court suit, Miller made yet a third *Bush*-related argument: as a matter of fairness, the rules for running an election should not be changed midstream. To do so not only upsets settled expectations; it also reeks of lawlessness and raises the possibility of manipulation by the people making the rules up as they go along. This "due process" argument echoed the subtext of the *Bush v. Gore* majority's discomfort with the recounting of punch card ballots in Florida. Changing the rules for counting write-ins could violate due process protections against arbitrary and disparate treatment by the government.

Because Murkowski's victory over Miller put the election beyond the margin of litigation, these issues did not get fully litigated. There was a similar situation in Minnesota in 2010. Initially, the race for governor between Democrat Mark Dayton and Republican Tom Emmer was too close to call. But although everyone feared another Coleman-Franken saga, Emmer conceded when the automatic recount showed him trailing by almost nine thousand votes.[25]

Both Murkowski-Miller and Dayton-Emmer show that since 2000, the easiest way to avoid protracted election litigation has been for one candidate to win decisively. Not better rules, better machines, or taking the high road. Instead, divine intervention following the Election Administrator's Prayer:

Lord, let this election not be close.
Amen.

6

Deus ex Machina

ail! to the victors valiant
Hail! to the conqu'ring heroes
Hail! Hail! to Michigan
the leaders and best
Hail! to the victors valiant
Hail! to the conqu'ring heroes
Hail! Hail! to Michigan,
the champions of the West![1]

ABSENTEE +
Military votes

Paul Stenbjorn, the technology guru of the Washington, D.C., elections and ethics board, was not amused, but many in Ann Arbor were. The University of Michigan's fight song, "The Victors," was playing through the board's computers. Go Blue!

The Wolverine hacking came in response to the board's 2010 invitation to computer geeks to "give it your best shot" at exposing vulnerabilities in an experimental system the board had set up to receive ballots from military and other overseas voters over the Internet.[2] "To be quite honest," Stenbjorn told the Associated Press, "I didn't listen to it. I was less concerned with what the file was. Just knowing it was there was enough." He added that there were no Michigan alumni on the elections board.

It was a noble experiment, and the Michigan hackers performed an important public service. For years, election boards have struggled to send blank ballots to voters who are outside the United States, for military, government, business, or other reasons, and get those marked ballots back, validated, and counted. Could the Internet be the answer?

As we saw in chapter 1, overseas ballots were one of the key factors pushing George W. Bush's Florida vote totals beyond Gore's reach in 2000, and reports that emerged only after Bush was declared president raised serious questions about how these ballots were handled and whose votes got counted. Military ballots have been a sensitive issue ever since.

After Congress passed the Help America Vote Act in 2002, with decidedly ambiguous results, national election reform stalled. While Democrats offered a host of proposals for election reform—including modernizing voter registration on a national scale—these measures had no support on the Republican side of the aisle. The only other piece of significant election reform legislation to emerge from Congress since Florida 2000 is the Military and Overseas Voters Empowerment (MOVE) Act, which made it easier for these voters to cast valid ballots. It took until 2009 to get this legislation passed.

It wasn't lost on anyone that Republicans would be more inclined to support legislation making it easier to vote if the legislation helped military voters. Aside from the general point of patriotism—those who risk their lives for our country should not face the prospect of disenfranchisement—a 2003 *Military Times* survey found that 57 percent of military members, and a whopping 66 percent of officers, considered themselves Republicans, and only 13 percent of military members, and 9 percent of officers, identified as Democrats. And so the MOVE Act was born, updating a 1986 law ensuring the counting of military and overseas votes, and maybe, if it worked, giving Republicans a boost at the polls.[3]

The measure called for a number of changes making it easier for military and overseas voters to cast a ballot, including a requirement that states transmit blank ballots to overseas voters at least forty-five days before a federal election, that ballot materials and registration forms be available electronically, and that states provide overseas voters electronic access to a fail-safe federal absentee write-in ballot in case the paper ballot materials do not arrive in time.

Like everything else related to the mechanics of elections since 2000, the MOVE Act has caused a partisan rift. A major area of contention has been the forty-five-day requirement for election officials to mail ballots overseas, which has forced some states to adjust their primary schedules and make other changes to the timing of their elections. The Department of Justice was given the power to waive compliance with the time limits and to enforce the law. The Obama Justice Department granted some waivers, denied others, and brought suit against some states for failing to comply with MOVE requirements. Many of those suits resulted in settlements, with states agreeing to change their procedures.[4]

Republicans have criticized the department for doing too little to protect military voting under the new law. In calling on the Justice Department to be more aggressive in 2012 to make states observe the forty-five-day limit, John Cornyn, the Republican U.S. senator from Texas, wrote to Obama attorney general Eric Holder in 2011 that "the November 2010 elections were marred by the Justice Department's grossly inadequate enforcement of federal laws designed to safeguard the voting rights of our military service members and their families."[5]

Hans von Spakovsky and former Justice Department voting rights attorney and current department critic J. Christian Adams have also been vocal about the Obama administration's efforts on behalf of military voters, fitting what they see as the department's lax enforcement of the MOVE Act into a broader pro–Democratic Party pattern: turn the other way on African-American-driven voter suppression efforts (think New Black Panthers) and rampant voter fraud (think ACORN), but suppress the (Republican) military vote. As Adams wrote in the *Washington Examiner,* "At DOJ, encouraging felons to vote is more important than helping a Marine understand her new rights."[6]

While these hyperbolic claims don't hold water, there is much to criticize about federal, state, and local efforts on military balloting.

It is hard to argue that the slow implementation of the MOVE Act was the Justice Department's fault. State and local election officials fight federal interference with election procedures at every turn, and it is fairly difficult for state and local governments to quickly change their procedures for preparing ballots. Often there is litigation about what goes on the ballot, or in what order, and the MOVE Act's forty-five-day limit ends up affecting a range of decisions and deadlines that local election officials must attend to. We will see how things go in the 2012 elections, when states and the department have had more experience working under the new deadlines.

Whether or not the Justice Department is to blame, the statistics on military voting, even after the 2010 rollout of the MOVE Act, are troubling. According to a study by the Military Voter Protection Project (MVPP) of two million military voters in twenty-four states, "only 4.6 percent of those voters cast an absentee ballot that counted in 2010. This percentage represents a significant decrease from the last mid-term election in 2006, when 5.5 percent of military and overseas voters were able to cast an absentee ballot that counted." According to the study, only 15.8 percent of military voters even requested an absentee ballot in 2010, also down from 2006. Taking into account in-person voting rates from 2006, the project estimated a military voting rate of about 11.6 percent.[7]

The Federal Voting Assistance Program, part of the Department of Defense, recently released a report painting a much rosier picture of military absentee voting than that described by the MVPP. The agency estimated a 46 percent military voting rate in 2010, although it acknowledged that the number of military voters who did not receive their requested absentee ballots increased from 16 percent in 2008 to 29 percent in 2010.[8]

Whether military turnout is abysmally low (as the Military Voter Protection Project suggests) or just poor (as the Federal Voting Assistance Program suggests), the country needs to do a much better job of ensuring that military voters and other overseas voters receive absentee ballots, can cast them, and can return them to have them counted. The MVPP report ends with a call for greater use of the Internet to cast overseas absentee ballots: "Congress should consider whether fax machines are a viable form of technology to meet the electronic delivery requirements under the MOVE Act. Given the outdated nature of this technology, as well as its limited use by overseas military voters, it may be time to require states to adopt either an online or email delivery mechanism to meet the electronic delivery requirements."

This brings us back to the Michigan fight song, which scuttled the Washington, D.C., experiment with Internet-based voting for military and overseas voters.

"Access versus integrity" is the phrase by which election law folks describe the battles over voter fraud and voter identification that we've seen earlier in this book. But it is an especially apt phrase for the wars over the use of the Internet to allow these hard-to-reach voters to cast a ballot, and it flips the usual pattern of Republicans arguing for greater integrity and Democrats for greater access. In this circumstance, at least some Republicans argue for greater access for military voters over the Internet, and computer scientists, good government groups, at least some Democrats, and a fair number of left-wing conspiracy theorists argue for integrity. For the time being, "The Victors" of Michigan have won the debate for the integrity side.

The MOVE Act requires that certain ballot materials, such as voter registration materials, be available electronically, and there has been some debate over whether the law allows (or mandates) a procedure for the electronic *return* of overseas ballots. According to a study by Candice Hoke and Matthew Bishop, "At least half of all States now offer some option of electronic transmission of marked ballots. A significant number of these States permit voted (marked) ballots to be returned by email."[9]

The D.C. board went even further, participating in a pilot project funded through the MOVE Act to test the wider use of Internet web browsers (such as Firefox, Safari, and Internet Explorer) in the overseas vote experience. To its credit, rather than rolling out untested technology, the board opened its proposed Internet voting website for public testing. Inviting hackers to try to break in was a terrific way to harness the power of crowds and a spirit of good-natured competitiveness to test a system about which many voters had their doubts. And if the experiment showed that election officials could create a secure Internet voting environment for overseas voters, it might create momentum to move to Internet voting more generally.

Instead, the test showed that the D.C. system was extremely vulnerable to attack. Here is how J. Alex Halderman, the Michigan computer scientist who led a team of students attempting the hack, described what they did, when, and how:

> D.C. launched the public testbed server on Tuesday, September 28. On Wednesday afternoon, we began to exploit the problem we found to demonstrate a number of attacks:
>
> - We collected crucial secret data stored on the server, including the database username and password as well as the public key used to encrypt the ballots.
> - We modified all the ballots that had already been cast to contain write-in votes for candidates we selected. (Although the system encrypts voted ballots, we simply discarded the encrypted files and replaced them with different ones that we encrypted using the same key.) We also rigged the system to replace future votes in the same way.
> - We installed a back door that let us view any ballots that voters cast after our attack. This modification recorded the votes, in unencrypted form, together with the names of the voters who cast them, violating ballot secrecy.
> - To show that we had control of the server, we left a "calling card" on the system's confirmation screen, which voters see after voting. After 15 seconds, the page plays the University of Michigan fight song. . . .
>
> Stealthiness wasn't our main objective, and our demonstration had a much greater footprint inside the system than a real attack would need. Nevertheless, we did not immediately announce what we had done, because we wanted to give the administrators an opportunity to exercise their intrusion detection and recovery processes—an essential part of any online voting system. Our attack remained active for two business days, until Friday afternoon, when D.C. officials took down the testbed server after several testers pointed out the fight song.[10]

Scary stuff for those concerned about the security of the vote.

Even worse for proponents of Internet voting were Halderman's conclusions about the D.C. system generally: "The specific vulnerability that we exploited is simple to fix, but it will be vastly more difficult to make the system secure. We've found a number of other problems in the system, and everything we've seen suggests that the design is *brittle:* one small mistake can completely compromise its security."

Halderman's conclusions support what many computer scientists have said: when it comes to voting, the Internet is simply not ready for prime time. Computer scientist (and leading Internet voting opponent) David Jefferson said of the Michigan hack: "Let there be no mistake about it: this is a major achievement, and supports in every detail the warnings that security community have been giving about Internet voting for over a decade now. After this there can be no doubt that the burden of proof in the argument over the security of Internet voting systems has definitely shifted to those who claim that the systems can be made secure."[11]

Speaking with *Time* magazine, MIT computer scientist Ron Rivest was similarly glum about the near-term prospects for Internet voting: "We don't have the technology yet to do this in a secure way, and we may not for a decade or more. [The worst case scenario is] elections that end up with a totally unclear result. . . . You may find the entire system taken over and trashed."[12]

Every day the news brings reports of cyberattacks and hacking on government and industry computers by private operatives and, likely, foreign governments. Halderman detected hack attempts from China and Iran in the D.C. experiment. In this poor security environment, it would be foolish to expect that Internet voting systems would not be targets, too. An Internet voting program that can gain the confidence of computer scientists may be out of reach.

Many people who are not computer experts are skeptical of the difficulties with Internet voting. After all, don't we engage in secure online banking transactions all the time without hacking? But this argument doesn't wash. First, banking is not anonymous, and there are numerous ways to check if there is an error and demand correction (wouldn't you notice if your checkbook balance changed unexpectedly?). In contrast, there is no way for a voter to verify that his or her vote was accurately counted. Second, and perhaps more important, the premise of the question is wrong. The banking industry loses billions each year to online thievery, but banks accept those losses as a cost of doing business and try to minimize public knowledge of the extent of Internet theft.[13]

What would we do if the group "Anonymous" claimed that it had hacked presidential election results broadcast over the Internet? Further, what would happen if that claim could not be proven or disproven? Financial transactions under questionable circumstances can be easily reversed in ways that election results cannot.

MILTARY / HACKING

Stenbjorn of the D.C. board vows to fight on. "With all due respect to Mr. Jefferson, the lesson learned is not to be more timid, but more aggressive about solving the problem in exactly the way that we have chosen. Our task is to continue pursuing a robust, secure digital means for overseas voters to cast their ballot rather than resorting to e-mail or fax. As Thomas Edison famously said, 'Nearly every man who develops an idea works at it up to the point where it looks impossible, and then gets discouraged. That's not the place to become discouraged.'"

Halderman's response to Stenbjorn's optimism? "Voting over the Internet is just so far from a good idea using today's technology that it's a little bit startling to me that jurisdictions are seriously considering it."[14]

Aside from the hacking, the D.C. system had other problems, including reports that compatibility issues led Mac users to submit blank ballots. That's not to say that Internet voting will never be ready technologically. Experiments like Washington's will need to be done repeatedly and show success to convince computer scientists that the system is hack-proof.[15]

Even then, there may be serious concerns with voter confidence that would caution against adopting such a system. We know from recent experience that conspiracy-minded people on the left and right would complain that unverifiable Internet votes were the deciding factor in a razor-thin election. "How do we know the votes weren't hacked?" will be the losers' fallback, stirring up foment that cannot be quelled with a statement from election officials like "Trust us." "Show me the code" will not be an adequate substitute for "Show me the ballots," especially when voting companies don't make their source code public. In short, even if we could overcome the technological problems, Internet voting carries too much political risk in this era of hyperpolarized politics.

At least in the near term, the failure of browser-based Internet voting means that electronic submission of marked ballots by overseas voters will be limited to fax and email. These technologies present serious security issues as well: how do we know that the emails are genuine, successfully arrived at election offices, and have not been hacked? Further, neither faxes nor emails preserve ballot secrecy. That alone gives reason for election experts to look to lower-tech solutions for the return of marked ballots.[16]

Military and overseas participation in elections is now so low that it can be improved substantially by low-tech means. As a country we can make an effort to encourage more than 15 percent of military voters to request an absentee ballot and more than 5 percent to actually vote in a federal election. Using the Internet to distribute blank ballots and materials is fine, but when it comes to returning ballots, more low-tech solutions should be offered, such as making sure that military mail service is expedited and handled carefully during election times. Increasing turnout is a more pressing need than experimenting with Internet voting.[17]

✔ *2006*
Most expensive race
in
house
history

Vern Buchanan and Christine Jennings were battling for the seat in Florida's thirteenth congressional district being vacated by Katherine Harris. Harris, who successfully ran for Congress after her famous stint as Florida's secretary of state, was leaving her congressional seat in 2006 to run for U.S. Senate. Although she won the Republican primary, incumbent Democratic U.S. senator Bill Nelson crushed her, 60 percent to 38 percent, in the general election.[18]

Things were much closer in the Buchanan-Jennings race. The Republican Buchanan led the Democrat Jennings on election night by about 400 votes out of more than 230,000 votes cast. Theirs was the most expensive House race in the country in 2006.[19]

The district sits on Florida's beautiful Gulf Coast. Half of it is the busy city of Sarasota, but the district comprises other areas, too, including some idyllic beach communities. According to the *Almanac of American Politics,* "Though some high-tech firms diversify the economy, the district as a whole remains a place of tourists and well-off retirees: 26% of its population is 65 and older, and it has 195,000 Social Security recipients, the second highest level of all congressional districts in Florida."[20]

As results rolled in on election night, a strange pattern emerged. The *Sarasota Herald Tribune,* which later provided essential coverage of the Buchanan-Jennings dispute, reported that "many people apparently chose not to vote in the District 13 race. About 8,000 to 10,000 fewer people voted in the race than in the other high-profile races for governor, attorney general and U.S. Senate." There were also absentee ballots that awaited counting. The race was too close to call.[21]

Undervote / voting Machines

Why would thousands of people apparently not vote in this hard-fought, high-profile election, especially when control of the entire United States House of Representatives was on the line? In this election Democrats nationally retook control of the House (only to lose it again in 2010), and everyone knew that any close House election could mean the difference between the next Congress having Speaker Dennis Hastert or Speaker Nancy Pelosi. Many Sarasota ballots had votes recorded in every high-profile race *but* this one.

Once the vote counting was done, the numbers coming out of Sarasota were even more startling. Buchanan led Jennings by 369 votes, but more than 18,000 Sarasota ballots lacked a valid vote in the congressional race. Suspicion turned immediately to the electronic voting machines that Sarasota County had adopted after dumping its punch card machines following the Florida 2000 debacle. Sarasota used touch-screen machines made by Election Systems & Software, bought at a cost of $4.5 million. Voters made their choices by touching the image of a box on the screen to the right of the candidate's name and party. The technology was familiar to anyone who has used an ATM.[22]

The undervote rate in the Buchanan-Jennings race in Sarasota County was an extremely high 13.9 percent for voters who voted on touch-screen machines on Election Day, and an even higher 17.6 percent for Sarasota touch-screen voters who took advantage of an "early voting" period in the days before the election. Yet Sarasota voters who used paper ballots (for example, to vote by absentee ballot) had an undervote rate of only 2.5 percent. The 13.9 percent figure also contrasted sharply with Sarasota's undervote rate in the 2002 congressional election (2.2 percent). Further, voters outside Sarasota County but within the thirteenth congressional district had much lower undervote rates in the 2006 Buchanan-Jennings race, ranging from 2.1 percent to 5.8 percent. As Jennings's lawyers later explained, Sarasotans made up only half the voters in the Buchanan-Jennings contest but accounted for 86 percent of the undervotes.[23]

What went wrong? Kathy Dent, the Sarasota County elections supervisor, initially claimed that the problem was deliberate undervoting by voters, a theory that made no sense when judged against the statistics. No plausible reason exists why Sarasota voters in the thirteenth district would be so much more likely to undervote than non-Sarasota voters in the same district, or why Sarasota voters who used paper absentee ballots would choose to vote in much higher numbers than electronic voters.[24]

Dent's claims also were belied by evidence of problems during early voting. Just before Election Day, the *Sarasota Herald-Tribune* reported: "Poll workers are to remind every voter to look out for the 13th Congressional District race on the electronic ballot after at least four people complained that their initial votes for Democrat Christine Jennings weren't recorded. Sarasota County Supervisor of Elections Kathy Dent gave the order by e-mail, calling it 'critical.' She told the *Herald-Tribune* she believes a very small number of the 24,000 early voters overlooked the 13th Congressional District race because it 'is sandwiched in between the Senate and the governor's race.'" "A very small number" turned out to be over 17 percent of early voters in Sarasota.

With voter choice ruled out, there remained two plausible explanations for the undervote: one, the one put forward by Jennings, was that something was wrong with the voting machines, either malicious code or some software bug. The other possibility, supported by voting machine maker ES&S, was poor ballot design. The congressional race appeared on the second of twenty-one screens on the Sarasota touch-screen machines, and the ballot layout made it very easy for hurried voters to miss the congressional race appearing at the top of the second screen above a large heading for state races, beginning with governor–lieutenant governor races. I have reprinted the ballot screenshots in black and white, but the color version makes it even easier to miss the congressional race at the top of the second screen.

As Jennings's lawyers later put it, "Jennings claimed that the machines malfunctioned, ES&S claimed that the voters malfunctioned, and Dent claimed that the candidates malfunctioned."[25]

Opponents of electronic voting machines (called DRE—direct recording electronic—machines by those in the voting technology business) fought against their adoption long before the Sarasota problem. In fact, in the same election as the Buchanan-Jennings race, Sarasota voters overwhelm-

OFFICIAL GENERAL ELECTION BALLOT
SARASOTA COUNTY, FLORIDA
NOVEMBER 7, 2006

CONGRESSIONAL

UNITED STATES SENATOR
(Vote for One)

Katherine Harris	REP ☐
Bill Nelson	DEM ☐
Floyd Ray Frazier	NPA ☐
Belinda Noah	NPA ☐
Brian Moore	NPA ☐
Roy Tanner	NPA ☐
Write-In	☐

Page 1 of 21	Next
Public Count: 0	Page

Screenshot of first screen on electronic ballot, Sarasota County, Florida, 2006

ingly approved an amendment to their county charter to bar the use of any voting technology that did not include a printout showing the voters' choices for each race on the ballot.

A so-called voter verified paper audit trail could be used in the event of a recount and to make sure that the machine recorded the votes as the voter intended. It is possible to design electronic voting machines with a paper printout to be saved by election officials in the event of a recount or to audit the vote totals to make sure the machines are working properly—some jurisdictions have such machines—but Sarasota did not.

Electronic voting machine critics raised issues similar to those with Internet voting: if everything is taking place inside the machines, what safeguards prevent malicious code inserted by a hacker or a software glitch

U.S. REPRESENTATIVE IN CONGRESS
13TH CONGRESSIONAL DISTRICT
(Vote for One)

Vern Buchanan	REP	☐
Christine Jennings	DEM	☐

STATE

GOVERNOR AND LIEUTENANT GOVERNOR
(Vote for One)

Charlie Crist Jeff Kottkamp	REP	☐
Jim Davis Daryl L. Jones	DEM	☐
Max Linn Tom Macklin	REP	☐
Richard Paul Dembinsky Dr. Joe Smith	NPA	☐
John Wayne Smith James J. Kearney	NPA	☐
Karl C.C. Behm Carol Castagnero	NPA	☐
Write-In		☐

Previous Page	Page 2 of 21 Public Count: 0	Next Page

Screenshot of second screen on electronic ballot, Sarasota County,
Florida, 2006

from affecting the vote totals? Of course, the potential for problems escalates when the voting technology is accessible over the Internet.

Even if not connected to the Internet, electronic voting machines present
additional challenges. Internet voting requires no special equipment beyond a computer with a web browser and Internet connection. Electronic
voting machines, on the other hand, are designed only for elections and
must be brought to polling places, set up, and managed by poll workers,
many of whom are older voters inexperienced with computers. If the machines must also have a printer set up and maintained with paper, potential
polling place issues multiply.

But for some electronic voting opponents, that printer is crucial. One
electronic voting opponent in California, Susan Weber, went so far as to sue the

California secretary of state and the registrar of voters in Riverside County in federal court to force election officials to bar the use of electronic voting machines without a paper trail. She claimed that the use of such machines deprived her of equal protection under *Bush v. Gore,* because she was less certain than other voters of casting a ballot that would actually be counted.[26]

Weber's concern was not necessarily that the machinery was unreliable, like punch card ballot machines, which California had decertified. Instead, she claimed that because of the potential for hacking or software glitches, there was no way to know that the electronic voting machine she voted on was accurately recording her choices.

The Ninth Circuit Court of Appeals easily rejected Weber's argument, saying the choice of voting equipment was one for the political branches of government:

> No balloting system is perfect. Traditional paper ballots, as became evident during the 2000 presidential election, are prone to overvotes, undervotes, "hanging chads," and other mechanical and human errors that may thwart voter intent. . . . Meanwhile, touchscreen voting systems remedy a number of these problems, albeit at the hypothetical price of vulnerability to programming "worms." . . . The unfortunate reality is that the possibility of electoral fraud can never be completely eliminated, no matter which type of ballot is used. . . . However, it is the job of democratically-elected representatives to weigh the pros and cons of various balloting systems. So long as their choice is reasonable and neutral, it is free from judicial second-guessing.

Although the Ninth Circuit did not find a constitutional problem with electronic voting machines lacking a paper trail, computer scientists and others continued to express serious reservations about their security. Bev Harris of Black Box Voting, a leading opponent of electronic voting machines, somehow obtained the source code for a machine made by Diebold, one of the largest makers of electronic voting machines, and posted it on her website, allowing everyone to see if it had security vulnerabilities. As MIT's Charles Stewart explains, "The analysis of the code by a team of computer scientists revealed an astonishing set of defects, including those that would allow voters to vote multiple times with forged smart cards and others that could give precinct workers virtually unfettered access to machines, allowing them to alter ballot definitions and vote tallies."[27]

Touch Screens vs electronic paper ballot

With all the controversy surrounding the machines, why would any jurisdiction want to adopt them? In usability testing, many voters liked them more than optical scans or other ballots; they were as easy to use as an ATM machine. Sarasota 2006 aside, electronic voting machines had among the lowest rates of undervotes of all types of voting machines. Fewer than 1 percent of Alameda County voters, who used electronic voting machines, failed to record a choice in the 2003 California gubernatorial recall, compared with 9 percent of Los Angeles punch card voters. The machines are designed to be accessible by some disabled voters, and the Help America Vote Act now mandates that each polling place have at least one disabled-accessible machine. Electronic voting machines also can be programmed to comply with the new HAVA requirement that the machinery be designed to notify voters in the event of an overvoted or undervoted ballot. The machines leave no "hanging chads." It is no surprise that many jurisdictions, in Florida and elsewhere, rushed in to buy electronic voting machines when political pressure and HAVA money made it the right time to get rid of bad, old voting technology.

Despite these benefits, opponents favor optically scanned ballots because they provide a paper trail that can be used to verify that the vote counting machines worked correctly and to perform a hand recount in a very close race like the Coleman-Franken race in Minnesota. Nonetheless, opponents of electronic voting have also raised questions about the security of the software running the machines that count optically scanned ballots. With software running all types of vote counting machines, hacking and software glitches are possible in every election.

As we will see, some critics have raised valid concerns. But others have moved into the realm of tinfoil-hat conspiracy theories. The paranoia began with the statement by former Diebold president Walden O'Dell in a fundraising letter that he would "deliver" Ohio's electoral votes for President Bush in his 2004 reelection battle. O'Dell was writing to raise funds for Bush, not to signal that the fix was in. If the Diebold machines really had a secret code in them to flip Democratic votes for Republicans, O'Dell would hardly have been so rash as to advertise it in a letter sent to hundreds of people asking for funds for Bush. It was a stupid letter for someone in his position to send, but there was never any proof that Diebold machines were rigged. Even Brad Friedman, one of the most ardent foes of Diebold and the use of electronic voting equipment, had to concede that "it hasn't been shown that Diebold has actually thrown any elections." That hasn't stopped the conspiracy theorists from throwing around allegations of stolen elections.[28]

The fringe left's equivalent to the Fraudulent Fraud Squad is out there making unsubstantiated claims (think of Robert F. Kennedy Jr.'s assertions, which we saw in chapter 3) but drawing far less attention than the squad. Among the machine conspiracy theorists, there is tremendous distrust of the voting machine companies and a belief, not backed up by any valid scientific proof I have seen, that the companies are involved in a conspiracy to manipulate election results to help Republicans. So far, fewer Democrats seem to buy into the right-wing conspiracy on voting machines than Republicans who buy into the left-wing voter fraud conspiracy, but that could change with the next election controversy.

Let's be clear: there is no more proof of a vast Republican conspiracy to steal elections through hidden software in voting machines than there is proof of a vast Democratic conspiracy to steal elections through voter impersonation fraud.

What's really going on with the voting machines? The story should by now be familiar: Hanlon's razor. Incompetence, not criminality.

In 2007, California secretary of state Debra Bowen, who has more technical knowledge than most elected secretaries of state, organized a "top to bottom review" of the voting machinery and software used in California counties. A number of computer scientists and other researchers, many from the University of California, found numerous flaws in the hardware and software of every voting machine tested. Unnecessarily open ports on equipment, outdated software, easy-to-open machines: Bowen's teams found all sorts of defects that could be exploited by hackers or cause inadvertent changes leading to the reporting of incorrect vote totals.[29]

Bowen decertified all the electronic voting machines then used by counties and decertified optical scan systems and other voting systems as well until the manufacturers could make hardware and software security enhancements. The decertification order caused some upheaval in California, as manufacturers and local election officials scrambled to put approved machines in place for the next elections.

Manufacturers claimed that Bowen's review was unrealistic. The researchers had unlimited access to private internal manuals and to all of the machinery, which normally would be protected by manufacturers and by election official security measures. The review not only made the manufacturers angry but also put Bowen at odds with county voting officials, who resented state interference with their control over voting technology. Bowen defended the tests on grounds that the machinery and software needed to be designed to prevent hacking or errors in the event of a security breach.[30]

Jennifer Brunner, the Ohio secretary of state, soon commenced a similar review, named EVEREST, in Ohio. Her task force found similar vulnerabilities and recommended changes to Ohio's voting equipment and procedures.[31]

Perhaps it was because both Bowen and Brunner are Democrats who received the John F. Kennedy Profile in Courage Award for their work on the security of voting technology. Perhaps it was because the conspiracy theories surrounding the voting machines thrived more on the left than the right. Or perhaps it was the Buchanan-Jennings fight itself that put the Democrats on the side of questioning the integrity of voting machine software.[32] For whatever reason, voting technology and security issues now sometimes have a partisan cast. Democrats are much more concerned about security questions of voting machines and vote counting machines than Republicans are. But Republicans could jump on that bandwagon, too, if a major Republican candidate finds him- or herself slightly behind in an election in which the security or accuracy of the voting technology could be called into question. It would a shame if this should develop into another partisan issue. There are legitimate questions that need to be asked and answered about our voting technology.

Back in Sarasota, elections supervisor Kathy Dent, a Republican, fought all the way to the Florida Supreme Court against the validity of the county charter amendment, put on the ballot by county voters, to block the use of voting machines without paper trails and to establish independent audits of her elections. It was certainly unusual for a local election official to claim that questions of how to run elections were matters for state, not local, control. But Dent had been battling Democrats and electronic voting machine opponents ever since the county spent millions on the new machines, and

Introfxd
★ a

the charter amendment expressed *voters'* views of how to run local elections, not those of local election officials.[33]

Dent eventually lost her appeal in the Florida Supreme Court, but long before that loss, she junked the new electronic voting machines in favor of optically scanned ballots. The Buchanan-Jennings controversy so soured Floridians on electronic voting machines that Governor Charlie Crist eventually signed legislation to outlaw their use statewide.[34]

After 2000, in an understandable rush to get rid of its punch card machines, Florida rushed headlong into buying shiny new electronic machines. And just as quickly, voter confidence in the machines plummeted, especially after the Buchanan-Jennings controversy. The state has now spent millions more on still newer voting machines, in a boon to the manufacturers and to the dismay of its taxpayers. Florida is trying desperately not to be the next Florida.

Members of Congress hold their seats for only two years, and the Buchanan-Jennings fight lasted well into the second year of Buchanan's term. He was certified the winner and took his seat in Congress provisionally, subject to Jennings's challenges. First, Jennings brought suit in state court, contesting the congressional election by claiming that an error in the ES&S software was to blame for her loss. This was her only hope in litigation; if the problem was bad ballot design, the court was not going to order a new election, just as the court in Palm Beach County did not order a new election in 2000 based on voter confusion over the butterfly ballot—though of course in Buchanan-Jennings the problem mercifully was not on a presidential scale.[35]

Jennings's lawyers had a daunting task. How could they prove that the problem was with the machine's code rather than with the ballot design? ES&S's code was not public. The company protected it as a "trade secret" so that competitors could not use it to build competing voting machines.

The key to Jennings's case was "discovery," the litigation tool that includes obtaining a court order for information from an opposing party (or a third party) that would be relevant to the investigation. ES&S resisted discovery, asserting a privilege when Jennings sought to examine the source code for the voting machines. Not every relevant piece of information is subject to discovery. For example, a party in litigation cannot use discovery to find out what a client told his or her lawyer, because doing so would violate attorney-client privilege. ES&S claimed a "trade secret" privilege to bar Jennings discovery of the source code.

Jennings offered to have her designated experts sign confidentiality agreements to protect the company's secrets. ES&S still refused to produce the code. After months of wrangling in the Florida courts—all with Buchanan (temporarily) serving and voting as the member of Congress for Florida's thirteenth congressional district—a Florida appeals court upheld the trial court's order denying Jennings's request. That effectively ended her case.

Jennings had one more chance to contest the election's outcome: going directly to the House of Representatives. The U.S. Constitution gives each house of Congress the ultimate power to resolve election disputes: "Each House shall be the Judge of the Elections, Returns and Qualifications of its own Members." The procedure is used more often than you might think. In 1985, the Democratic House reversed the results of an Indiana House of Representatives race between incumbent Democrat Frank McCloskey and challenger Republican Richard McIntyre, finding that McCloskey won by four votes. The decision was very controversial; 179 House Republicans stormed off the floor in protest, believing that Democrats had stolen the election for McCloskey. Then in 1996, Republican incumbent Bob Dornan tried to challenge a declaration that Democratic challenger Loretta Sanchez had won the Orange County, California, congressional district. Dornan claimed that Sanchez benefited from illegal votes by Latino noncitizens. The House investigated and found some evidence of noncitizen voting, but not enough to overturn the result.[36]

With the Buchanan-Jennings dispute in the House, Republicans first dragged their feet in appointing members to the task force to review Jennings's allegations. They claimed that the state proceedings should conclude first, but of course the longer Buchanan stayed in his seat, the better it was for them. Eventually the House Administration Committee formed a bipartisan task force to investigate, with two Democrats and a Republican (at this time Democrats had control of the House and therefore an extra member on the task force).

The task force voted two to one to investigate Jennings's claims (the two Democrats voting for investigation, the one Republican voting against), but they unanimously agreed to appoint as investigators the Government Accountability Office, an independent, nonpartisan agency that works for Congress. Buchanan wanted no investigation at all and Jennings wanted a broader investigation, not conducted by the agency. The GAO investigation was a good compromise because the agency has a stellar reputation for independence and integrity.

Over many months, the GAO first looked into what tests of voting equipment might be appropriate to investigate Jennings's allegations. The state of Florida, meanwhile, conducted its own investigation. The agency eventually agreed to conduct three tests on the equipment, much less than the comprehensive examination of software code that Jennings wanted, but enough to satisfy the two Democrats on the task force.[37]

The agency then issued a report, which provided enough information to the task force for it to vote to unanimously dismiss Jennings's complaint:

> Based on the results of these tests, we have obtained increased assurance, but not absolute assurance that the iVotronic DREs used in Sarasota County's 2006 general election did not contribute to the large undervote in the Florida-13 contest. Absolute assurance is impossible to achieve because we are unable to recreate the conditions of the election in which the undervote occurred. Although the test results cannot be used to provide absolute assurance, we believe that these test results, combined with the other reviews that have been conducted by the State of Florida, GAO, and others, have significantly reduced the possibility that the iVotronic DREs were the cause of the undervote. At this point, we believe that adequate testing has been performed on the voting machine software to reach this conclusion and do not recommend further testing in this area. Given the complex interaction of people, processes, and technology that must work effectively together to achieve a successful election, we acknowledge the possibility that the large undervote in Florida's 13th Congressional District race could have been caused by factors such as voters who intentionally undervoted, or voters who did not properly cast their ballots on the iVotronic DRE, potentially because of issues relating to interaction between voters and the ballot.

Another study, published in the *Election Law Journal,* concluded that it was almost certainly poor ballot design that caused the large number of undervotes in the Jennings-Buchanan race. Among other things, the study found two other counties, Charlotte and Lee, with similarly unexplained

STATE

GOVERNOR & LIEUTENANT GOVERNOR
(Vote For One)

Charlie Crist / Jeff Kottkamp	REP	☐
Jim Davis / Daryl L. Jones	DEM	☐
Max Linn / Tom Macklin	REF	☐
Richard Paul Dembinsky / Dr. Joe Smith	NPA	☐
John Wayne Smith / James J. Kearney	NPA	☐
Karl C.C. Behm / Carol Castagnero	NPA	☐
Write-In		☐

ATTORNEY GENERAL
(Vote For One)

Bill McCollum	REP	☐
Walter "Skip" Campbell	DEM	☐

| Previous Page | Page 3 of 15 | Next Page |

Screenshot of screen with attorney general's race on electronic ballot, Charlotte County, Florida, 2006

undervotes in the same election. But in those counties, they occurred not in the congressional race but in the race for attorney general. The ballot design, used only in those counties, made it very easy for voters to miss that race. It was similar to the Sarasota layout for the Buchanan-Jennings race.[38]

If you look at the screenshot of a page from the Charlotte County ballot, it is very easy to miss the attorney general race at the bottom of the ballot screen. Charlotte's undervote rate in this race was four times the state average. A recent experiment using ballots similar to the Charlotte and Sarasota ballots showed that the most important reason voters tended to skip those races was the presence of two races on the same screen—this was more significant than the color headers or the placement of the race at the top or bottom of the ballot. The lesson: one race, one screen.[39]

Although Jennings's supporters may never fully accept the ballot design theory, the privacy of ES&S's source code prevented her side from fully examining the claim that a software glitch was at fault. My guess is that discovery would have revealed nothing in the software to explain the undervote, although it likely would have revealed other flaws.

Despite the lingering disagreement on the cause of the undervote, the experts seem to agree that more voters in Florida's thirteenth congressional district *wanted* to vote for Jennings over Buchanan. Without the flawed ballot design (or whatever caused the undervote), experts believe that Jennings would have won the election by about three thousand votes. That's probably no more consolation to Jennings than similar news was to Al Gore, who likely was the actual choice of more Florida voters in 2000.

Unlike Gore, Jennings had a chance for a do-over. In 2008, voters again had a choice to vote for Jennings or Buchanan, this time on optically scanned ballots. But incumbency is a powerful thing. Buchanan won more than 55 percent of the vote.[40]

Meanwhile, Kathy Dent had a rough time moving her county from electronic voting machines to optically scanned ballots. The county put the election system up for bid, and ES&S, which came out looking terrible in the Bowen review, the Sarasota litigation, and elsewhere, underbid Diebold by about $1 million. The Sarasota County Commissioners nonetheless chose Diebold (since renamed Premier), awarding the company a $3.5 million contract. County Commissioner Jon Thaxton said he had "totally lost" confidence in ES&S. "If it costs me a million dollars to restore the voters' faith in our election system, I'll write that check tomorrow."[41]

According to the *Herald-Tribune,* the problem with ES&S ultimately was not its machines but its lack of candor. "'In 2007, bidders were asked to describe problems their elections systems had experienced in the past and all ES&S wrote was that its system got few complaints,' said Jono Miller, who chaired the citizens advisory panel that recommended the county switch to Premier. 'They needed to explain, they needed to recognize there had been a problem,' he said. But they did not."

Nonetheless, ES&S was soon back in Sarasota. The company bought Premier and ended up with the contract after all. "ES&S' purchase earlier this month of Premier Election Solutions means the company will now provide

outrageous!

the voting machines, software and services to 68 percent of the precincts in the United States, and 65 of 67 counties in Florida, including both Sarasota and Manatee," the *Herald-Tribune* reported.

The sale led to a federal antitrust investigation and a Department of Justice order that ES&S sell its Premier assets to another company so as to diversity the voting machine market. Meanwhile, ES&S has made payments to a number of jurisdictions, including two hundred thousand dollars to troubled Cuyahoga County, Ohio, for problems with the performance of its voting equipment.[42]

With all the churn over voting systems and companies in the decade since *Bush v. Gore,* it was possible to lose sight of some good news. In 2000, the Caltech-MIT Voting Technology Project estimated the number of "lost votes" nationwide from faulty voting equipment at between four and six million. By 2004, thanks in part to improvements in voting technology (including the phase-out of punch card and lever voting machines), about one million fewer votes were lost. Professor Stewart of the Caltech-MIT Voting Technology Project estimated another three hundred thousand fewer lost votes in 2008.[43]

Meanwhile, Kathy Dent continued to tangle with skeptics. A provision of that Sarasota charter amendment required her to put in place an independent auditor to check her election results. She didn't put the audit in place for an election decided soon after the Florida Supreme Court upheld the authority of Sarasota voters to impose the requirement on her, causing her critics to come after her once again, but she promised to do it in later elections.

It was a good thing she did. An audit of a 2009 election revealed a ballot counting problem that tipped a race, and in 2011 another election was decided by fourteen votes. With margins like this, all the voting machines and procedures, as well as partisan election officials who administer the systems, will remain under the microscope for years to come.[44]

Tweeting the Next Meltdown

Wisconsin Unions [handwritten annotation]

*E*lection Day, August 2011. Following the contentious Wisconsin Supreme Court race and the controversy over Waukesha County clerk Kathy Nickolaus's handling of the ballots in that race, it was time for another vote.

Justice David Prosser, the ultimate winner in that earlier race and a former Republican legislative leader, did what everyone expected: he cast the deciding vote on the state Supreme Court to uphold the Wisconsin law limiting the collective bargaining rights of public sector unions against a challenge that the state legislature did not follow proper procedures in passing it. Few doubt that had Democrat Joanne Kloppenburg won the election, the court decision would have come out the other way.

The collective bargaining rights case was so contentious at the Wisconsin Supreme Court that during the drafting of the opinions, Prosser and Justice Ann Walsh Bradley got into a physical altercation at the courthouse, with Bradley claiming that Prosser put his hands around her neck and Prosser claiming that he was moving defensively against an attack by Bradley. The state police were called to investigate, but a special prosecutor declined to file charges.[1]

Things were just as heated outside the courthouse. Labor unions and Democrats, angry with Republican governor Scott Walker and the Republican legislature, started recall campaigns against state senators in an effort to flip the state senate to the Democrats.[2]

They succeeded in qualifying six recalls for the state ballot. Republicans, not to be outdone, qualified two recall elections against Democrats for the following week. Parties and groups spent at least thirty million dollars on campaign ads for and against the recall efforts. To capture control of the state senate, Democrats needed to win three seats in the first election and hold their other two a week later. Republicans ran phony Democratic candidates in recall primaries "to buy time for Republican state senators subject to recalls." In the end, the Democrats netted two seats, leaving the Republicans with a one-vote margin in the senate.[3]

The time leading up to the election saw its share of voting controversies. A group affiliated with the conservative Koch brothers, Americans for Prosperity, sent absentee ballot applications to Democratic areas asking recipients to send in their requests for absentee ballots two days *after* the election was to be held. The requests were to be mailed to a post office box shared with other conservative organizations. Liberal blogs and groups publicized the mailing as an effort at voter suppression; an Americans for Prosperity spokesman called it a "typo" and added, "I'm sure the liberals will try to make a mountain out of a molehill in an attempt to distract voters' attention from the issues."[4]

On Election Day, the group Election Defense Alliance sent out volunteers to conduct "exit polls." This is the group, profiled in chapter 3, that claims—without convincing evidence—that the machinery used to cast and count votes is programmed with a "red shift" to systematically aid Republican candidates.[5] Rather than use clipboards and oral interviews, as most exit pollers do, the volunteers passed out paper with the candidates' names on them and asked exiting voters to mark their choice and put it in a box—a kind of shadow election. Some election officials said that the group's methods violated the ban on "electioneering," which prevents the dissemination of anything in writing with a candidate's name close to the polling place.

Results began to roll in shortly after 8:00 p.m., when the Wisconsin polls closed. MSNBC's *Ed Show* broadcast from Madison (even though no Madi-

son residents were voting in these recall elections). The show's host, Ed
Schultz, was a cheerleader for the Democratic efforts. After a few hours,
when it became clear that Republicans were going to keep three seats and
lose two, the mood turned glum on the liberal television channel. Control
of the state senate hung on the race in Senate District 8, pitching incumbent Republican Alberta Darling against Democratic state representative
Sandy Pasch.[6]

For much of the night, the election results did not move. Pasch had a
small lead over Darling, but ten of eleven precincts from Kathy Nickolaus's
Waukesha County had not yet reported, and twelve of fifty-one Milwaukee
precincts had not reported either.[7]

Soon the Twitterverse lit up with conspiracy theories. Twitter allows users
to instantly post messages of up to 140 characters for anyone in the world
to see who chooses to follow those messages. Someone tweeting about the
Wisconsin recall could use the hashtag (or symbol) "#wirecall" as part of
their message so that other Twitter users searching for all posts on the topic
could easily find them.

From the left, Twitter messages sporting the #wirecall hashtag were
quick to accuse Nickolaus of criminally interfering with the election outcomes: "Kathy #Nickolaus should be jailed for vote tampering and voter
intimidation by proxy." "Waukesha County Clerk Kathy #Nickolaus is either THE most incompetent clerk or a lying cheat!" "Will state of #WI get
out their pitchforks&torches if Kathy #Nickolaus rigs ANOTHER election?"
"#WTF Is up with Waukesha county #WI I SMELL A ROTTEN FISH! #Wiunion
#Wirecall #FRAUD ! FIRE KATHY N NOW!"[8]

The paranoia spread beyond Twitter. After Nickolaus reported most of
Waukesha's numbers, putting Darling comfortably over the top, a state Democratic Party official told the news media, "We believe there's dirty tricks
afoot." The state chair released this statement on the party's website: "The
race to determine control of the Wisconsin Senate has fallen in the hands
of the Waukesha County clerk, who has already distinguished herself as
incompetent, if not worse. She is once more tampering with the results of
a consequential election and in the next hours we will determine our next
course of action. For now, Wisconsin should know that a dark cloud hangs
over these important results."[9]

The paranoia on the right was just as great, but it was directed against the Democrats and the outstanding votes in Milwaukee. "Amusing that no-bodys asking about MKE County being late. County with recent election #fraud convictions. Waukesha is smoke screen #wirecall." "Wait for the ACORN recounts and the absentee-voter #fraud in #wirecall." "Remember wisconsin, not only must we get more voters to vote, we have to win beyond the margin of liberal vote #fraud. #wigop #tcot #wirecall."[10]

Pasch conceded after midnight, when it was clear the election was lost. By morning, Democrats had retracted their charges of vote tampering and removed the incendiary statement from their website. The state chair re-leased a new statement: "Though we believe that Sandy Pasch was able to battle Alberta Darling to a virtual tie, on her turf, we will not pursue ques-tions of irregularities. Those heat-of-the-moment statements came in light of the uncertainties that arose from a recent election, known too well."[11]

Not everyone approved of this capitulation. Provocateur Brad Friedman wrote on his Brad Blog: "Lame, Dems. You don't charge election tampering and evidence of fraud when you ain't got none. Want some? Try counting the actual ballots in Wisconsin rather than relying on oft-failed, easily-manipulated computers to do so. You might be amazed at what you find." It was the in-nuendo of conspiracy again. But no proof.[12]

Things were even less temperate on Twitter. One person, amid an online shouting match, tweeted about wanting Nickolaus dead: "I wish I had a missile to shove up her fat ass! So I pray someone closer to her gets Wiscon-sin some justice! Now FUCK OFF!" To which his opponent responded with false incredulity: "Let's be clear, you are actively plotting the death of Kathy #Nickolaus via missle or hiring a contract killer?"[13]

Election administration expert Doug Chapin seemed to have understated it that morning when he posted Kathy Nickolaus's picture with the follow-ing bit of wisdom: "Right now, anyone working in the field of elections in today's highly-charged political environment—with a political class newly aware of (if not terribly knowledgeable about) election administration—has to assume that she or he is one close vote away from becoming front page news."[14]

A small bit of sanity came from Curt Rees, an elementary school princi-pal in Wisconsin. Around midnight on election night, just as the Associated Press was about to call the race for Darling and confirm that Republicans had kept the Wisconsin senate, Principal Rees tweeted a call for a timeout: "Looks like stupidity and hatred are winning in the #wirecall thread right now. Very sad. Chill out and grow up people."[15]

As for Nickolaus's apparent delay in posting the results, the next day she told the *Milwaukee Journal Sentinel* that timing was out of her hands because of even more localized control.[16]

> Nickolaus explained that the final three wards from Menomonee Falls came in at 11:41 P.M. and were posted on the county clerk's website at 11:47 P.M. Most of the village's 29 wards in 10 reporting units were called in earlier, at 10:39 P.M., according to the village clerk. Nickolaus said she had those partial results posted at 10:47 P.M.
>
> "It's just a matter of understanding the process," Nickolaus said. "I don't touch ballots on election night. I stay in my office and have to wait for poll workers to get results to the municipal clerk, and for the municipal clerk to get them to me. I don't run elections on election day. What I do is report the results after the election."

Let us leave aside the fact that the county election clerk should have more control over local entities and should be responsible for training and supervising municipal clerks and poll workers so that he or she actually is in control on election night and can assure timely returns. The key point is that even though Nickolaus may be incompetent, there is no indication whatsoever that she is engaged in criminal activity to steal the election.

But Democrats saw no reason to give Nickolaus the benefit of the doubt. The fact-checking organization Politifact rated the Wisconsin state chair of the Democratic Party's election night statements about Nickolaus's alleged "dirty tricks" as "pants on fire." Only with Darling's victory safely beyond the margin of litigation did Democrats dial back the rhetoric.[17]

"Nowadays, when I am asked 'could Florida happen again?' I answer, 'We won't have any more problems of hanging chad, but I actually think the chance of a large-scale meltdown in many parts of the country are *greater* now than they were. I at least expect "another Florida" in my lifetime.'"[18]

The speaker was MIT political scientist Charles Stewart, one of the founders of the Caltech-MIT Voting Technology Project, whose research has been crucial in trying to fix the problems with elections since 2000. Stewart is one of the most astute observers of election problems in the United States today, and we should take his warnings seriously. His statement and the story of Wisconsin's recent elections raise two questions: How likely is it that another razor-thin presidential election will go into overtime in our lifetime? And if we do have a presidential election in overtime, will the nation handle it better, as badly, or worse than we did Florida 2000?

It is hard to assess fully the odds of "another Florida" on a presidential scale, but they seem relatively small.

First, an election dispute would have to arise in a state in which the difference between the Democratic and Republican presidential candidates is less than a few thousand votes. Alternatively, some major technological snafu with voting equipment or other disaster would have to prevent the casting or counting a significant portion of votes in the state.

Second, the tiny margin or major problem would have to take place in a state whose electoral votes were pivotal. If one presidential candidate is leading another by five electoral votes and the dispute arises in a state with only three votes, the dispute would not provoke a national crisis.

Third, the candidate who is behind in the count would have to decide if it is worth pursuing postelection remedies, such as a recount, contest, or litigation, rather than conceding and trying for a better result next time. In short, we would need a perfect storm, once again.

Let's take each of these apart, beginning with the likelihood of another razor-thin election. Since 2000, there have been several close, high-profile statewide elections, most prominently Rossi-Gregoire in Washington State and Coleman-Franken in Minnesota. In a number of others, there were enough questions about how the election was run—either technologically or through the decisions of election officials—to make postelection remedies plausible. Think of the dispute over how to count misspelled write-in votes for Lisa Murkowski in the Alaska U.S. Senate race, or the Buchanan-Jennings clash over the eighteen thousand unexplained undervotes in Sarasota County, Florida.

Overall, postelection recounts have been relatively rare. According to an analysis by the group FairVote, "Out of the 2,884 statewide general elections in the 2000 to 2009 decade, there were 18 statewide recounts, 11 of which were deemed 'consequential' (with an original victory margin no more than 0.15 percent). In other words, there was one recount for every 160 statewide elections and one consequential recount for every 262 statewide elections." Of those "consequential" recounts, only three led to reversals of results.[19]

By the numbers, then, there seems less than a 1 percent chance that a statewide election for president will be within the margin of litigation. If we factor in the fact that the state where the margin has to be so close must also be *pivotal* for the outcome of the election, the chance that a presidential election will lead to another national meltdown appears quite small.

On the other hand, the fact that it is a *presidential* election increases the chances for a razor-thin result. Presidential elections get the most attention and the most money, and they are the hardest-fought contests in those close "battleground" states where either party has a reasonable chance of winning. With both parties pouring tremendous resources into these states, with the media and other attention lavished on them, and with voters more likely to cast ballots in presidential races than in any other, the chances of a razor-thin election on a presidential level seem at least a bit higher as each side battles to the end for the voters in the middle. It seems plausible that the fight over each vote will have the tendency to make close elections closer.

There is also more than a negligible chance of some kind of disaster preventing a state from casting ballots on Election Day, which would create a different type of election meltdown. Hurricane, earthquake, terrorist attack: all of these are unlikely but possible on or just before the first Tuesday of November in a presidential election year. (The 9/11 attacks actually did scuttle a primary in New York City.) They are even less likely to take place in a state whose electoral votes are pivotal in the election.

We are left with a small but real risk that another presidential election will be close enough to go into overtime in our lifetimes. And just as we should prepare for the low risk of a catastrophic meltdown at a nuclear power plant, we should prepare for the low risk of a catastrophic meltdown of our electoral system.

This brings us to the question whether a presidential candidate in a close election would choose to fight on (through a recount or litigation) or concede. First there must be something to fight *about*. Even if the margin is very close, if there is no plausible complaint, the public pressure on the candidate to concede will be great.

As for election technology, Stewart is right to begin with the happy fact that the hanging chads are gone. We know, thanks to his and his colleagues' work, that many fewer votes are lost now that election officials have junked the worst machines. There have also been improvements in poll worker training. Early voting, which is spreading across the country, sometimes gives election officials a chance to see problems early. (We should not overstate the benefits of the early warning. It did not help Kathy Dent in Sarasota avoid the problems in the Buchanan-Jennings congressional race in 2006.)

Nonetheless, there has been so much churn in election technology since 2000, and so many changes to both the means of casting votes and the technology with which election officials count them, that technological issues may provide fertile ground for a postelection challenge. Stewart explains:

> Innovation in the core technology of voting has failed to keep up with the challenges of the voting environment. At the same time, the 'new' machines purchased with HAVA money have proven to have shorter life spans than initially estimated. Just as the pregnant chad problem was caused by the failure to keep up the maintenance of old technology that inevitably degrades, the 'next Florida' is likely to come when a cash-strapped county somewhere in America lets its maintenance contract lapse, or fails to update its software in time. (This is in addition to worrying about voting tabulation systems that were originally written in [outdated computer programming languages like] Cobol or FORTRAN, and are now just marking time.)

Although Stewart sees the greatest potential for meltdown coming from a technology problem, I believe a more likely scenario is a dispute over the rules for counting of provisional or absentee ballots. The lack of uniformity in these rules is a serious problem. We have already seen such issues play out in *Coleman v. Franken* in Minnesota, and in *Hunter,* the 2010 juvenile judge race in Ohio that got the Sixth Circuit to expand the scope of the meaning of the *Bush v. Gore* case.

If this type of dispute arose on the presidential level, there would be ample grounds for a candidate to vigorously pursue an election challenge. Even though few cases have relied on *Bush v. Gore* to push the line that the procedures for running elections need to be (1) established in advance and (2) uniform within the entire jurisdiction, the *norm* of uniformity and advance rules seems well entrenched. A candidate in a very tight election who finds some disparity in the way election officials handled similarly situated ballots will have a ready-made issue for a recount, an election contest, or litigation. This is not to say that the candidate behind in the count can win with such arguments; *Bush v. Gore* leaves plenty of room for courts to reject uniformity under most circumstances. But it provides a reasonable basis for a candidate to go on if he or she wants to.

And if there is a plausible basis for contesting the race without conceding, there will be tremendous pressure from party faithful to fight to the finish.

To begin with, for a variety of reasons that would take us far afield from the subject of this book, the United States is in a period of intense partisan polarization. Gary Jacobson of the University of California at San Diego has been tracking political polarization for many years and has created a simple but ingenious way to illustrate the amount of polarization over time. Jacobson has charted, from President Eisenhower to President Obama, the difference between the president's approval rating (as measured by the Gallup polling organization) by those in the president's party compared to his approval rating by those in the other party.

Aside from a narrowing for George W. Bush after the 9/11 attacks, the partisan gap has increased steadily since the Clinton years. George H. W. Bush's approval gap averaged under 39 percent. Clinton's was just under 56 percent. George W. Bush's was over 61 percent. Through the summer of 2011, Obama's gap was over 62 percent. This high level of political polarization means that partisans would push strongly for the candidate slightly behind not to concede the race, just as they pushed Al Gore to fight on in 2000.

But there is a big difference between Gore's situation in 2000 and the situation facing a similarly situated candidate in a future meltdown. The past decade's Voting Wars have made partisans less likely to trust the results of a close election and more likely to believe that litigation could suc-

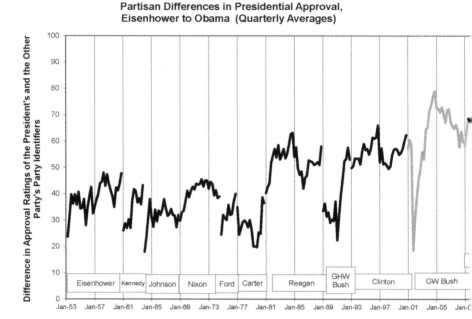

Partisan Differences in Presidential Approval, Eisenhower to Obama (Quarterly Averages) (Courtesy Professor Gary Jacobson, University of California, San Diego)

ceed in reversing the losing candidate's fortunes. Florida 2000 still reverberates among the political elite.

The pretext could be voting machinery, vote counting machinery, partisan election officials, provisional ballots, absentee ballots, claims of voter fraud or suppression (or both), unclear rules, discretionary decisions by political and nonpolitical actors—everything would be up for grabs. And the fight would be happening in a battleground state, where emotions would already be high because the election contest would have been fought the hardest there.

We should not forget the emotional aspect of these disputes. There is a feedback loop between close elections and the Voting Wars. The Voting Wars undermine voter faith in election results, especially among partisans. This makes it more likely that candidates will see a smaller downside in pursuing postelection remedies. The pursuit of those remedies exposes more flaws in how we conduct our elections and raises partisan emotions. This further undermines faith in the elections and makes candidates even more willing to pursue postelection remedies.

Social media, including Twitter and interactive political blogs, increase both the chance that a candidate would litigate rather than concede in the razor-thin election and the likelihood of extreme nastiness in that postelection period.

One may be either optimistic or pessimistic about the relation between political polarization and social media. The optimistic story has those on the left and right reading and commenting on each other's blog posts and Twitter feeds. The use of common hash tags facilitates political dialogue, allowing people to challenge others' assumptions and their own and thus to find some common ground. It is a story of constructive dialogue overcoming legitimate political differences in a respectful way. Candidates, parties, and partisans can learn of potential election problems and cure misinformation quickly and effectively over social media.

The pessimistic story is the "enclave" story told by Cass Sunstein: Modern media and the Internet allow people to get their news only from like-minded sources that reinforce their existing world view. These media inhibit the democratic deliberation necessary for political compromise. For conservatives it is Fox News, Red State, and the Daily Caller. For liberals it is MSNBC, Daily Kos, and Talking Points Memo.[20]

Social media seem to exacerbate the dangers of the enclave mentality. Back in 2000, when the Florida story was at its height, it took what felt like an interminably long time for any news outlet to post the Supreme Court's opinion in *Bush v. Gore,* which I accessed slowly over a dial-up connection. I eventually sent a *Washington Post* link to the opinion out to a "listserv" of a few hundred election law professors and others. Opinions about the controversial opinion were formed slowly and disseminated by elites: the major television and cable news networks and the leading national newspapers.

Today, the Internet provides many more outlets for individual expression. Anyone can have a Facebook page, blog, or Twitter account. Many important political blogs allow users to have publicly available "Diaries."

Comments appear on virtually all of these media. Everyone is a publisher; everyone is a critic.

Although these are politically healthy developments that allow diverse voices to be heard, the open nature of social media could create serious problems in a heated postelection dispute. The technology for mass publication about these disputes has emerged just as trust in mainstream media has decreased and partisanship increased.[21]

Some people have always held extreme opinions and paranoia about how elections are run, but those opinions were often sent as letters to the editor that never saw the light of day. Now anyone with a cell phone can broadcast to the world that the Waukesha County elections clerk should have a missile shoved up her ass. The enclave can be ugly, and it allows people with extreme opinions to reinforce and legitimate each other.

Even when not personal and offensive, social media can influence public opinion during election disputes. The Internet allows for a kind of crowd-sourcing of every decision made by every election official and judge. People can second-guess every challenged ballot, piece of voting machinery, election official delay, and judicial opinion. Although it sounds democratizing, much of this analysis is neither thoughtful nor well-considered. In a world in which it is increasingly hard for people to accept objective truth—think of the idea that President Obama is a Muslim or that President Bush caused 9/11—a million comments about an election meltdown in partisan echo chambers sounds scary.

In the optimistic story, then, the next election meltdown is less severe. In the pessimistic story, it is much worse.

Count me with the pessimists.

Admittedly, my views here are based more on my sense of the political atmosphere than on hard evidence. I remember organizing a conference in 1999 on "Internet Voting and Democracy," in which political pundit Dick Morris predicted an era when Congress would make decisions based on the votes of millions of individuals cast over the Internet—think of it as *American Idol* governance. Not every Brave New World prediction comes true. We can be grateful that Morris's has not.

Perhaps my prediction will prove equally wrong. But there are some disturbing signs.

A study by scientists at the Center for Complex Networks and Systems Research at Indiana University examined more than 250,000 tweets on politics from the six weeks leading up to the 2010 U.S. congressional elections. The researchers found some interesting patterns. Twitter users used "retweets" (reposting someone else's message) in a highly partisan way. Approximately 93 percent of right-leaning tweeters and 80 percent of left-leaning tweeters retweeted from other users with whom they agreed.[22]

Tweets that included "Mentions" of other people (which were far less frequent than retweets) linked to a more ideologically balanced group of tweeters—Democrats would mention Republican tweets and vice-versa. The use of common hashtags by Democrats and Republicans (like #wirecall in this chapter's example) had the effect of exposing users to ideas with which they were likely to disagree. The study shows that some parts of the Twitterverse are an echo chamber while other parts show some cross-ideological interaction.

What to make of it? The echo chamber effect can only increase the enclave mentality, providing more confirming selective information for the home team.

The study's findings of cross-ideological Twitter mentions might at first encourage someone like Sunstein, who believes that the sharing of ideas on the Internet could make people deliberate more and be less partisan. But the Indiana authors found that exchanging messages across the ideological divide did not lead to moderation. Instead, the authors saw what I saw in the #wirecall thread: "Qualitatively speaking, our experience with this body of data suggests that the content of political discourse on Twitter remains highly partisan. Many messages contain sentiments more extreme than you would expect to encounter in face-to-face interactions, and the content is frequently associated with disparaging of the identities and views associated with users across the partisan divide. . . . These interactions might actually serve to exacerbate the problem of polarization by reinforcing preexisting political biases."

Truly, during a political battle, to know you is to hate you, especially behind the relative anonymity of the Internet.

Twitter's 140-character limit may further exacerbate political tensions. In a study of relevant tweets following the assassination of Kansas abortion doctor George Tiller, Sarita Yardi and danah boyd found that "the kinds of interactions we observed suggest that Twitter is exposing people to multiple diverse points of view, but that the medium is insufficient for reasoned discourse and debate, instead privileging haste and emotion."[23]

It is a mistake to dismiss the emotional content of political tweets and blog posts as merely people without influence blowing off steam. The ideological echo chamber of Twitter, political blogs, and other social media reverberates to elites in the mainstream media, campaigns and elsewhere, fueling greater partisanship. When the Democratic chair in Wisconsin retracted his statements in the August 2011 recall accusing Waukesha County election official Kathy Nickolaus of "dirty tricks," he excused his initial comments as "heat-of-the-moment" responses.[24]

Twitter and other social media make the heat of the moment even hotter. I am sure that the Democratic chair in Wisconsin that evening had been checking his mobile phone, iPad, or computer, getting tweets and text messages expressing unfounded outrage against Nickolaus. Without these constant prompts, the chair likely would have thought twice before accusing her of dirty tricks.

Political commentary on these social media sites matters to election officials, too. In a semiofficial account of the Rossi-Gregoire dispute published as *An Election for the Ages: Rossi vs. Gregoire, 2004,* Washington secretary of state Sam Reed is quoted several times as complaining about the intemperate comments of those on the Internet criticizing him and other election officials. Similarly, at a press conference announcing the date of the New Hampshire primary, New Hampshire secretary of state Bill Gardner acknowledged he followed a series of humorous tweets about him using the hashtag #BillGardnerFacts. It's hard to believe that most election officials are not keeping up with what's written about them on social media sites.[25]

Social media can play another role as well, allowing for the organization of live (not virtual) social protest. From the failed Iranian revolution to the successful Egyptian one to the London riots, in the past few years people have used Twitter, Blackberry Messenger, and text messaging to organize real social protests. Short of shutting down the Internet and phone lines (which occurred Tehran, Cairo, and San Francisco, and was contemplated in London), central authorities can do little to stop communication during times of political or civil unrest.[26]

This goes well beyond the "Brooks Brothers riot" at the Miami-Dade election offices in 2000, which was organized top-down by Republican political operatives flying in staff from Washington, D.C. The chance of large decentralized social protests accompanying any future presidential election dispute is real and substantial. It is not clear that a candidate's pleas against public protests, if made, would be heeded. As Thomas Johnson and David Perlmutter document in their study of the "Facebook Election" of 2008, social media tools now make it much harder for candidates to control their message even on their own sites and feeds.[27]

What is to be done about the nightmare scenario? If we had the political will, we could take many steps to minimize the chances of an election meltdown.[28]

The core problems with how American elections are run are no secret: they are partisanship and localism. As Richard Pildes of New York University Law School noted in 2004 in the *Harvard Law Review,* "The background institutional context to *Bush v. Gore* . . . involved partisan elected county canvassing boards and elected state officials who chaired the presidential campaigns for each party. Such a partisan and decentralized structure is a peculiarly American means to resolve disputed elections."[29] Indeed, there seems to be a near-consensus among law professors who write in this area that partisan discretion, lack of uniformity, and inadequate training on the local level are this country's most serious problems with running elections.

We need nonpartisan, professionalized election administration at the federal, state, and local levels, with more power in the hands of the federal government than state government and more power in the hands of the states than localities. Neutral election officials, whose allegiance is not to a political party or candidate but to a fair election system, must be the norm.

These officials should be professional and technically competent to deal with the difficult task of running a complex election process and everything that it entails: contracting with election vendors; understanding the software and hardware; organizing a large-scale, short-term operation on Election Day; conducting poll worker training; establishing procedures for transparency and competence in counting and recounting votes; providing vital, timely, and clear communication with the public; and much more. Running a smooth election is no easy job, even without a meltdown.

Nonpartisanship is a common-sense necessity: to the extent possible, the people running our elections should not have a vested interest in their outcome. In thirty-three states, the secretary of state (or other statewide official charged with responsibilities as the chief elections officer of the state) is chosen through a partisan election process. No state currently uses a nonpartisan election, although Wisconsin recently moved from a bipartisan state elections board to a new board made up of six retired state court judges appointed by the governor and confirmed by the state legislature on a two-thirds vote.[30]

The remaining states use an appointment process. Many states let the governor appoint the chief elections officer, sometimes subject to confirmation of one or both houses of the state legislature. Some states use various appointment measures for boards or commissions to run elections. Most of these commissions use a bipartisan model that either splits representation evenly between the two major parties or gives an advantage to the majority party in the state, as in Ohio, where the partisan secretary of state sits as a tie-breaker on each bipartisan county elections board.

There is even greater variation in how officials are chosen at the county level. Some officials are more partisan than others; some are more competent than others. Some election agencies get many more government resources than others.

"Let a thousand flowers bloom" should not be the model for how we run our elections. We should follow the path of other mature democracies. A nonpartisan election czar or panel of three should run our national elections, with political insulation and a long term of service. The czar should impose uniformity, competence, and discipline on the election process.

If used on a national scale, the president would make the nomination subject to a two-thirds or three-fourths confirmation vote by both houses of Congress. The large supermajority requirement would ensure that the person picked is a consensus candidate who cannot be easily manipulated by political forces. The election czar (or committee) should have the power to impose uniform standards on federal elections. Ideally, a voter should be able to walk into any polling place, anywhere in the country, and see the same voting equipment and same ballot format. Election boards with balanced representation from both parties should have the power to monitor operations conducted by the nonpartisan official, with ample protection for either party to call for grand jury investigations if there are allegations of partisanship or incompetence.

Some may reject the idea of nonpartisan election officials as naive, Pollyannaish, or "adding another government bureaucracy." It might be that we are in too partisan a moment for it to work nationally. But it has worked on the local level in California, and I have seen it work in such democracies as Australia and Canada. Neutral administrators whose allegiance is to the running of free and fair elections, free of fraud and mismanagement, and whose actions are monitored by a bipartisan board of elections, are the best hope to restore faith in the integrity of elections.

There should be uniform standards for how to deal with absentee ballots and provisional ballots. Election laws should be updated so that the rules are clear and established in advance. States should conduct periodic election law audits to ensure that laws are up to date, clear, and match current voting technology. Uniformity not only minimizes the grounds for a potential postelection contest but benefits all voters by ensuring a fair process.

The registration rolls should be uniform as well. The federal government should be in the business of registering all voters, paying all costs associated with registration and voter verification. Registration should begin when someone graduates from high school (or drops out), and voter registration should follow citizens wherever they go with a unique voter identification number (which would differ from a Social Security number). The government should provide a voter identification card to each voter, but voters lacking identification would have the choice of using a thumbprint or other means to verify their identity.

Voting machine hardware and software should have government approval. The source code and hardware should undergo rigorous independent testing and full disclosure to government officials before rollout and implementation. Manufacturers should not be able to frustrate efforts to improve security by claiming that the source code is proprietary.

Forget everything you just read. None of it is going to happen. Despite the Florida debacle, states have not moved toward greater nonpartisan election administration. Florida did get rid of its partisan elected secretary of state. But now the position is appointed by the governor, without the supermajority confirmation requirement that would keep the office apolitical. Neither Democrats nor Republicans see much benefit in giving up the chance to have one of their own as the state's chief election officer.

More generally, the Voting Wars have shown the parties the virtue of manipulating election rules for their advantage. The parties have a vested interest in keeping some partisan control. And local election officials fight for power against state officials, while both fight against federal control. There's no strong lobby for change. The window for change following 2000 closed quickly with the half-measure of the Help America Vote Act.

Nor is there support for mandatory, government-paid national voter registration with a voter identification—much less with biometric information like a fingerprint. When I first proposed such a system, in 2005, I managed the nearly impossible feat of uniting the two political parties around an idea. Unfortunately, they were united in opposition. Republicans oppose federal control, oppose another government program, and oppose government control on principle. Democrats oppose voter identification requirements, even if the government pays for it and goes out and registers voters, even though a large majority of the public supports such identification. Civil libertarians don't like the government having your thumbprint. Barring a much worse meltdown than 2000, nationalizing our elections won't happen in our lifetimes.

The Help America Vote Act made some positive moves toward uniformity and empowered state officials against local election officials, at least when it comes to voter registration efforts. Still, the registration systems are a mess.

Partisan election officials can make choices in the registration process that can help either Democrats or Republicans. How often should a voter purge be done, and by what criteria? How much outreach to government offices, including welfare offices as mandated by the 1993 motor-voter law, should election officials do to increase voter registration? How tough should the rules be for outside groups that submit voter registration forms? There is too much discretion and too little uniformity.

Even my noncontroversial suggestion for "election law audits" has fallen on deaf ears. The 2003 California recall is a case in point. There were more than twenty lawsuits concerning various aspects of the recall rules, including litigation over the rules for nominating petitions for candidates to replace Governor Davis. One part of the state elections code provides that the rules for nominating candidates during a recall shall be made "in the manner prescribed for nominating a candidate to that office in a regular election." But those usual nomination provisions explicitly state that they do not apply to recall elections.

California's secretary of state nonetheless applied those rules, thereby granting anyone with sixty-five signatures and thirty-five hundred dollars a place on the recall ballot. The California Supreme Court refused to consider whether to overturn the secretary's decision or to defer to his administrative judgment. The result was a ballot with 135 potential replacements for Governor Davis.

Even in the face of such a blatant conflict, more than eight years after the embarrassing recall the California legislature has not fixed this obvious internal inconsistency in the state code, much less taken steps to minimize all the other problems that emerged in the recall election, whose recurrence could easily be avoided by rewriting the rules.

It is often said that society plans for the last disaster. After the terrible meltdowns at Japan's Fukushima nuclear power plants in 2011, engineers and regulators went back to examine the sea walls and other steps meant to minimize the risk of nuclear meltdowns at oceanfront reactors in the event of very large earthquakes and tsunamis. Planning for the last disaster is not ideal—we should be planning to prevent the next—but planning for the last disaster at least helps prevent its repetition.

In the election law field, things are worse. We are not even planning for the last disaster. Aside from junking the hanging chads, the chances of "another Florida" are all too real. And political provocateurs, now aided by social media, have spent the past decade fighting the Voting Wars in a way that will ensure our next disaster will be far worse.

NOTES

Introduction: The Next Meltdown

1. Patrick Marley, Larry Sandler, & Mike Johnson, *Prosser Wins Recount in Wisconsin Supreme Court Race*, Milwaukee Journal Sentinel, May 20, 2011, http://www.jsonline.com/news/statepolitics/122364728.html.

2. John Fund, *Recount Likely in Wisconsin Court Race*, Wall Street Journal, Apr. 6, 2011, http://online.wsj.com/article/SB10001424052748704013604576246821949372388.html ("Any recount will be scrutinized for irregularities and possible vote fraud."). On the Dane County allegations, see Fund's interview on this "Opinion Journal" video embedded in this Talking Points Memo story: http://tpmdc.talkingpointsmemo.com/2011/04/conservative-pundit-sees-vote-fraud-in-wisconsin-supreme-court-race-video.php.

3. Mark Memmott, *How Did Wisconsin Miss 14,000 Votes? Someone Didn't Click Save*, The Two-Way (NPR News Blog), Apr. 8, 2011, http://www.npr.org/blogs/thetwo-way/2011/04/08/135235107/how-did-wisconsin-miss-14–000-votes-someone-didnt-click-save.

4. Ian Milhiser, *Wisconsin Republican County Clerk Claims She Misplaced 7,500 Votes for Judge Prosser, Her Former Boss*, Think Progress Blog, Apr. 8, 2011, 11:55 am, http://thinkprogress.org/2011/04/08/kathy-nickolaus-crook-or-idiot/.

5. The original statement on the Waukesha County Democratic Party website is no longer posted. It was available at http://www.orchidforchange.com/parties/waukeshadems.com/ht/display/ArticleDetails/i/1343504. Excerpts from the statement appear at these links: http://thepoliticalcarnival.net/2011/04/11/waukesha-dem-member-of-the-board-of-canvassers-shocking-somewhat-appalling-i-feel-like-i-must-speak-up/; http://www.jsonline.com/news/waukesha/119627189.html; and http://electionlawblog.org/archives/019215.html.

6. Patrick Marley, *Supreme Court Tensions Boil Over*, Milwaukee Journal Sentinel, Mar.

19, 2011, http://www.jsonline.com/news/statepolitics/118310479.html. To view the ad, go to http://www.slate.com/blogs/blogs/weigel/archive/2011/04/01/wisconsin-unions-attack-prosser-for-calling-a-judge-a-total-bitch.aspx. See footnote 3 of Judge Conley's opinion in *Wisconsin Right to Life Political Action Committee v. Brennan*, 09-cv-764-wmc (W.D. Wis. Mar. 31, 2011), http://www.scribd.com/doc/52022373/Wrtl-Judges.

7. Journal Sentinel Politifact Wisconsin rated Kloppenburg's "anomalies" claim "barely true." *Joanne Kloppenburg Says Anomalies Were Widespread During State Supreme Court Race*, April 29, 2011, http://www.politifact.com/wisconsin/statements/2011/apr/29/joanne-kloppenburg/joanne-kloppenburg-says-anomalies-were-widespread-/. Bill Glauber, *Baldwin Calls for Federal Investigation of Waukesha County Vote Reporting*, All Politics Blog, Milwaukee Journal Sentinel, April 9, 2011, http://www.jsonline.com/blogs/news/119532844.html.

8. *Crawford v. Marion County Election Board*, 472 F.3d 949, 954 (7th Cir. 2007) (Evans, J., dissenting), *aff'd*, 553 U.S. 181 (2008).

9. *Massachusetts "Show ID" Billboards Irks Latino Activists*, Fox News Latino, April 12, 2011, http://latino.foxnews.com/latino/news/2011/04/12/billboard-irks-latino-activists/; Karoun Demirjian, *Man Behind Ad Urging Latinos Not to Vote Is a Longtime GOP Operative*, Las Vegas Sun, Oct. 21, 2010, http://www.lasvegassun.com/news/2010/oct/21/de-posadas-gop-influence-deep/.

10. Heather K. Gerken, *The Democracy Index: Why Our Election System Is Broken and How to Fix It* 84–85 (Princeton: Princeton University Press 2009).

11. Richard L. Hasen, *The Untimely Death of* Bush v. Gore, 60 Stanford Law Review 1, 26 (2007).

12. Samuel Issacharoff, *The Court's Legacy for Voting Rights*, New York Times, Dec. 14, 2000, at A39; Steven J. Mulroy, *Lemonade from Lemons: Can Advocates Convert* Bush v. Gore *into a Vehicle for Reform?*, 9 Georgetown Journal on Poverty Law and Policy 357 (2002).

13. Bob Mahlburg & Maurice Tamman, *Dist. 13 Voting Analysis Shows Broad Problem*, Herald-Tribune, Nov. 9, 2006, http://www.heraldtribune.com/article/20061109/NEWS/611090343.

14. Paul Krugman, *Hack the Vote*, New York Times, Dec. 2, 2003, http://www.nytimes.com/2003/12/02/opinion/hack-the-vote.html.

Chapter 1: All I Really Need to Know I Learned in Florida

1. The account in this chapter is drawn mainly from court documents, newspaper articles, and the following books: Correspondents of the *New York Times*, *36 Days: The Complete Chronicle of the 2000 Presidential Election Crisis* (New York: Times Books 2001) ("*36 Days*"); Howard Gillman, *The Votes That Counted: How the Court Decided the 2000 Presidential Election* (Chicago: University of Chicago Press 2001) ("Gillman"); Abner Greene, *Understanding the 2000 Election: A Guide to the Legal Battles That Decided the Presidency* (New York: NYU Press 2001) ("Greene"); Martin

Merzer and the Staff of the *Miami Herald, The Miami Herald Report: Democracy Held Hostage* (New York: St. Martin's Press 2001) ("Merzer"); Political Staff of the *Washington Post, Deadlock: The Inside Story of America's Closest Election* (New York: Public Affairs 2001) (*"Deadlock"*); Jeffrey Toobin, *Too Close to Call: The Thirty-Six-Day Battle to Decide the 2000 Election* (New York: Random House 2001) ("Toobin"); and Charles L. Zelden, Bush v. Gore: *Exposing the Hidden Crisis in American Democracy* (Kansas: University Press of Kansas, abridged and updated edition 2010) ("Zelden").

This chapter is also based on my recollection of events. I provided extensive media commentary and analysis during the controversy. I also played a peripheral role late in the Florida litigation, giving informal advice to the Gore campaign in one of its lawsuits (at this point in time, I cannot recall which one).

You can listen to the audio of the oral argument in *Bush v. Gore* and read a full transcript thanks to the Oyez Project at Chicago-Kent College of Law: http://www .oyez.org/cases/2000–2009/2000/2000_00_949/argument (*Bush v. Gore* oral argument).

2. The chronology here is laid out best in *36 Days, Deadlock,* and Zelden. *36 Days* at 22 reports the 200-vote gap.

3. Roy G. Saltman, *The History and Politics of Voting Technology: In Quest of Integrity and Public Confidence* 7–8, 10 (New York: Palgrave Macmillan 2006, 2008). Salman provides the greatest detail on the technological issues.

4. *Deadlock* at 101.

5. Fla. Stat. § 101.5614(5) (Supp. 2001).

6. Bush v. Gore, 531 U.S. 98, 119 (Rehnquist, C.J., concurring) (2000), http://supreme .justia.com/us/531/98/.

7. The Caltech/MIT Voting Technology Project, *Residual Votes Attributable to Technology: An Assessment of the Reliability of Existing Voting Equipment,* v. 2, March 30, 2001, http://vote.caltech.edu/drupal/files/working_paper/vtp_wp2.pdf.

8. Richard L. Hasen, *The California Recall Punch Card Litigation: Why Bush v. Gore Does Not "Suck,"* in *Clicker Politics: Essays on the California Recall* 170–81 (New Jersey: Prentice Hall, Shaun Bowler & Bruce E. Cain, eds. 2006).

9. NORC at the University of Chicago, Florida Ballot Project, http://www.norc.org/ projects/Florida+Ballots+Project.htm.

10. Merzer at 7, 66, 78–80.

11. *36 Days* at 10–13.

12. The *New York Times* attributed the "Jews for Buchanan" expression to Representative Barney Frank. *36 Days* at 36. See also John Nichols, *Jews for Buchanan: Did You Hear the One About the Theft of the American Presidency?* (New York: New Press 2001). Merzer at 43 (Arafat quotation). There were ten candidates, thanks to a reform to loosen the state's ballot access laws, making it among the easiest in the country for presidential candidates. Merzer at 37. On the 2,800 votes, see Jonathan Wand et al., *The Butterfly Did It: The Aberrant Vote for Buchanan in Palm Beach County, Florida,* 95 American Political Science Review 793, 795 (2001), http://wand .stanford.edu/research/apsr2001.pdf. On the controversy over Buchanan's views

on Jews and Israel, see *Is Pat Buchanan Anti-Semitic?*, Newsweek, Dec. 22, 1991, http://www.thedailybeast.com/newsweek/1991/12/23/is-pat-buchanan-anti-semitic.html.

13. ABC News, *Butterfly Ballot Designer Speaks Out*, Dec. 21, 2010, http://abcnews.go.com/Politics/story?id=122175&page=1. Reports that she was apolitical appear in *Deadlock* at 67; and Merzer at 39.

14. The description of the Duval problem is drawn from *36 Days* at 91–92; Merzer at 37–38; and Toobin at 172–76. Toobin also points out that claims of roadblocks in African American neighborhoods turned out to be unproven. Toobin at 168–69.

15. Chemerinksy's own recollection appears in Erwin Chemerinksy, *The Conservative Assault on the Constitution* 238–48 (New York: Simon & Schuster 2010). The trial court's order is unreported but posted at Stanford University's repository on the Florida election controversy at http://election2000.stanford.edu/fladell1120.pdf. The Florida Supreme Court appeal is *Fladell v. Palm Beach County Canvassing Board*, 772 So.2d 1240 (Fla. 2000).

16. Justin Martin, *Nader: Crusader Spoiler Icon* 272 (New York: Basic Books 2003) ("not a dime's worth of difference" quotation). On the Nader voting statistics, see http://www.fec.gov/pubrec/2000presgeresults.htm.

17. You can see the full extent of potential remedies for election problems in Steven F. Huefner, *Remedying Election Wrongs*, 44 Harvard Journal on Legislation 265 (2007).

18. Richard A. Posner, *Breaking the Deadlock: The 2000 Election, the Constitution and the Court* (Princeton: Princeton University Press 2001).

19. Federal Election Commission, *2000 Presidential Popular Vote Summary for All Candidates Listed on at Least One State Ballot* (updated 12/2001), http://www.fec.gov/pubrec/fe2000/prespop.htm (500,000 vote margin).

20. *36 Days* at 181–82, 336–37.

21. *36 Days* at 113–14; *Deadlock* at 96.

22. Richard L. Hasen, *Beyond the Margin of Litigation: Reforming U.S. Election Administration to Avoid Electoral Meltdown*, 62 Washington & Lee Law Review 937 (2005); Merzer at 133 (co-chair).

23. *Deadlock* at 85.

24. Alec Ewald, *The Way We Vote: The Local Dimension of Election Suffrage* 3 (Nashville: Vanderbilt University Press 2009).

25. *36 Days* at 330.

26. *Deadlock* at 85–86; see also Toobin at 67–69. Toobin said that he "was to be Katherine Harris's minder." See also *36 Days* at 341 on the secretary of state's office contacts with the Bush team. On the pizza boxes, see *Deadlock* at 104; see also Merzer at 131–32, recounting Harris's later testimony at the U.S. Commission on Civil Rights Hearing, where she said that she did not "have expertise in the management of these activities."

27. Fla. Stat. Ann. § 102.166(5) (Supp. 2001). The interpretation from Roberts appears at http://election.dos.state.fl.us/opinions/new/2000/deo011.pdf. The Rehnquist opinion appears at 531 U.S. 119: "No reasonable person would call it 'an

error in the vote tabulation,' Fla. Stat. Ann. § 102.166(5) (Supp.2001), or a 'rejection of . . . legal votes,' § 102.168(3)(c), when electronic or electromechanical equipment performs precisely in the manner designed, and fails to count those ballots that are not marked in the manner that these voting instructions explicitly and prominently specify."

28. *Deadlock* at 104; Merzer at 58–59.

29. Richard L. Hasen, *The Democracy Canon,* 62 Stanford Law Review 69 (2009), http://papers.ssrn.com/sol3/papers.cfm?abstract_id=1344476.

30. *Deadlock* at 63, 99–100. You can find the Butterworth opinion at: http://abcnews .go.com/Politics/story?id=122506&page=1.

31. Toobin at 50–52; *Deadlock* at 81.

32. *Deadlock* at 156–57, 249–50.

33. *Deadlock* at 127–28.

34. *36 Days* at 97.

35. *Deadlock* at 127–29.

36. *36 Days* at 101.

37. *Deadlock* at 131–33.

38. *Deadlock* at 133.

39. Diane H. Mazur, *The Bullying of America: A Cautionary Tale About Military Voting and Civil-Military Relations,* 4 Election Law Journal 105 (2005), http://www.lieber tonline.com/doi/abs/10.1089/elj.2005.4.105.

40. David Barstow & Don Van Natta, Jr., *Examining the Vote: How Bush Took Florida: Mining the Overseas Absentee Vote,* New York Times, July 15, 2001, http://www .nytimes.com/2001/07/15/us/examining-the-vote-how-bush-took-florida-min ing-the-overseas-absentee-vote.html.

41. Mazur at 111.

42. Michael P. McDonald & Justin Levitt, *Seeing Double Voting: An Extension of the Birthday Problem,* 7 Election Law Journal 111 (2008), http://www.liebertonline .com/doi/abs/10.1089/elj.2008.7202.

43. Most of this information comes from the U.S. Commission on Civil Rights Report, *Voting Irregularities in Florida During the 2000 Presidential Election (June 2001),* http://www.usccr.gov/pubs/vote2000/report/main.htm, especially chapter 5. The commission was deeply divided on partisan lines, and to this day it does not include the Dissent from the report written by Commissioner Abigail Thernstrom. Her dissent is available at: http://www.manhattan-institute.org/pdf/final_dissent .pdf. For more on DBT, see Greg Palast, and Merzer at 107; Robert. E Pierre, *Botched Name Purge Denied Some the Right to Vote,* Washington Post, May 31, 2001, at A01; and Scott Hiassen et al., *Felon Purge Sacrificed Innocent Voters,* Palm Beach Post, May 27, 2001, http://www.palmbeachpost.com/news/content/news/election 2000/election2000_felons2.html. Palast takes a provocative and controversial look at DST and the felon voting purge in chapter 1 of *The Best Democracy Money Can Buy: The Truth About Corporate Cons, Globalization, and High-Finance Fraudsters* (New York: Plume expanded electoral edition 2004). The Florida legislature,

acting after the 1997 Miami mayoral scandal, mandated that a private company create the purge list for the secretary of state. See Lorraine C. Minnite, *An Analysis of Voter Fraud in the United States* 10 (Demos, n.d. [adapted from the 2003 report, *Securing the Vote* by L. Minnite & D. Callahan, with updates]), www.demos. org/pubs/analysis.pdf.

44. Guy Stuart, *Databases, Felons, and Voting: Bias and Partisanship of the Florida Felons List in the 2000 Elections,* 119 Political Science Quarterly 453 (2004). LePore, quoted in chapter 5 of the report of the U.S. Commission on Civil Rights.

45. Hiassen et al.

46. Stuart at 462.

47. Merzer at 8, 97–106, 108.

48. For the best treatment of the problems of partisanship and inconsistent standards on the county canvassing boards, see Roy A. Schotland, *In Bush v. Gore, Whatever Happened to the Due Process Ground?,* 34 Loyola University of Chicago Law Journal 211 (2002). For the best history of the Miami-Dade board, see *Deadlock* at 124–126, 137–41.

49. *36 Days* at 40.

50. Toobin at 185.

51. *36 Days* at 134–35.

52. Al Kamen, *Miami "Riot" Squad: Where Are They Now?,* Washington Post, Jan. 24, 2005, http://www.washingtonpost.com/wp-dyn/articles/A31074-2005Jan23.html; *Deadlock* at 139–43.

53. Zelden at 40–44; *Deadlock* at 86–89, 119–21.

54. *Deadlock* at 135–36. For more on Broward, see *Deadlock* at 122–24.

55. Einer Elhauge, *Florida 2000: Bush Wins Again,* Weekly Standard, November 26, 2001, http://www.weeklystandard.com/Content/Public/Articles/000/000/000/ 554teojk.asp.

56. Toobin at 208–9, *Deadlock* at 183. For more on the Martin and Seminole controversies, see *36 Days* at 188–89, 253–54, 271–72.

57. The case is at 772 So.2d 1220 (Fla. 2000). The U.S. Supreme Court opinion reversing and remanding is at 531 U.S. 70 (2000). On remand, the Florida Supreme Court issued almost the identical opinion, simply deleting the reference to the Florida state constitution and not expressly acknowledging the concerns raised by the U.S. Supreme Court. 772 So.2d 1273 (Fla. 2000). This surely irked the conservative Justices of the Supreme Court and added to concern about whether the Florida Supreme Court was out of control.

58. Judge Sauls's trial court opinion on the contest was oral. Stanford has posted a copy at: http://election2000.stanford.edu/00-2431_transcript.pdf. The Florida Supreme Court opinion in *Gore v. Harris* is at 772 So.2d 1243 (Fla. 2000). The U.S. Supreme Court's stay order is at 531 U.S. 1046 (2000), and the *Bush v. Gore* opinion is at 531 U.S. 98 (2000).

59. There were twice as many overvotes as undervotes in Florida. Merzer at 188. For more on the ruling, see *Deadlock* at 199–200.

60. Ford Fessenden & John M. Broder, *Study of Disputed Florida Ballots Finds Justices Did Not Cast the Deciding Vote,* New York Times, Nov. 12, 2001, http://www.ny times.com/2001/11/12/politics/recount/12VOTE.html.

61. Gillman at 125.

62. See Merzer at 13, 55; *36 Days* at 223–24 (on chads during recounts). The Bush team stay request is posted at http://election2000.stanford.edu/emappforstay bushvvore.pdf. Its supplemental memorandum is at http://election2000.stan ford.edu/supp00-a504.pdf. Gore's lawyers did not dispute the degradation point in their opposition to the stay. In their brief on the merits, in footnote 18 they did so. That brief is posted at: http://election2000.stanford.edu/gore949brief.pdf. *36 Days* also includes an article dated Nov. 27, 2000 (weeks before the *Bush v. Gore* case), which includes the following: "That state count showed 4,000 more votes than the first one. Election officials say such an increase is standard fare mostly because partially detached chads on punch-card ballots fall off the second time through, allowing the machines to see votes they had previously missed."

63. Toobin at 264–65. The opinion appears at 531 U.S. 98 (2000).

Chapter 2: The Fraudulent Fraud Squad

1. The title of this chapter comes from a column I wrote for *Slate:* Richard L. Hasen, *The Fraudulent Fraud Squad: The Incredible Disappearing American Center for Voting Rights,* Slate, May 18, 2007, http://www.slate.com/id/2166589/. My editor on the piece, Dahlia Lithwick, came up with the title, as she did with most witty lines appearing in my pieces during the time she edited my *Slate* columns.

   On Gallegos's illness, see Gary Scharrer, *Lawmaker Risks Health to Stop Voter ID Bill: A Hospital Bed Was Set Up for Sen. Mario Gallegos in Case He Was Needed,* Houston Chronicle, May 22, 2007, http://www.chron.com/disp/story.mpl/special/07/legislature/4824361.html.

2. Ben Philpott, *Texas GOP Works to Remove Senate's Two-Thirds Rule,* Texas Tribune, Nov. 10, 2010, http://www.texastribune.org/texas-senate/texas-senate/texas-gop-works-to-remove-senates-two-thirds-rule/. For the statistics on the partisan breakdown of the state senate, see this page from the Legislative Reference Library of Texas: http://www.lrl.state.tx.us/legeLeaders/members/memberStatistics.cfm.

3. Gary Scharrar, *Gallegos Thanks Colleagues for "Standing with Me,"* Houston Chronicle, May 24, 2007, http://www.chron.com/disp/story.mpl/special/07/legislature/4831556.html.

4. Queblog, "Texas Republicans Still Carrying Torch for Contrived Voter Fraud Issue," *San Antonio Current,* Jan. 30, 2009, http://www.sacurrent.com/blog/que blog.asp?perm=69438.

5. Reeve Hamilton, *Perry Declares More Emergency Items, Including Voter ID,* Texas Tribune, Jan. 20, 2011, http://www.texastribune.org/texas-legislature/texas-legislature/perry-emergency-items-including-voter-id/; Daniel Setiawan, *After Six-Year Fight, Perry Signs Voter ID into Law,* Texas Observer, May 27, 2011, http://www.texas

observer.org/component/k2/item/17879-voter-id-signed-into-law; Office of the Governor Rick Perry, Press Release, *Gov. Perry: SB 14 Takes a Major Step in Securing the Integrity of the Electoral Process; Signs Legislation Requiring Voters to Present Photo ID at Polling Places,* May 27, 2011, http://www.governor.state.tx.us/news/press-release/16189/. Elise Foley, *Rick Perry: South Carolina Is at War with the Government on Voter ID,* Huffington Post, Jan. 16, 2012, http://www.huffington post.com/2012/01/16/rick-perry-immigration-voter-id_n_1209485.html; Patrik Jonsson, *Partisan Feud Escalates over Voter ID Laws in South Carolina, Other States,* Christian Science Monitor, Jan. 11, 2012, http://www.csmonitor.com/USA/Poli tics/2012/0111/Partisan-feud-escalates-over-voter-ID-laws-in-South-Carolina-other-states.

6. Brief *Amici Curiae* of Historians and Other Scholars in Support of Petitioners, United States Supreme Court, Crawford v. Marion County Elections Board, Nos. 07-21, 07-25, November 2007, http://www.brennancenter.org/dynamic/subpages/download_file_50874.pdf.

7. Martin Wiskcol, *Armey Wants to Transform Congressional GOP,* Orange County Register, Sept. 7, 2010, http://www.ocregister.com/news/armey-264883-gop-party .html.

8. Jane Mayer, *Covert Operations: The Billionaire Brothers Who Are Waging War Against Obama,* New Yorker, Aug. 30, 2010, http://www.newyorker.com/reporting/2010/08/30/100830fa_fact_mayer (Freedomworks funded by Koch brothers).

9. The video of the exchange appears at: http://tpmmuckraker.talkingpointsmemo .com/2010/10/dick_armey_so_many_dems_are_voting_early_because_t.php as part of a post, *Dick Armey: Many Dems Are Voting Early to Commit Voter Fraud* (VIDEO), Oct. 21, 2010.

10. Michelle Malkin, *The Left's Voter Fraud Whitewash,* Oct. 27, 2010, http://michelle malkin.com/2010/10/27/62680/.

11. Hearne no longer works for that law firm, but a copy of the brochure is posted on the Brad Blog, at http://www.bradblog.com/Docs/LathropGage_THOR_Insert.pdf.

12. Lorraine C. Minnite, *The Myth of Voter Fraud* 100 (Ithaca: Cornell University Press 2010). The recounting of the Saint Louis controversy in the next few paragraphs tracks Minnite's analysis appearing in her book at 99–102.

13. National Voter Registration Act of 1993 ("NVRA"), 42 U.S.C. 1973gg et seq.

14. Minnite at 101 n.48, citing Jo Mannies & Jennifer LaFleur, *City Mislabeled Dozens as Voting from Vacant Lots: Property Records Appear to Be in Error, Survey Finds; Just 14 Ballots Are Found Suspect,* St. Louis Post-Dispatch, Nov. 5, 2001, at A1.

15. *Missouri v. Baker,* 34 S.W. 3d 410 (Mo. App. 2000), http://caselaw.findlaw.com/mo-court-of-appeals/1406459.html.

16. Minnite at 101, quoting Dirk Johnson, *The 2000 Elections: The Swing States: Judge Delays Closing of Polls in St. Louis Amid Unexpectedly Heavy Turnout,* New York Times, Nov. 8, 2000, B10, http://www.nytimes.com/2000/11/08/us/2000-elections-swing-states-judge-delays-closing-polls-st-louis-amid.html.

17. Minnite at 135 and n. 34.

18. Help America Vote Act of 2002, 42 U.S.C. 15301 et seq.; Minnite at 135.

19. Minnite at 101. For the report itself, see Matt Blunt, *Mandate for Reform: Election Turmoil in St. Louis, November 7, 2000*, Office of Missouri Secretary of State, July 24, 2001, at 36–37, http://web.archive.org/web/20061228014132/http://bond.senate.gov/mandate.pdf. Hearne bragged about his testimony in his biography once posted on the website of the American Center for Voting Rights and available now via the Internet Wayback Machine: http://web.archive.org/web/20050324134516/http://www.ac4vr.com/news/biography.html.

20. Office of the Missouri State Auditor, Board of Election Commissioners, City of St. Louis, Missouri, Report No. 2004-40, May 26, 2004, http://www.auditor.mo.gov/press/2004-40.pdf. The Missouri voter registration numbers by county from 2000 to 2006 appear on the secretary of state's website, http://www.sos.mo.gov/elections/registeredvoters.asp?rvmID=0006.

21. Minnite at 102.

22. Greg Gordon, *2006 Missouri's Election was Ground Zero for GOP*, McClatchy Newspapers, May 2, 2007, http://www.mcclatchydc.com/2007/05/02/16224/2006-missouris-election-was-ground.html.

23. Minnite at 11 n. 31, quoting Murray Waas, *Legal Affairs—The Scales of Justice*, National Journal, June 2, 2007, http://www.nationaljournal.com/magazine/legal-affairs-the-scales-of-justice-20070602?print=true.

24. The next few paragraphs rely on the Brad Blog, *Special Coverage: Thor Hearne's "American Center for Voting Rights" (ACVR) GOP "Voter Fraud" Scam*, http://www.bradblog.com/?page_id=4418; and Hasen, *Fraudulent Fraud Squad*.

25. Susan Schmidt & James V. Grimaldi, *Ney Pleads Guilty to Corruption Charges: Lawmaker's Conviction is 8th in Abramoff Probe*, Washington Post, Oct. 14, 2006, http://www.washingtonpost.com/wp-dyn/content/article/2006/10/13/AR2006101300169.html. On the lack of a website, see the Brad Blog, http://www.bradblog.com/?p=1276.

26. You can view what the website looked like at: http://web.archive.org/web/20050324102250/http://www.ac4vr.com/.

27. Minnite at 249–50 n. 37 describes what was known about the finances of ACVR.

28. Richard L. Hasen, *Implausible Deniability: The Internet Foils Fudging by Three "Voter Fraud" Warriors*, Slate, June 13, 2007, http://www.slate.com/id/2168350/; Rick Hasen, *And the American Center for Voting Rights Domain Name Goes to . . .*, Election Law Blog, May 2, 2007, http://electionlawblog.org/?p=7640.

29. You can find Arent Fox's application posted at: http://wedrawthelines.ca.gov/downloads/march_documents/arent_vra_20110311.pdf.

30. Eric Lipton & Ian Urbina, *In 5-Year Effort, Scant Evidence of Voter Fraud*, New York Times, Apr. 12, 2007, http://query.nytimes.com/gst/fullpage.html?res=9E0CE5D8123FF931A25757C0A9619C8B63 ("The Justice Department stand is backed by Republican Party and White House officials, including Karl Rove, the president's chief political adviser. The White House has acknowledged that he relayed Republican complaints to President Bush and the Justice Department that some

prosecutors were not attacking voter fraud vigorously. In speeches, Mr. Rove often mentions fraud accusations and warns of tainted elections").

31. Minnite at 227, app. 3, table A3.1.

32. Ian Urbina, *Fraudulent Voting Reemerges as a Partisan Issue*, New York Times, Oct. 26, 2010, http://www.nytimes.com/2010/10/27/us/politics/27fraud.html.

33. Wayne Slater, *Texas AG Fails to Unravel Large-Scale Voter Fraud Schemes in His Two-Year Campaign*, Dallas Morning News, May 18, 2008, http://www.dentonrc.com/sharedcontent/dws/news/texassouthwest/stories/051808dnpolvotefraud.3c75dcb.html; Tova Andrea Wang, *A Rigged Report on U.S. Voting?*, Washington Post, Aug. 30, 2007, http://www.washingtonpost.com/wp-dyn/content/article/2007/08/29/AR2007082901928.html. The *Election Law Journal* later published the draft report coauthored by Wang. Job Serebrov & Tova Wang, *Voting Fraud and Voter Intimidation*, [Draft] Report to the U. S. Election Assistance Commission (EAC) on Preliminary Research and Recommendations (2006), 6 Election Law Journal 330 (2007).

34. The chronology and quotations in this section come from the 392-page OIG report: U.S. Department of Justice Office of the Inspector General and Office of Professional Responsibility, *An Investigation into the Removal of 9 U.S. Attorneys in 2006*, September 2008, http://www.justice.gov/oig/special/s0809a/final.pdf.

35. Dan Eggen & Amy Goldstein, *Voter-Fraud Complaints by GOP Drove Dismissals*, Washington Post, May 14, 2007, http://www.washingtonpost.com/wp-dyn/content/article/2007/05/13/AR2007051301106.html.

36. Richard Roesler, *No Evidence of Election Crime, Former U.S. Attorney Says*, Spokesman Review, May 20, 2007, http://www.spokesmanreview.com/breaking/story.asp?ID=9951.

37. Charlie Savage, *Missouri Attorney a Focus in Firings; Senate Bypassed in Appointment of Schlozman*, Boston Globe, May 6, 2007, http://www.boston.com/news/nation/washington/articles/2007/05/06/missouri_attorney_a_focus_in_firings/; Waas; U.S. Department of Justice Office of the Inspector General and Office of Professional Responsibility, *An Investigation of Allegations of Politicized Hiring and Other Improper Personnel Actions in the Civil Rights Division*, July 2, 2008 (released publicly January 13, 2009), http://www.justice.gov/oig/special/s0901/final.pdf; Dan Eggen, *Ex-Prosecutor Says He Didn't Think Charges Would Affect Election*, Washington Post, June 6, 2007, http://www.washingtonpost.com/wp-dyn/content/article/2007/06/05/AR2007060502352.html.

38. Michael P. McDonald & Justin Levitt, *Seeing Double Voting: An Extension of the Birthday Problem*, 7 Election Law Journal 111 (2008). For a detailed, step-by-step analysis of supposed voter fraud claims that fall apart when they are given any scrutiny, see the Brennan Center for Justice's website, The Truth About Fraud, http://www.truthaboutfraud.org. Justin Levitt, who is now a professor at Loyola Law School in Los Angeles, was largely responsible for the material in the website when he worked at the Brennan Center.

39. 169 F.3d 723 (11th Cir. 1999).

40. Jac C. Heckelman, *The Effect of the Secret Ballot on Voter Turnout Rates*, 82 Public Choice 107 (1995), http://www.wfu.edu/~heckeljc/papers/published/PC1995.pdf.

41. Supreme Court Oral Argument in *Crawford v. Marion County Election Board*, http://www.supremecourt.gov/oral_arguments/argument_transcripts/07-21.pdf.

42. Hans A. von Spakovsky, *Smoke of Registration Fraud Leads to Election Fires*, Fox News, Oct. 31, 2008, http://www.foxnews.com/story/0,2933,445805,00.html. The longer version of the report is Hans von Spakovsky, *Stolen Identities, Stolen Votes: A Case Study in Voter Impersonation*, The Heritage Foundation, Legal Memorandum #22, Mar. 10, 2008, http://www.heritage.org/Research/Reports/2008/03/Stolen-Identities-Stolen-Votes-A-Case-Study-in-Voter-Impersonation.

43. Sydney H. Schanberg, *New York; Mississippi for a While*, New York Times, Oct. 26, 1982, http://www.nytimes.com/1982/10/26/opinion/new-york-mississippi-for-a-while.html ("The evidence powerfully suggested that the forgeries were carried out not on Election Day but later, over the Columbus Day weekend, when Beatty operatives swarmed into the skeleton-staffed Board of Elections office in Brooklyn, ostensibly to check over the voter records for irregularities. Handwriting experts testified that sometimes the same forger was responsible for signatures in election districts that are ethnically and geographically far apart - some of them eight miles apart. Which conjures the image of either the fastest roadrunner in Central Brooklyn or a sedentary criminal scribbling names at leisure into the books at the Board of Elections after the primary while officials there, all appointed by the party organization, looked the other way."); Frank Lynn, *Boss Tweed Is Gone But Not His Vote*, New York Times, Sept. 9, 1984, http://www.nytimes.com/1984/09/09/weekinreview/boss-tweed-is-gone-but-not-his-vote.html; *Brooklyn Grand Jury Finds Fraud in 8 Primaries*, New York Times, Sept. 5, 1984, http://www.nytimes.com/1984/09/05/nyregion/brooklyn-grand-jury-finds-fraud-in-8-primaries.html. For links to Jim Sleeper's past and current thoughts on the grand jury report, see the links at: http://electionlawblog.org/?p=20039.

44. Ryan J. Reilly, *Election Expert Can't Find Report on 1984 Voter Impersonation Case Cited by von Spakovsky*, TPMMuckraker, June 20, 2011, http://tpmmuckraker.talkingpointsmemo.com/2011/06/election_expert_cant_find_report_on_1984_voter_impersonation_case_cited_by_von_spakovsky.php. I have posted the 1984 grand jury report at http://electionlawblog.org/wp-content/uploads/1984_grand_jury_report-r84-11.pdf. For more, see Rick Hasen, *1984 New York Grand Jury Report on Voter Fraud Now Available*, Election Law Blog, June 23, 2011, http://electionlawblog.org/?p=19560.

45. Hasen, *Implausible Deniability*.

46. Rick Hasen, *More Hans v. Reality*, Election Law Blog, June 28, 2011, http://electionlawblog.org/?p=20953; Rick Hasen, *I Guess von Spakovsky Reads My Blog*, Election Law Blog, June 28, 2011, http://electionlawblog.org/?p=21016.

47. *Crawford v. Marion County Election Board*, 128 S.Ct. 1610 n.11 (2008).

48. Rick Hasen, *Vintage Vadum*, Election Law Blog, Sept. 3, 2011, http://electionlawblog.org/?p=22585.

49. Joe Mahr, *Voter Fraud Case Traced to Defiance County Registrations Volunteer,* Toledo Blade, Oct. 19, 2004, http://www.toledoblade.com/Politics/2004/10/19/Voter-fraud-case-traced-to-Defiance-County-registrations-volunteer.html; CNN Justice, *Mary Poppins Prompts Investigation,* Oct. 19, 2004, http://articles.cnn.com/2004-10-18/justice/mary.poppins.registers.to.vote_1_voter-registration-naacp-national-voter-fund-legal-status?_s=PM:LAW; AP, *Man Pleads Guilty to Mary Poppins Voter Registration,* USA Today, Feb. 19, 2005, http://www.usatoday.com/news/offbeat/2005-02-19-poppins_x.htm.

50. Mahr.

51. Minnite at 7–11; see also Spencer A. Overton, *Voter Identification,* 105 Michigan Law Review 631, 649 n. 94 (2007).

52. Mathew Vadum, *Registering the Poor to Vote is Un-American,* American Thinker, Sept. 1, 2011, http://www.americanthinker.com/2011/09/registering_the_poor_to_vote_is_un-american.html; Rick Hasen, *Beyond the Pale,* Election Law Blog, Sept. 1, 2011, http://electionlawblog.org/?p=22531.

53. Cara McCoy, *Ex-ACORN Official Gets Probation for Voter Registration Plan,* Las Vegas Sun, Nov. 23, 2009, http://www.lasvegassun.com/news/2009/nov/23/ex-acorn-official-gets-probation-voter-registratio/.

54. The press release is posted on my Election Law Blog as an update to Election Law Blog, "*Criminal Charges Filed Against ACORN, Two Employees,*" May 4, 2009, http://electionlawblog.org/?p=12596.

55. Francis McCabe, *ACORN Defendant Gets Probation,* Las Vegas Review-Journal, Jan. 10, 2011, http://www.lvrj.com/news/last-individual-in-acorn-voter-registration-case-gets-probation-113245739.html; Francis McCabe, *ACORN Pleads Guilty to Felony Compensation for Registration of Voters,* Las Vegas Review-Journal, Apr. 7, 2011, http://www.lvrj.com/news/acorn-pleads-guilty-to-felony-compensation-for-registration-of-voters-119367839.html.

56. Michael Falcone & Michael Moss, *Group's Tally of New Voters Was Vastly Overstated,* New York Times, Oct. 23, 2008, http://www.nytimes.com/2008/10/24/us/politics/24acorn.htm.

57. Stephanie Strom, *Acorn Report Raises Issues of Legality,* New York Times, Oct. 21, 2008, http://www.nytimes.com/2008/10/22/us/22acorn.html.

58. McCain made the comment at the October 15, 2008, debate. The transcript is posted at: http://www.debates.org/index.php?page=october-15-2008-debate-transcript.

59. Office of the California Attorney General, Press Release, *Brown Releases Report Detailing a Litany of Problems with ACORN, But No Criminality,* Apr. 1, 2010, http://oag.ca.gov/news/press_release?id=1888&p=3&y=2010&m=; Daniel Massey, *ACORN Files for Bankruptcy,* Crain's New York Business, Nov. 3, 2010, http://www.crainsnewyork.com/article/20101103/FREE/101109948; U.S. Government Accountability Office, Report to Congressional Addressees, *ACORN: Federal Funding and Monitoring,* GAO Report 11–484, as revised June 17, 2011, http://www.gao.gov/new.items/d11484.pdf.

60. 549 U.S. 1 (2006).

61. Stephen Ansolabehere & Nathaniel Persily, *Vote Fraud in the Eye of the Beholder:*

The Role of Public Opinion in the Challenge to Voter Identification Requirements, 121 Harvard Law Review 1737 (2008).

62. http://truethevote.org; Urbina, New York Times, Oct. 26, 2010; Ed Barnes, *Citizens' Group Helps Uncover Alleged Rampant Voter Fraud in Houston*, Fox News, Sept. 25, 2010, http://www.foxnews.com/politics/2010/09/23/voter-fraud-houston-tea-party-truethevote-texas/; Chris Moran, *Vasquez, Group Hurl Voter Registration Accusations: "Attack" Alleged on Local Voter Rolls*, Houston Chronicle, Aug. 25, 2010, http://www.chron.com/disp/story.mpl/metropolitan/7170826.html; Morgan Smith, *Partisan Battles Plague Voter Registration Drive*, Texas Tribune, Oct. 6, 2010, http://www.texastribune.org/texas-politics/texas-political-news/partisan-battles-plague-voter-registration-drive/; Morgan Smith, Texas Tribune, TribBlog, *Democrats Sue Houston Area Tea Party Group*, Texas Tribune, Oct. 18, 2010, http://www.texastribune.org/texas-politics/texas-political-news/democrats-sue-houston-area-tea-party-group/; Dave Fehling, *Harris County Attorney Investigates Allegations of Voter Intimidation at Polls*, Texas Tribune, Oct. 21, 2010, http://www.khou.com/home/Harris-County-Attorney-addresses-allegations-of-voter-intimidation-at-polls-105362988.html; Pam Fessler, *Efforts to Prevent Voter Fraud Draw Scrutiny*, NPR News, Oct. 26, 2010, http://www.npr.org/templates/story/story.php?storyId=130822279&; Ryan J. Reilly, *True the Vote Documents Show Hidden Donations, Republican Ties*, TPMMuckraker, Oct. 29, 2010, http://tpmmuckraker.talkingpointsmemo.com/2010/10/true_the_vote_documents_show_hidden_donations_republican_ties-vote_fraud_players.php; Patrick Brendel, *King Street Patriots Set Fundraising Goal of $500K*, Washington Independent, Apr. 5, 2011, http://washingtonindependent.com/107557/king-street-patriots-set-fundraising-goal-of-500k; Patrick Brendel, *King Street Patriots Reach Out to Non-Texans, Minorities*, American Independent, May 26, 2011, http://www.americanindependent.com/185717/king-street-patriots-reach-out-to-non-texans-minorities; Rachel Slajda, *In Texas' Biggest County, A Minority Registration Drive Is Crippled by Fraud Allegations*, TPMMuckraker, Oct. 5, 2010, http://tpmmuckraker.talkingpointsmemo.com/2010/10/in_texas_biggest_county_a_minority_registration_dr.php.

63. John Fund, *How the Obama Administration Threatens to Undermine Our Election* 27 (New York: Encounter Books 2009).

64. Aaron Deslatte, *Elections Bill Prompts League of Women Voters to Stop Registration*, Orlando Sentinel, Central Florida Political Pulse, May 9, 2011, http://blogs.orlandosentinel.com/news_politics/2011/05/elections-bill-prompts-league-of-women-voters-to-stop-registration.html.

Chapter 3: ¡No Votes!

1. I transcribed the advertisement from the English-language version made by Latinos for Reform and posted at Ben Smith's *Politico* Blog, Oct. 8, 2010, http://www.politico.com/blogs/bensmith/1010/AntiReid_group_to_Hispanic_voters_Dont_Vote.html?showall.

2. Finn is listed as having contributed $45,000 to the group in its 2008 year-end

filing with the Internal Revenue Service, http://forms.irs.gov/politicalOrgs
Search/search/Print.action?formId=33911&formType=E72; J. T. Finn, "Pro-Life
Hero Dies; John Edward Finn, 1937–2009," Pro-Life.com, http://www.prolife.
com/DadLegacy.html (last visited June 29, 2011).

3. Huma Khan, *Sharron Angle's Campaign Denounces "Don't Vote" Ad in Nevada;
Backer Linked to the GOP,* ABC News, Oct. 20, 2010, http://abcnews.go.com/
Politics/vote-2010-election-vote-ad-nevada-targeting-hispanics/story?id=1192
7768.

4. Brian Beutler, *Maker of Ad Telling Latinos Not to Vote Has Long History in GOP,*
TPM DC, Oct. 19, 2010, http://tpmdc.talkingpointsmemo.com/2010/10/maker-
of-ad-telling-latinos-not-to-vote-has-long-history-in-gop-and-conservative-advo
cacy.php.

5. Beutler; Andrea Nill Sanchez, *BREAKING: Univision Will Not Air GOP Group's Ad
Telling Latinos Not to Vote,* Think Progress, Oct. 19, 2010, http://thinkprogress.
org/politics/2010/10/19/125117/latinos-for-reform-swift-boat/.

6. KRNV Reno, *Where Does Sharron Angle Stand on Immigration?,* June 3, 2010,
http://www.clipsyndicate.com/video/play/2643847/where_does_sharron_
angle_stand_on_immigration_6_3; Karoun Demirjian, *Ad Discouraging Hispanics
from Voting May Backfire on Republicans,* Las Vegas Sun, Oct. 21, 2010, http://
www.lasvegassun.com/news/2010/oct/21/backlash-ballot/; Tim Gaynor, *Hispanic Voter May Decide Tight Nevada Senate Race,* Reuters, Oct. 21, 2010, http://
www.reuters.com/article/2010/10/21/us-usa-elections-nevada-idUSTRE69K4PR
20101021.

7. Adam Burke, *Number of Latino Voters in Nevada Jumps,* NPR's Day to Day, Jan. 18,
2008, http://www.npr.org/templates/story/story.php?storyId=18218552; Mark
Hugo Lopez, *Latinos and the 2010 Elections: Strong Support for Democrats; Weak
Voter Motivation,* Pew Hispanic Center, Oct. 5, 2010, http://pewhispanic.org/re
ports/report.php?ReportID=127.

8. Lopez; Sanchez: Christine Pelosi, *GOP Voter Suppression Ad Fails as Pro-Immi-
grant Americans Refuse to Sit Down and Shut Up,* Huffington Post, Oct. 19, 2010,
http://www.huffingtonpost.com/christine-pelosi/gop-voter-suppression-ad-b
_768536.html.

9. Peter Overby, *Political Ad's Message to Latinos: "Don't Vote,"* NPR, Oct. 21, 2010,
http://www.npr.org/templates/story/story.php?storyId=130715322.

10. Pew Research Center, *The Latino Vote in the 2010 Elections,* Nov. 3, 2010 (updated
Nov. 17, 2010), http://pewresearch.org/pubs/1790/2010-midterm-elections-exit-
poll-hispanic-vote.

11. U.S. Commission on Civil Rights Report, *Voting Irregularities in Florida During the
2000 Presidential Election* (June 2001), ch. 1, http://www.usccr.gov/pubs/vote2000/
report/ch1.htm.

12. *Debbie Wasserman Schultz Compares GOP-Backed Voting Bills to Jim Crow,* St. Pe-
tersburg Times/Politifact.com, June 9, 2011, http://www.politifact.com/truth-o-
meter/statements/2011/jun/09/debbie-wasserman-schultz/debbie-wasserman-
schultz-compares-gop-backed-votin/.

13. Benjy Sarlin, *Bill Clinton: GOP Voting Crackdown Worst Since Jim Crow,* TPMDC, July 6, 2011, http://tpmdc.talkingpointsmemo.com/2011/07/bill-clinton-accuses-gop-of-disenfranchising-minorities.php?ref=fpblg.

14. The solicitation email letter dated June 28, 2011, is posted at: http://talking pointsmemo.com/documents/2011/06/donna-brazile-extremists-trying-to-pass-restrictive-voting-laws-that-target-democratic-voters.php?page=1.

15. *Crawford v. Marion County Election Bd.,* 472 F.3d 949, 954 (7th Cir. 2007). You can find links to the materials in the case throughout the federal judiciary, including the opinions of the judges in the district court, Seventh Circuit, and Supreme Court at the Election Law@Moritz website, http://moritzlaw.osu.edu/election-law/litigation/indy-dems.php. The statistics on the partisan splits among the judges in the election law cases appears in the amicus brief I filed in the case in the U.S. Supreme Court supporting the challengers. That brief is posted at the Moritz site at http://moritzlaw.osu.edu/electionlaw/litigation/documents/Rokita-BriefamicuscuriaeofProfessorRichardLHasen11-13-07.pdf.

16. Richard L. Hasen, *A Voting Test for the High Court,* Washington Post, Sept. 19, 2007, http://www.washingtonpost.com/wp-dyn/content/article/2007/09/18/AR 2007091801572.html.

17. Deborah Hastings, *Indiana Nuns Lacking ID Denied at Poll by Fellow Sister,* AP, May 6, 2008, http://www.breitbart.com/article.php?id=D90GBCNO0&show_article=1.

18. Michael J. Pitts & Matthew D. Neumann, *Documenting Disfranchisement: Voter Identification During Indiana's 2008 General Election,* 25 Journal of Law and Politics 329, 340–43 (2009), http://papers.ssrn.com/sol3/papers.cfm?abstract_id=1465529.

19. Press Release, *Secretary of State Statement on New Photo ID Lawsuit,* Official Website of the Indiana Secretary of State, June 20, 2008, http://www.in.gov/sos/elec tions/2850.htm; Justin Levitt, *Still Jumping to Conclusions,* Brennan Center for Justice Blog, Jan. 30, 2009, http://www.brennancenter.org/blog/archives/still_jumping_to_conclusions.

20. Robert S. Erikson & Lorraine C. Minnite, *Modeling Problems in the Voter Identification-Voter Turnout Debate,* 8 Election Law Journal 85 (2009), http://www.columbia.edu/~rse14/erikson-minnite.pdf.

21. Rachel V. Cobb, D. James Greiner, & Kevin M. Quinn, *Can Voter ID Laws Be Administered in a Race-Neutral Manner? Evidence from the City of Boston in 2008,* Quarterly Journal of Political Science (forthcoming), http://papers.ssrn.com/sol3/papers.cfm?abstract_id=1625041.

22. Thomas B. Edsall, *GOP Official Faces Sentencing in Phone-Jamming,* Washington Post, May 17, 2006, http://www.washingtonpost.com/wp-dyn/content/article/2006/05/16/AR2006051601712.html.

23. *United States v. Tobin,* 480 F.3d 53 (1st Cir. 2007), http://caselaw.findlaw.com/us-1st-circuit/1294865.html.

24. Allen Raymond with Ian Spiegelman, *How to Rig an Election: Confessions of a Republican Operative* 175 (New York: Simon & Schuster Paperbacks 2008).

25. Email from Ken Gross to author dated July 5, 2011, on file with the author. In a follow-up email to me dated July 6, 2011, Gross provided me with additional details: "My only association with Allen Raymond was through the Republican Leadership Council (RLC). I was doing some legal work for it and Allen, at some point, became its Executive Director. It wasn't for long. It was only in that context that I even knew him or ever talked with him. I only found out later, when the news came out about him getting into trouble, that he had a telemarketing business at that time. I have zero recollection of talking to him about any such issues. It certainly had nothing to do with the RLC. Thus, I never represented Allen personally nor any business venture of his much less tell him that it was legally OK to jam phones lines. It seems to me that it is more an FCC issue than an election law issue anyway. So I have no idea what he is talking about and that is exactly what I told the DOJ lawyers who were prosecuting him when they called me from New Hampshire during the trial. Neither Allen nor his lawyer ever tried to call me doing his prosecution, trial, or writing of his book to see if I would vouch for him or mitigate his liability. (Which I would not have.) While I am still not familiar with the details of what he actually did, from what I have read it seems what he did was a serious violation of law and I don't know how a lawyer would advise otherwise. Although I understand that an appeals court ended up questioning one of the related prosecutions."

26. TPMMuckraker Reference Section, Shaun Hansen, http://tpmmuckraker.talking pointsmemo.com/hansen.php.

27. *United States v. Tobin*; Raymond at 202; Edsall.

28. Raymond at 191.

29. *United States v. Tobin*, 552 F.3d 29 (1st Cir. 2009). Documents posted on the court's docket in the Hansen case (which I have on file) show the government's motion to dismiss the indictment against Shaun Hansen in light of the second ruling of the First Circuit in *Tobin*.

30. Thomas B. Edsall & David A. Fahrenthold, *2002 N.H. Scandal Shadows GOP Anew*, Washington Post, Apr. 14, 2006, http://www.washingtonpost.com/wp-dyn/content/article/2006/04/13/AR2006041301673.html.

31. Andrew Miga, Associated Press, *Feds Drop Phone-Jamming Case; Hodes: Questions Still Not Answered*, May 31, 2009, http://www.concordmonitor.com/article/feds-drop-phone-jamming-case.

32. Associated Press, *N.H. Republicans Settle Phone-Jamming Lawsuit*, Dec. 3, 2006, http://www.signonsandiego.com/uniontrib/20061203/news_1n3jamming.html.

33. Gilda R. Daniels, *Voter Deception*, 43 Indiana Law Review 343, 344 (2010), http://papers.ssrn.com/sol3/papers.cfm?abstract_id=1591803.

34. Aaron Nathans, *GOP Fliers Give Wrong Voting Info; UW Tries to Alert Students*, Capital Times, Oct. 3, 2004, at 1A. The graphic of the flyer is courtesy of Professor Justin Levitt.

35. Nathans.

36. Deceptive Practices and Voter Intimidation Prevention Act of 2007, S. 453, http://www.gpo.gov/fdsys/pkg/BILLS-110s453rs/pdf/BILLS-110s453rs.pdf.

37. Justin Levitt, *A Devil in the Details of Florida's Early Voting Law,* Election Law Blog, May 23, 2011, http://electionlawblog.org/?p=18296; *New Florida Voting Law: Voting Ban on Final Sunday,* June 25, 2011, http://www.theledger.com/article/201106 25/EDIT01/110629619?Title=New-Florida-Voting-Law-Voting-Ban-On-Final-Sunday-.

38. Steve Freeman & Joel Bleifuss, *Was the 2004 Election Stolen? Exit Polls, Election Fraud, and the Official Count* (New York: Seven Stories Press 2006).

39. Jonathan D. Simon, *Believe It (or Not): The Massachusetts Special Election for U.S. Senate,* Aug. 27, 2010, http://electiondefensealliance.org/files/BelieveIt_OrNot _100904.pdf.

40. Jonathan D. Simon, *"Creating Reality": The Method Soros Et Al Seem Determined to Overlook* (letter to the editor, New York Review of Books, June 10, 2011), http://electiondefensealliance.org/Letter.

41. Robert F. Kennedy, Jr., *Was the 2004 Election Stolen?,* Rolling Stone, June 1, 2006. An archived copy appears at the Common Dreams website, http://www.commondreams.org/views06/0601-34.htm. Farhad Manjoo, *Was the 2004 Election Stolen? No,* Salon, June 3, 2006, http://www.salon.com/news/feature/2006/06/03/kennedy. Kennedy's response and Manjoo's reply appear at *Was the 2004 Election Stolen? Robert F. Kennedy, Jr. and Farhad Manjoo Face Off,* Salon, June 6, 2006, http://www.salon.com/news/opinion/feature/2006/06/06/rfk_responds. Manjoo's two responses deal as well with the long lines point and the exit polls issue. For additional responses on the exit polls from 2004, see *Evaluation of Edison/Mitofsky Election System 2004 Prepared by Edison Media Research and Mitofsky International for the National Election Pool (NEP) Embargoed for Release at 10AM ET January 19, 2005,* http://abcnews.go.com/images/Politics/EvaluationofEdison MitofskyElectionSystem.pdf.

42. Lawrence Norden, *About That "Flipping" Vote—What You Should Know,* Brennan Center for Justice Blog, Oct. 29, 2008, http://www.brennancenter.org/blog/archives/about_that_flipping_vote_what_you_should_know/. The staff of staunch Democratic representative John Conyers issued a report for a House Judiciary Committee on Ohio 2004, finding no evidence supporting the conspiracy theories. "Preserving Democracy: What Went Wrong in Ohio," Status Report of the House Judiciary Committee Democratic Staff, Jan. 5, 2005, http://www.iwant myvote.com/lib/downloads/references/house_judiciary/final_status_report.pdf.

43. The video of the event is posted on YouTube at: http://www.youtube.com/watch? v=neGbKHyGuHU&feature=player_embedded. The best accounts of the incident and aftermath appear in the *Washington Post* and in an investigative report by the Department of Justice's Office of Professional Responsibility. Jerry Markon and Krissah Thompson, *Dispute Over New Black Panthers Case Causes Deep Divisions,* Washington Post, Oct. 22, 2010, http://www.washingtonpost.com/wp-dyn/content/article/2010/10/22/AR2010102203982.html; Department of Justice,

Office of Professional Responsibility, Report, Investigation of Dismissal of Defendants in *United States v. New Black Panther Party for Self-Defense, Inc., et al.*, No. 2:09cv0065 (E.D. Pa. May 18, 2009), Mar. 17, 2011, http://www.scribd.com/doc/52515892/Department-of-Justice-OPR-Report-on-the-New-Black-Panther-Party-Matter ("OPR NBPP Report"). (The report was first posted by Democrats on the House Judiciary Committee: http://democrats.judiciary.house.gov/sites/democrats.judiciary.house.gov/files/OPR%20Report_0.pdf.) A second, broader report on the Department of Justice's handling of voting rights issues by the Department of Justice's Office of the Inspector General remains forthcoming.

44. Jonathan Martin, *Rudy's Team*, Jonathan Martin's blog, *Politico*, Feb. 14, 2007, http://www.politico.com/blogs/jonathanmartin/0207/Rudys_Team.html. The Election Journal website is www.electionjournal.org.

45. *REPORT: Fox News Has Hyped Phony New Black Panther Scandal at Least 95 Times*, Media Matters for America, July 16, 2010, http://mediamatters.org/research/201007160038.

46. Carrie Johnson, *Holder Confirmed as Nation's First Black Attorney General; He Overcame Objections of Some in GOP*, Washington Post, Feb. 3, 2009, http://www.washingtonpost.com/wp-dyn/content/article/2009/02/02/AR2009020202581.html.

47. The account of the Ike Brown controversy comes from Markon and Thompson; the OPR NBPP Report; and *United States v. Brown*, 494 F.Supp.2d 440 (S.D. Miss. 2007).

48. OPR NBPP Report at 75.

49. Ryan J. Reilly, *DOJ Attorney Fights to Testify About Black Panthers*, Main Justice, Dec. 2, 2009, http://www.mainjustice.com/2009/12/02/doj-attorney-fights-to-testify-about-black-panthers/.

50. Markon and Thompson.

51. U.S. Commission on Civil Rights, *Race Neutral Enforcement of the Law? The U.S. Department of Justice and the New Black Panther Party Litigation: An Interim Report*, Nov. 23, 2010, http://www.usccr.gov/NBPH/USCCR_NBPP_report.pdf.

52. Markon and Thompson; Mary Jacoby, *Ex-DOJ Voting Section Chief Now Representing South Carolina in Voter ID Fight*, Main Justice, Jan. 11, 2012, http://www.mainjustice.com/2012/01/11/ex-doj-voting-section-chief-now-representing-south-carolina-in-voter-id-fight.

53. Abigail Thernstrom, *The New Black Panther Case: A Conservative Dissent*, National Review Online, July 6, 2010, http://www.nationalreview.com/articles/243408/new-black-panther-case-br-conservative-dissent-abigail-thernstrom; Abigail Thernstrom, *Yes, the Black Panther Case Is Small Potatoes*, National Review Online, July 27, 2010, http://www.nationalreview.com/articles/243545/yes-black-panther-case-small-potatoes-abigail-thernstrom.

Chapter 4: Who Counts?

1. Richard L. Hasen, *Beyond the Margin of Litigation: Reforming U.S. Election Administration to Avoid Electoral Meltdown*, 62 Washington & Lee Law Review 937 (2005),

http://papers.ssrn.com/sol3/papers.cfm?abstract_id=698201; Mark Rollenhagen, *Brunner Experienced with Elections; Ohio's Secretary of State Brings Relevant Professional Background to the Job,* Cleveland Plain Dealer, May 7, 2007.

2. The quotation appears at the beginning of an advertisement run by the Ohio Republican Party and posted on YouTube at http://www.youtube.com/watch?v=niEF3Z3l_Ac. Below the video itself appears the quotation about Brunner being partisan.

3. Sarah Laskow, *Scoring Secretary of State Seats for Dems,* The Center for Public Integrity iWatch News, Sept. 8, 2008, http://www.iwatchnews.org/2008/09/08/3065/scoring-secretary-state-seats-dems. In a blog posting at the secretary of state's website, the group claimed to have raised even more: "We raised over $200,000 for Brunner, helping her replace Ken Blackwell. This equaled nearly 10 percent of her budget and close to the $220,000 fundraising advantage she achieved over her Republican opponent." Becky Bond, *Support Secretaries of State Who Will Protect the Election,* Secretaries of State Project Blog, Apr. 23, 2008, archived at: http://web.archive.org/web/20090618002121/http://www.secstateproject.org/blog/our_plans_for_2008.html. For more on the project, see Avi Zenilman, *Secretaries of State Give Dem Firewall,* Politico, Nov. 2, 2008, http://www.politico.com/news/stories/1008/15105.html. In 2011, I received an "Access Denied" message when I went to the Secretary of State Project website. My query about the current status of the group to Becky Bond, one of the founders of the group who works for Credo Mobile, went unanswered.

4. Chuck Neubauer, *Soros and Liberal Groups Seeking Top Election Posts in Battleground States,* Washington Times, June 23, 2011, http://www.washingtontimes.com/news/2011/jun/23/section-527-works-to-seat-liberals-as-election-ove/?page=1.

5. The fundraising data appear at the "Follow the Money" website of the National Institute on Money in State Politics and appear here: http://www.followthemoney.org/database/StateGlance/candidate.phtml?c=123413. A search of contributions or spending benefitting O'Shaughnessy on the Ohio Secretary of State website revealed no contributions from the Secretary of State Project or ActBlue, and no independent spending benefitting O'Shaughnessy. The election results appear at the secretary's website at: http://www.sos.state.oh.us/SOS/elections/electResultsMain/2010results/20101102sos.aspx.

6. *State ex rel. Myles v. Brunner,* 899 N.E.2d. 120 (Ohio 2008), http://scholar.google.com/scholar_case?case=5018033797971301418&hl=en&as_sdt=2&as_vis=1&oi=scholarr.

7. Cass Sunstein, *Of Law and Politics,* in *The Vote: Bush, Gore, and the Supreme Court* 6–7 (Chicago: University of Chicago Press, Cass Sunstein & Richard A. Epstein, eds. 2001).

8. *State ex. rel. Colvin v. Brunner,* 896 N.E.2d 979 (Ohio 2008), http://www.sconet.state.oh.us/rod/docs/pdf/0/2008/2008-ohio-5041.pdf.

9. Dennis Cauchon, *Ohio, Hit Economically, Votes Obama,* USA Today, Nov. 5, 2008, http://www.usatoday.com/news/politics/election2008/oh.htm; Catherine Candisky, *A Third of New Voters Must Be Verified, Brunner Says,* Columbus Dispatch, Oct. 15, 2008, http://www.dispatch.com/content/stories/local/2008/10/15/fraud_followup.html.

10. The case is *Ohio Republican Party v. Brunner*. The district court's opinion is at 582 F.Supp.2d 957 (S.D. Ohio 2008) and available at: http://moritzlaw.osu.edu/elec tionlaw/litigation/documents/R52Order.pdf. The original opinion of a panel of Sixth Circuit judges is not good law, because the en banc court order hearing the case took away its precedential value. It can be read at: http://moritzlaw.osu.edu/ electionlaw/litigation/documents/ORPvBrunnerOct10.pdf.

The order of the entire Sixth Circuit sitting en banc and reversing the panel decision is at 544 F.3d 711 (6th Cir. 2008) (en banc) and is available at: http:// scholar.google.com/scholar_case?case=10067678243758169013&hl=en&as _sdt=2&as_vis=1&oi=scholarr. The U.S. Supreme Court's opinion is at 555 U.S. 5 (2008) and is available at: http://scholar.google.com/scholar_case?case=5729624 462900804934&hl=en&as_sdt=2&as_vis=1&oi=scholarr. The facts and quotations in the next few paragraphs come from these court decisions.

11. A chart of the president nominating each judge appears in Wikipedia: http:// en.wikipedia.org/wiki/United_States_Court_of_Appeals_for_the_Sixth_Circuit #Current_composition_of_the_court. The only exceptions to the partisan pattern are Judge Ronald Gilman, a Clinton appointee who has turned out to vote with conservatives on election law issues and Judge Helene White, who was originally a Clinton nominee but whose nomination was stalled in the Senate. President George W. Bush renominated White as part of a package to break the Senate log-jam on judicial appointments. Press Release, Senator Patrick Leahy, *Leahy Helps Solve Impasse on Sixth Circuit Judicial Nominations*, Apr. 15, 2008, http://leahy.senate .gov/press/press_releases/release/?id=93e8c8d6–28d8–4aa0–9883–8b4a6b6 68770. For more on HAVA mismatches, see Candice Hoke & David Jefferson, *Voting and Registration: Technology Issues: Lessons from 2008*, in *America Votes! Supplement*, ch. 3, http://apps.americanbar.org/abastore/index.cfm?section=main& fm=Product.AddToCart&pid=5330200PDF.

12. *Alexander v. Sandoval*, 532 U.S. 275 (2001), http://scholar.google.com/scholar_case? case=6907411608837736130&hl=en&as_sdt=2&as_vis=1&oi=scholarr. In this case, the conservative justices of the U.S. Supreme Court interpreted the language of Title VI of the Civil Rights Act of 1964 narrowly, holding that no private right of action existed for an individual to challenge the English-only administration of driver's license examinations. The liberal justices interpreted Title VI broadly in dissent, writing that such a private right of action would further the congressional purposes of Title VI.

13. Edward B. Foley, *Running Elections in Cuyahoga County Next Year*, Free and Fair, Election Law @ Moritz, Apr. 10, 2007, http://moritzlaw.osu.edu/electionlaw/news/ articles.php?ID=137.

14. Cuyahoga Election Review Panel, Cuyahoga, OH, Final Report, July 20, 2006, at 8, available at: http://www.acluohio.org/issues/votingrights/cerp_final_report_2006 07.pdf.

15. Jean Dubail, *Bennett Loses a Round; Swings Back at Brunner*, Cleveland Plain Dealer, Apr. 4, 2007, http://blog.cleveland.com/openers/2007/04/bennett_loses_a_round

_swings_b.html; Jesse Watters, *The Worst Judge Ever?*, BillOReilly.com, Mar. 24, 2006, http://www.billoreilly.com/blog?action=viewBlog&blogID=-265515387107 576531.

16. Mark Niquette, *Bennett Resigns from Cleveland Board of Elections*, Columbus Dispatch, Apr. 12, 2007, http://www.dispatch.com/content/stories/local/2007/04/11/resigned.html.

17. Press Release, Ohio Secretary of State, *Brunner Swears in New Cuyahoga County Board*, May 8, 2007, http://www.sos.state.oh.us/PressReleases/2007%20Press%20Releases/Brunner%20Swears%20In%20New%20Cuyahoga%20County%20Board.aspx.

18. Daniel P. Tokaji, *Ohio's Primary: What Will Go Wrong?*, Equal Vote Blog, Mar. 2, 2008, http://moritzlaw.osu.edu/blogs/tokaji/2008/03/ohios-primary-what-will-go-wrong.html.

19. Joan Mazzolini, *10 Percent of Cuyahoga County's Voting Machines Fail Pre-Election Tests*, Cleveland Plain Dealer, Apr. 14, 2010, http://blog.cleveland.com/metro/2010/04/some_cuyahoga_countys_voting_m.html.

20. Heather K. Gerken, *The Democracy Index: Why Our Election System Is Broken and How to Fix It* (Princeton: Princeton University Press 2009). On the pollworker error, see http://electionlawblog.org/?p=29505.

21. Daniel P. Tokaji, *Early Returns on Election Reform: Discretion, Disenfranchisement, and the Help America Vote Act*, 73 George Washington Law Review 1206, 1249–50 (2005), http://moritzlaw.osu.edu/electionlaw/election06/Tokaji-EarlyReturns-Final.pdf. The account of the "Box 10" episode comes from pages 1226–27 of the Tokaji article.

22. The case is *Lucas County Democratic Party v. Blackwell*. The district court's opinion is at 341 F. Supp. 2d 861, 863 (N.D. Ohio 2004), and information about the case is available from Election Law @ Moritz at http://moritzlaw.osu.edu/electionlaw/litigation/lucas.php.

23. Jim Siegel, *New Election Law Spurs Repeal Push*, Columbus Dispatch, July 15, 2011, http://www.dispatch.com/live/content/local_news/stories/2011/07/15/new-election-law-spurs-repeal-push.html; Editorial, *New Florida Voting Law: Voting Ban on Final Sunday*, Ledger, June 25, 2011, http://www.theledger.com/article/20110625/EDIT01/110629619?Title=New-Florida-Voting-Law-Voting-Ban-On-Final-Sunday-; Justin Levitt, *A Devil in the Details of Florida's Early Voting Law*, Election Law Blog, May 23, 2011, http://electionlawblog.org/?p=18296.

24. Joe Vardon, *Husted Draws Line Against Party Over Photo IDs at Voting Booths*, Columbus Dispatch, June 25, 2011, http://www.dispatch.com/content/stories/local/2011/06/25/husted-draws-line-against-party.html; Rick Hasen, *A Courageous Statement on Voter ID Bill from Republican Ohio Secretary of State*, Election Law Blog, June 24, 2011, http://electionlawblog.org/?p=19628.

25. Jim Siegel, *Bill Edits Overhaul of State Election Laws*, Columbus Dispatch, July 14, 2011, http://www.dispatch.com/live/content/local_news/stories/2011/07/14/bill-edits-overhaul-of-state-election-laws.html.

26. *Fair Elections Ohio Turns in First 1,000 Signatures for HB 194 Referendum*, Progress

Ohio Blog, July 18, 2011, http://www.progressohio.org/blog/2011/07/fair-elections-ohio-turns-in-first-1000-signatures-for-hb194-referendum.html; *Ed Fitzgerald Says Cuyahoga Will Fight Back,* WTAM—Local News, Aug. 28, 2011, http://www.wmms.com/cc-common/news/sections/newsarticle.html?feed=122520&article=9032968; Joe Vardon, *Husted Will Send Absentee Ballots to Voters Statewide Next Year,* Columbus Dispatch, Sept. 2, 2011, http://www.dispatch.com/content/stories/local/2011/09/02/husted-will-send-absentee-ballots-to-voters-statewide-next-year.html.

27. Martinez's biography appears on page 19 of an EAC presentation to a House committee, posted at: http://www.eac.gov/assets/1/Page/Congressional%20Testimony%20before%20House%20Administration%20Committee%20June%2017%202004.pdf; Pamela Coloff, *Go Ask Alice: What Happened to the Ballot Box That Saved Lyndon Johnson's Career?,* Texas Monthly, November 1998, http://www.texasmonthly.com/1998–11–01/reporter.php.

28. Dr. Buster Soaries, The Grable Group, http://thegrablegroup.com/speakers/dr-buster-soaries-popular-speaker-agent-change/; Max Pizarro, *Soaries Recommended Pinkett for LG,* PolitickerNJ, July 14, 2009, http://www.politickernj.com/max/31371/soaries-recommended-pinkett-lg; David W. Chen, *In Person: A Crowd-Pleaser, With a Mission,* New York Times, May 7, 1995, http://www.nytimes.com/1995/05/07/nyregion/in-person-a-crowd-pleaser-with-a-mission.html.

29. Tim Dickinson, *The Voice of Voting Reform: 2004 Election Interview: The Rev. DeForest Soaries,* Rolling Stone (blog), June 6, 2006, http://www.rollingstone.com/politics/blogs/national-affairs/the-voice-of-voting-reform-20060606.

30. Ray Martinez III, *Improving Our Elections: A View from the Front Lines,* 8 Election Law Journal 239, 241 (2009), http://www.liebertonline.com/doi/pdfplus/10.1089/elj.2009.8309.

31. Position Statement, Commissioner Ray Martinez III, July 10, 2006, *On the Matter Regarding EAC Tally Vote Dated July 6, 2006, "Arizona's Request for Accommodation,"* at 7, http://www.eac.gov/assets/1/News/Vice%20Chairman%20Ray%20Martinez%20III%20Position%20Statement%20Regarding%20Arizona's%20Request%20for%20Accomodation.pdf.

32. Leonard M. Shambon, *Implementing the Help America Vote Act,* 3 Election Law Journal 424, 428 (2004).

33. National Association of Secretaries of State, *NASS Position on Funding and Authorization of U.S. Election Assistance Commission, Adopted on February 26, 2005, Extended Until the 2010 Summer Conference on February 1, 2010, Renewed at the 2010 Summer Conference on July 20, 2010 (until summer conference 2015),* http://www.nass.org/index.php?option=com_docman&task=doc_download&gid=906&Itemid; Ben Pershing, *House Votes to End Public Funding for Presidential Campaigns,* "2 Chambers" blog, Washington Post, Dec. 1, 2011, http://www.washingtonpost.com/blogs/2chambers/post/house-votes-to-end-public-funding-for-presidential-campaigns/2011/12/01/gIQAc8SaHO_blog.html.

34. Ian Urbina, *U.S. Panel Is Said to Alter Finding on Voter Fraud,* New York Times, Apr. 11, 2007, http://www.nytimes.com/2007/04/11/washington/11voters.html.

35. Tova Andrea Wang, *A Rigged Report on U.S. Voting?*, Washington Post, Aug. 30, 2007, http://www.washingtonpost.com/wp-dyn/content/article/2007/08/29/AR 2007082901928.html.

36. U.S. Election Assistance Commission Office of the Inspector General, *Report of Investigation: Preparation of the Voter Fraud and Voter Intimidation Report*, Report No. I-IV-EAC-02–08, March 2008, http://www.eac.gov/assets/1/Page/Report%20of %20Investigation%20-%20Preparation%20of%20the%20Voter%20Fraud%20 and%20Voter%20Intimidation%20Report.pdf. The Inspector General of the EAC had no investigators on staff. The IG asked the Inspector General's office of the Interior Department to conduct the investigation.

37. J. Gerald Hebert, *"He Said, She Said" at the EAC*, Campaign Legal Center Blog, Mar. 13, 2008, http://www.clcblog.org/blog_item-216.html; Kenneth P. Doyle, *Former EAC Member Says Von Spakovsky Pressured Him to Advance Republican Agenda*, BNA Money & Politics Report, Mar. 14, 2008, http://news.bna.com/mpdm/ MPDMWB/split_display.adp?fedfid=7100336&vname=mpebulallissues&wsn= 503692000&searchid=14982179&doctypeid=1&type=date&mode=doc&split=0 &scm=MPDMWB&pg=0; Gerry Hebert, *Hans Von Spakovsky's Culture of Corruption*, Campaign Legal Center Blog, July 3, 2007, http://www.clcblog.org/index.php? option=com_content&view=article&id=257:hans-von-spakovskys-culture-of-corruption; Dan Tokaji, *A Worrisome Nominee to the EAC*, Equal Vote Blog, Sept. 15, 2006, http://moritzlaw.osu.edu/blogs/tokaji/2006/09/worrisome-nominee-to-eac .html.

38. Rick Hasen, *Tova Wang Issues Comment on EAC IG Report*, Election Law Blog, Mar. 14, 2008, http://electionlawblog.org/?p=9532.

39. Rick Hasen, *Picture of the Day: Election Administration Edition*, Election Law Blog, Jan. 25, 2012, http://electionlawblog.org/?p=28623.

40. *Commentary: Deforest B. Soaries Jr.*, in *Making Every Vote Count: Federal Election Legislation in the States*, app. A 113–18 (Essays and commentary sponsored by the Policy Research Institute for the Region at the Woodrow Wilson School of Public and International Affairs at Princeton University, the Brennan Center for Justice at New York University School of Law, and the Fels Institute of Government at the University of Pennsylvania, Andrew Rachlin, ed. 2006), http://wws.princeton. edu/research/prior-publications/conference-books/vote.pdf.

Chapter 5: Margin of Litigation

1. Jay Weiner, *This Is Not Florida: How Al Franken Won the Minnesota Senate Recount* 15–16 (Minneapolis: University of Minnesota Press 2010).

2. For the best legal account of the Franken-Coleman dispute, see Edward B. Foley, *The Lake Wobegone Recount: Minnesota's Disputed 2008 U.S. Senate Election*, 10 Election Law Journal 129 (2011) ("Foley, *Lake Wobegone*"), and Edward B. Foley, *How Fair Can Be Faster: The Lessons of Coleman v. Franken*, 10 Election Law Journal 187 (2011) ("Foley, *Lessons*"). See also the fifteen-page appendix to Foley's *Lake Wobegone* article, posted at http://moritzlaw.osu.edu/electionlaw/docs/foley-eljapp.pdf. The

account of the Minnesota controversy in this chapter draws on Foley's two articles and Weiner's *This Is Not Florida*.

3. Foley, *Lake Wobegone*, at 142.

4. James Baker, Statement, Transcript, Nov. 11, 2000, http://dir.salon.com/politics/feature/2000/11/11/baker_text/index.html.

5. Edward B. Foley, *The Founder's* Bush v. Gore: *The 1792 Election Dispute and Its Continuing Relevance*, 44 Indiana Law Journal 23 (2010), http://indylaw.indiana.edu/ilr/pdf/vol44p23.pdf.

6. *In re The Matter of Protest of Election Returns and Absentee Ballots in the Nov. 4, 1997 Election for the City of Miami, Fla.*, 707 So. 2d 1170, 1171 (Fla. 3d Dist. Ct. App. 1998), rev. denied, 725 So 2d 1108 (Fla. 1998). The trial court had ordered a new election.

7. The next few paragraphs draw on Richard L. Hasen, *Beyond the Margin of Litigation: Reforming U.S. Election Administration to Avoid Electoral Meltdown*, 62 Washington & Lee Law Review 937, 957–59 (2005).

8. *Bush v. Gore*, 531 U.S. 98 (2000), http://supreme.justia.com/us/531/98/.

9. Nixon recounted his reasons for conceding in an autobiography: a "recount would require up to half a year, during which time the legitimacy of Kennedy's election would be in question"; moreover, "the effect could be devastating to America's foreign relations. I could not subject the country to such a situation." See the quotations in R.W. Apple, *The 2000 Elections: News Analysis; Recipe for a Stalemate*, New York Times, Nov. 9, 2000, http://www.nytimes.com/2000/11/09/us/the-2000-elections-news-analysis-recipe-for-a-stalemate.html?pagewanted=all&src=pm. For a view that Nixon gave up the challenge only when it looked fruitless, see David Greenberg, *It's a Myth That Nixon Acquiesced in 1960*, Los Angeles Times, Nov. 10, 2000, http://articles.latimes.com/2000/nov/10/local/me-49741.

10. Chad Flanders, Bush v. Gore *and the Uses of "Limiting,"* 116 Yale Law Journal 1159 (2007).

11. Richard L. Hasen, *The Supreme Court's Shrinking Election Law Docket, 2001–2010: A Legacy of* Bush v. Gore *or Fear of the Roberts Court,* 10 Election Law Journal 325 (2011).

12. Steven J. Mulroy, *Lemonade from Lemons: Can Advocates Convert* Bush v. Gore *into a Vehicle for Reform?*, 9 Georgetown Journal on Poverty Law and Policy 357 (2002); Samuel Issacharoff, Op-Ed, *The Court's Legacy for Voting Rights*, New York Times, Dec. 14, 2000, at A39.

13. Richard L. Hasen, Bush v. Gore *and the Future of Equal Protection Law in Elections*, 29 Florida State Law Review 377 (2001). The next few paragraphs draw on Richard L. Hasen, *The Untimely Death of* Bush v. Gore, 60 Stanford Law Review 1, 10–14 (2007). The citations to the punch card cases discussed in the text appear in the article.

14. Foley, *Lake Wobegone*, at 133.

15. Jessica Mador, *Why Would Someone Vote for Lizard People?*, Minnesota Public Radio, Nov. 24, 2008, http://minnesota.publicradio.org/display/web/2008/11/23/so_why_would_someone_for_the_lizard_people/.

16. Weiner at 112.

17. *Coleman v. Ritchie*, 758 N.W.2d 306 (Minn. Jan. 5, 2009).

18. *In re Contest of General Election Held on November 4, 2008, for the Purpose of Electing a United States Senator from the State of Minnesota*, 767 N.W.2d 453 (Minn. 2009).

19. On the culture of "niceness" in Minnesota compared to a more contentious elections-related culture in Ohio, see Steven F. Huefner et al., *From Registration to Recounts Revisited: Developments in the Election Ecosystems of Five Midwestern States* viii–ix (2011), http://moritzlaw.osu.edu/electionlaw/projects/registration-to-recounts/2011 edition.pdf.

20. 635 F.3d 219 (6th Cir.), stay denied, 131 S.Ct. 2149 (2011).

21. Trova Heffernan, *An Election for the Ages: Rossi vs. Gregoire, 2004* 147–48 (Pullman: Washington State University Press 2010). Heffernan is a staff member for Washington secretary of state Sam Reed, and the book tells the story of the 2004 controversy from Reed's perspective. The trial court gave an oral decision, the transcript of which was published in the Election Law Journal. *Borders v. King County*, No. 05-2-00027-3, Verbatim Report of Proceedings, June 6, 2005, http://www.liebertonline.com/doi/pdfplus/10.1089/elj.2005.4.418. The quotations and citations in this section come from these two sources.

22. *McDonald v. Reed*, 103 P.3d 722 (Wash. 2004).

23. Hasen, *Margin*, at 943–44.

24. The next few paragraphs draw on Richard L. Hasen, *Alaska's Big Spelling Test: How Strong Is Joe Miller's Argument Against the Leeza Markovsky Vote?*, Slate, Nov. 11, 2010, http://www.slate.com/id/2274556/. The Alaska Supreme Court opinion in the case is *Miller v. Treadwell*, 245 P.3d 867 (Alaska 2010). The federal district court opinion is also named *Miller v. Treadwell*, 736 F.Supp.2d 1240 (D. Alaska 2010). On the "Lisa M." votes, see Rick Hasen, *Will "Lisa M. Lackey" Ruin Sen. Murkowski's Chances of a Successful Write-in Vote?*, Election Law Blog, Oct. 29, 2010, http://electionlawblog.org/?p=16424.

25. Elizabeth Dunbar & Tom Scheck, *Mark Dayton Declared Winner, Finally*, Minnesota Public Radio, Dec. 8, 2010, http://minnesota.publicradio.org/display/web/2010/12/08/emmer-recount-concession/.

Chapter 6: Deus ex Machina

1. Michigan Athletics, Michigan Fight Song, http://www.mgoblue.com/genrel/062 909aaa.html.

2. Mike DeBonis, *Hacking Infiltration Ends D.C. Online Voting Trial*, Mike DeBonis on Local Politics Blog, *Washington Post*, Oct. 4, 2010, http://voices.washingtonpost .com/debonis/2010/10/hacker_infiltration_ends_dc_on.html; Jessica Gresko, *Michigan Students Get DC Vote Site to Play Song*, Associated Press, Oct. 6, 2010, http:// www.washingtontimes.com/news/2010/oct/5/michigan-students-get-dc-vote-site-to-play-song/.

3. Brock N. Meeks, *Military Vote Softens But Doesn't Shift; Pentagon Scrambles to As-*

sure Absentee Ballot Count, MSNBC.com, Sept. 15, 2004, http://www.msnbc.msn.
com/id/5964655/ns/politics/t/military-vote-softens-doesnt-shift/#.Tjrew2FPBJs;
Military and Overseas Voters Empowerment Act, Pub. L. No. 111-84, Subtitle H, §§
575–589, 123 Stat 2190, 2318–2335 (2009), *amending* Uniformed and Overseas Citizens Absentee Voting Act, 42 USC §§ 1973ff–1973ff-7. See S. Candice Hoke & Matthew A. Bishop, *Essential Research Needed to Support UOCAVA-MOVE Act Implementation at the State and Local Levels,* Cleveland State University Research Paper
10-197 (October 2010), http://ssrn.com/abstract=1697848; Clair Whitmer, *What
the Move Act Means for You,* Overseas Vote Foundation, Jan. 16, 2010, https://
www.overseasvotefoundation.org/node/282.

4. U.S. Department of Justice, Office of Public Affairs, *Fact Sheet: MOVE Act,* Oct.
27, 2010, http://www.justice.gov/opa/pr/2010/October/10-crt-1212.html.

5. Senator John Cornyn to Attorney General Eric Holder, July 19, 2011, http://www
.scribd.com/doc/60372120/SJC-Letter-to-AG-Re-Mil-Voting-Rights-in-2012-Elec
tion-JUL-2011-Signed-Scanned; The Republican Lawyer Blog, *Cornyn Calls Attention to Military Voter Disenfranchisement,* Republican National Lawyers Association,
July 19, 2011, http://rnla.org/Blogs/blogs/public/archive/2011/07/19/cornyn-calls-
attention-to-military-voter-disenfranchisement.aspx ("Two of the speakers, Hans
von Spakovsky and Christian Adams, are RNLA members. Christian Adams
mentioned that in addition to the legal issues involved [such as the fact no Section
1983 suit has been filed], the DOJ is not taking adequate efforts to find out whether
states are in compliance, does not have personnel with this as a priority, does not
communicate information for military voters as it has for civilians, and filed lawsuits too late").

6. J. Christian Adams, *Obama's Bumblers Damage Military Voting Rights,* Washington
Examiner, July 13, 2011, http://washingtonexaminer.com/opinion/op-eds/2011/
07/obamas-bumblers-damage-military-voting-rights#ixzz1UANpJMrd.

7. Eric Eversole, *Military Voting in 2010: A Step Forward, But a Long Way to Go, A
Study Published By* Military Families United's Military Voter Protection Project
and AMVETS Legal Clinic at the Chapman University School of Law 1, 4 (n.d.),
http://www.mvpproject.org/MVPProject_study_download.pdf.

8. Federal Voting Assistance Program, Department of Defense, *2010 Post-Election
Survey Report to Congress* iv (September 2011), http://www.fvap.gov/resources/
media/2010report.pdf. Eversole criticized the methodology of the FVAP report.
Eric Eversole, Guest Post, *Eversole Responds on Discrepancy in Military Voter Turnout Data, Questions FVAP Data,* Election Law Blog, Oct. 20, 2011, http://election
lawblog.org/?p=24491.

9. Hoke and Bishop at 4.

10. J. Alex Halderman, *Hacking the D.C. Internet Voting Pilot,* Freedom to Tinker, Oct. 5,
2010, https://freedom-to-tinker.com/blog/jhalderm/hacking-dc-internet-voting-pilot.

11. Paul Stenbjorn, *DC BOEE Lessons Learned from Digital Vote by Mail Hacking,* District of Columbia Board of Elections & Ethics, http://dcboee.us/dvm/ps_hacker
_response.htm.

12. Alex Altman, *Will Online Voting Turn into an Election Day Debacle?*, Time, Oct. 15, 2010, http://www.time.com/time/politics/article/0,8599,2025696,00.html.

13. David Jefferson, *If I Can Shop and Bank Online, Why Can't I Vote Online?*, http://electionlawblog.org/wp-content/uploads/jefferson-onlinevoting.pdf (attachment posted as supplement to http://electionlawblog.org/?p=24849, Nov. 1, 2011); U.S. General Accounting Office, *Elections: Perspectives on Activities and Challenges Across the Nation* 322 (GAO-02-3) (2001), http://books.google.com/books?id=xSkqezf_nSs C&pg=PA322#v=onepage&q&f=false.

14. Mike DeBonis, *Michigan Prof Explains How D.C. Online Voting System Was Hacked*, Mike DeBonis on Local Politics Blog, *Washington Post*, Oct. 6, 2010, http://voices .washingtonpost.com/debonis/2010/10/prof_explains_how_dc_online_vo.html.

15. DeBonis, *Hacker Infiltration.*

16. See David Jefferson, *Email Voting: A National Security Threat in Government Elections*, Verified Voting Blog, June 20, 2011, http://blog.verifiedvoting.org/2011/06/20/1375.

17. On the success of military postal voting, see Military Postal Service Agency, *The 2010 Analysis of the Military Postal System Compliance with the MOVE Act*, http://www.fvap.gov/resources/media/2010_MPSA_after_action_report.pdf.

18. National Public Radio, *Election 2006: Full U.S. Senate Race Results*, http://www .npr.org/news/specials/election2006/results/full_senate_results.html#fl.

19. Jessica Ring Amunson & Sam Hirsch, *The Case of the Disappearing Votes: Lessons from the* Jennings v. Buchanan *Congressional Election Contest*, 17 William & Mary Bill of Rights Journal 397, 398 (2008), http://www.jenner.com/files/tbl_s20Publ ications%5CRelatedDocumentsPDFs1252%5C2365%5CHirschAmunson.pdf.

20. National Journal, *Almanac of American Politics*, Florida 13th District, http://www. nationaljournal.com/almanac/area/fl/13.

21. Jeremy Wallace, *Democrats Seize House; Crist In; Buchanan Leads; Uncounted Votes Delay Outcome for Buchanan, Jennings*, Sarasota Herald Tribune, Nov. 8, 2006, http://www.accessmylibrary.com/coms2/summary_0286–28955654_ITM.

22. The Governor's Select Task Force on Election Procedures, Standards, and Technology, *Revitalizing Democracy in Florida* 32 (Mar. 1, 2001), http://www.collinscen ter.org/resource/resmgr/Election-Reform/Revitalizing_Democracy_in_Fl.pdf; Toni Whitt, *Touch-Screen Voting Was Supposed to Be Foolproof*, Sarasota Herald Tribune, Nov. 9, 2006, http://www.accessmylibrary.com/article-1G1–154211419/ touch-screen-voting-supposed.html.

23. Amunson & Hirsch at 399–400.

24. Todd Ruger, *Voting Glitch Prompts Warning*, Sarasota Herald Tribune, Nov. 5, 2006, http://www.accessmylibrary.com/coms2/summary_0286–24151731_ITM.

25. Amunson & Hirsch at 400.

26. Weber v. Shelley, 347 F.3d 1101 (9th Cir. 2003), http://scholar.google.com/scholar_ case?case=14102962181186073285&hl=en&as_sdt=2&as_vis=1&oi=scholarr.

27. Charles Stewart III, *Voting Technologies*, 14 Annual Review of Political Science 353 (2011), http://www.annualreviews.org/doi/pdf/10.1146/annurev.polisci.12.053007

.145205. Stewart provides a readable and comprehensive overview of voting technology issues since 2000, and the general statements in this section of the chapter about voting technology draw from Stewart's analysis.

28. Brad Friedman, *"Diebold Election Systems, Inc" Is No More! (At Least in Name)*, Huffington Post, Aug. 16, 2007, http://www.huffingtonpost.com/brad-friedman/diebold-election-systems-_b_60778.html.

29. Detailed information about the methodology and findings of Bowen's top-to-bottom review appear at California Secretary of State Debra Bowen, Top-to-Bottom Review, http://www.sos.ca.gov/voting-systems/oversight/top-to-bottom-review.htm.

30. AP, *Companies Say California Voting-Machine Review Unrealistic*, July 30, 2007, http://www.kcra.com/news/13785934/detail.html; Hector Becerra, *Registrar of L.A. County to Retire*, Los Angeles Times, Aug. 29, 2007, http://articles.latimes.com/2007/aug/29/local/me-registrar29.

31. Marc Kovac, *Capital News: More Volleys Over Brunner's Project Everest*, News Leader, June 11, 2008, http://www.the-news-leader.com/news/article/3921731.

32. John F. Kennedy Presidential Library and Museum, Award Announcement, "Election Integrity Spotlighted at JFK Profile in Courage Awards; California and Ohio Secretaries of State Join Former Governor of Mississippi as Honorees," May 12, 2008, http://www.jfklibrary.org/Events-and-Awards/Profile-in-Courage-Award/Award-Recipients/Debra-Bowen-2008.aspx?t=2.

33. *Sarasota Alliance for Fair Elections, Inc. v. Browning*, 28 So.3d 880 (Fla. 2010), http://caselaw.findlaw.com/fl-supreme-court/1507783.html.

34. Marc L. Songini, *Florida Bans Touch-Screen Voting Machines*, Computerworld, May 22, 2007, http://www.pcworld.com/article/132138/florida_bans_touchscreen_voting_machines.html.

35. The next few paragraphs draw from the description of the litigation in Amunson and Hirsch.

36. Angie Welborn, *House Contested Election Cases: 1933 to 2000* 105–6, 121–22 (New York: Novinka Books 2003); Dexter Filkins & Peter M. Warren, *Disputed 1984 Indiana Vote a Bad Omen for Sanchez?*, Los Angeles Times, May 11, 1997, http://articles.latimes.com/1997-05-11/news/mn-57795_1_indiana-vote; Guy Gugliota, *Dornan Challenge to Sanchez Rejected*, Washington Post, Feb. 5, 1998, http://www.washingtonpost.com/wp-srv/politics/campaigns/keyraces98/stories/cahouse020598.htm.

37. U.S. Government Accountability Office, *Results of GAO's Testing of Voting Systems Used in Sarasota County in Florida's 13th Congressional District; Statement of Nabajyoti Barkakati, Ph.D. Acting Chief Technologist Applied Research and Methods*, GAO-08-425T (2008), http://www.gao.gov/new.items/d08425t.pdf.

38. Laurin Frisina et al., *Ballot Formats, Touchscreens, and Undervotes: A Study of the 2006 Midterm Elections in Florida*, 7 Election Law Journal 25 (2008), http://www.liebertonline.com/doi/abs/10.1089/elj.2008.7103.

39. Matthew Doig & Maurice Tamman, *Analysis Suggests Undervote Caused by Ballot Design*, Sarasota Herald Tribune, Nov. 15, 2006, http://www.heraldtribune.com/

article/20061115/NEWS/611150751?p=4&tc=pg; Kristen K Greene, Effects of Multiple Races and Header Highlighting on Undervotes in the 2006 Sarasota General Election: A Usability Study and Cognitive Modeling Assessment (n.d.), http://chil.rice.edu/research/pdf/Greene_10.pdf.

40. Jeremy Wallace, *Getting Set to Try for House,* Sarasota Herald Tribune, July 16, 2009, http://www.accessmylibrary.com/article-1G1–204011463/getting-set-try-house.html.

41. Doug Sword, *3 Years After Vote Furor, Machine Vendor Is Back,* Sarasota Herald Tribune, Sept. 24, 2009, http://www.accessmylibrary.com/article-1G1–208424352/3-years-after-vote.html.

42. U.S. Department of Justice, Office of Public Affairs, *Justice Department Requires Key Divestiture in Election Systems & Software/Premier Election Solutions Merger,* Mar. 8, 2010, http://www.justice.gov/opa/pr/2010/March/10-at-235.html; Patrick O'Donnell, *Ballot-Scanning Company Election Systems & Software Agrees to Give Cuyahoga County $200,000,* Cleveland Plain Dealer Metro Blog, Mar. 22, 2011, http://blog.cleveland.com/metro/2011/03/ballot_scanning_company_electi.html.

43. Caltech-MIT Voting Technology Project, *Voting: What Is, What Could Be* 3 (2001), http://vote.caltech.edu/drupal/files/report/voting_what_is_what_could_be.pdf; Charles Stewart III, *Residual Vote in the 2004 Election,* 5 Election Law Journal 158 (2006), http://www.liebertonline.com/doi/pdfplus/10.1089/elj.2006.5.158; Charles Stewart III, *What Hath HAVA Wrought? Consequences, Intended and Not, of the Post-Bush v. Gore Reforms, i21,* Caltech-MIT Voting Technology Project, VTP Working Paper # 102 (Apr. 7, 2011), http://vote.caltech.edu/drupal/files/working_paper/wp_102_pdf_4dadc8a267.pdf.

44. J. David McSwane, *Election Is Settled, But Clapp Is Not,* Sarasota Herald Tribune, Mar. 12, 2011, http://www.heraldtribune.com/article/20110312/ARCHIVES/103121043.

Chapter 7: Tweeting the Next Meltdown

1. Crocker Stephenson, Cary Spivak, & Patrick Marley, *Justices' Feud Gets Physical; Prosser, Bradley Clashed on Eve of Union Ruling,* Milwaukee Journal-Sentinel, June 25, 2011, http://www.jsonline.com/news/statepolitics/124546064.html; Jason Stein & Larry Sandler, *Special Prosecutor: No Charges for Prosser, Bradley in Fracas,* Milwaukee Journal Sentinel, Aug. 25, 2011, http://www.jsonline.com/news/statepolitics/128389748.html.

2. Shushannah Walshe, *$30 Million Pouring in to Influence Wisconsin Recall Elections,* ABC News, Aug. 4, 2011, http://abcnews.go.com/Politics/30-million-pouring-influence-wisconsin-recall-elections/story?id=14235471.

3. Tom Tolan, *6 Fake Democrats Fall, Setting Stage for GOP Recalls,* Milwaukee Journal Sentinel, July 12, 2011, http://www.jsonline.com/news/statepolitics/125464393.html.

4. Daniel Bice, *Conservative Group Sends Absentee Ballot with Late Return Date,* No Quarter Blog, Milwaukee Journal Sentinel, Aug. 1, 2011, http://www.jsonline.com/

blogs/news/126530753.html; Brad Friedman, *"National Director" of Koch's "Americans for Prosperity" Created Mysterious WI "Gun Group," Coordinated on Misleading Absentee Ballot Mailings,* Brad Blog, Aug. 8, 2011, http://www.bradblog.com/?p=8658&utm_source=twitterfeed&utm_medium=twitter.

5. Mike Johnson, *Exit Pollsters Draw Complaints from Voters,* Milwaukee Journal Sentinel, July 12, 2011, http://www.jsonline.com/news/statepolitics/125432878.html.

6. Video from the Aug. 9, 2011, episode appears at: http://ed.msnbc.msn.com/?videoDate=20110809.

7. Josh Marshall, *Home Stretch, Part 2!,* Talking Points Memo, Aug. 9, 2011, http://www.talkingpointsmemo.com/archives/2011/08/home_stretch_part_2.php?ref=fpblg.

8. https://twitter.com/#!/Maliheh_/status/101196438524006401; https://twitter.com/#!/craftyme25/status/101157003161907200; https://twitter.com/#!/flossofer/status/101148807525437440; https://twitter.com/#!/slackadjuster/status/101140128600305664.

9. Larry Sandler, *Dem Spokesman Accuses GOP of Tricks in Waukesha Vote Count,* Milwaukee Journal Sentinel All Politics Blog, Aug. 9, 2011, http://www.jsonline.com/blogs/news/127434893.html. The state chair's statement is reprinted on the Election Law Blog at Rick Hasen, *The Wisconsin Recall Election Comes Down to Waukesha,* Election Law Blog, Aug. 9, 2011, http://electionlawblog.org/?p=21660.

10. https://twitter.com/#!/Charlie_Golf/status/101144756914106368, https://twitter.com/#!/charliemax/status/101121547925848064, https://twitter.com/#!/judsonphillips/status/100269611823546368.

11. *Darling Declares Victory,* Milwaukee Journal Sentinel, Aug. 10, 2011, http://www.jsonline.com/news/127435773.html; Larry Sandler, *Dems Back Off Vote-Tampering Charges,* Milwaukee Journal Sentinel All Politics Blog, Aug. 10, 2011, http://www.jsonline.com/blogs/news/127437863.html.

12. Brad Friedman, *Wisconsin GOP Recall Election—Open Thread,* Brad Blog, Aug. 9, 2011, http://www.bradblog.com/?p=8662.

13. https://twitter.com/#!/kline_m/status/101423017065852928, https://twitter.com/#!/Skye820/status/101436562327347201.

14. Doug Chapin, *Quick Lesson from the Wisconsin Recalls: Election Officials Are Public Figures,* University of Minnesota Humphrey School of Public Affairs, Program for Excellence in Election Administration Blog, Aug. 10, 2011, http://blog.lib.umn.edu/cspg/peea/2011/08/quick_lesson_from_the_wisconsi.php.

15. https://twitter.com/#%21/WiscPrincipal/status/101149221733924864.

16. Laurel Walker, *Waukesha Clerk Denies Delaying Voting Results,* Milwaukee Journal Sentinel, Aug. 10, 2011, http://www.jsonline.com/news/waukesha/127457003.html.

17. *Democratic Party of Wisconsin Chairman Mike Tate Says Waukesha County Clerk Kathy Nickolaus Has "Screwed Up Counting the Vote" in Two Consecutive Elections,* Politifact Wisconsin, Aug. 11, 2011, http://www.politifact.com/wisconsin/statements/2011/aug/11/state-democratic-party-wisconsin/democratic-party-wisconsin-chairman-mike-tate-says/.

18. Charles Stewart III, *Where Are the Cool Gadgets?*, in R. Michael Alvarez, Charles Stewart III, & Ron Rivest, *Reflections on the VTP's Contributions to Science, Policymaking and Education,* Caltech-MIT Voting Technology Project, VTP Working Paper # 100 (September 2010), http://vote.caltech.edu/drupal/files/working_paper/wp100_pdf_4cab501223.pdf.

19. Rob Richie & Emily Hellman, *A Survey and Analysis of Statewide Election Recounts, 2000–2009* 1 (April 2011), http://www.fairvote.org/assets/Uploads/Recounts2011Final.pdf.

20. Cass Sunstein, *Republic 2.0* (2008). See also Natalie Jomini Stroud, *Media Use and Political Predispositions: Revisiting the Concept of Selective Exposure,* 30 Political Behavior 341 (2007), http://www.springerlink.com/content/pl751r585356425/.

21. Jonathan McDonald Ladd, *The Role of Media Distrust in Partisan Voting,* 32 Political Behavior 567 (2010), http://www9.georgetown.edu/faculty/jml89/LaddMediaVoting.pdf.

22. M.D. Conover et al., *Political Polarization on Twitter,* Proceedings of the Fifth International AAAI Conference on Weblogs and Social Media (2011), http://truthy.indiana.edu/site_media/pdfs/conover_icwsm2011_polarization.pdf. See also Younghwan Kim, *The Contribution of Social Network Sites to Exposure to Political Difference: The Relationships Among SNSs, Online Political Messaging, and Exposure to Cross-Cutting Perspectives,* 27 Computers in Human Behavior 971 (2011), http://www.sciencedirect.com/science/article/pii/S0747563210003687; Jennifer Brundidge, *Encountering "Difference" in the Contemporary Public Sphere: The Contribution of the Internet to the Heterogeneity of Political Discussion Networks,* 60 Journal of Communication 680 (2010), http://onlinelibrary.wiley.com/doi/10.1111/j.1460-2466.2010.01509.x/abstract; Thomas J. Johnson, Shannon L. Bichard, & Weiwu Zhang, *Communication Communities or "CyberGhettos?": A Path Analysis Model Examining Factors That Explain Selective Exposure to Blogs,* 15 Journal of Computer-Mediated Communication 60 (2009), http://onlinelibrary.wiley.com/doi/10.1111/j.1083-6101.2009.01492.x/full.

23. Sarita Yardi & danah boyd, *Dynamic Debates: An Analysis of Group Polarization Over Time on Twitter,* 30 (5) Bulletin of Science, Technology & Society 316, 325 (2010), http://bst.sagepub.com/content/30/5/316.abstract.

24. Henry Farrell & Daniel W. Drezner, *The Power and Politics of Blogs,* 134 Public Choice 15 (2008), http://danieldrezner.com/research/blogpaperfinal.pdf. See also Matthew W. Ragas & Spiro Kiousis, *Intermedia Agenda-Setting and Political Activism: MoveOn.org and the 2008 Presidential Election,* 13 Mass Communication and Society 560 (2010), http://www.tandfonline.com/doi/abs/10.1080/15205436.2010.515372#preview.

25. Trova Heffernan, *An Election for the Ages:* Rossi vs. Gregoire, 2004 147–48 (Pullman: Washington State University Press 2010). On the Bill Gardner statements, see the tweets of *Politico* reporter Reid Epstein at https://twitter.com/#!/reidepstein/status/131752810852253697 and https://twitter.com/#!/reidepstein/status/131752181643755520.

26. Eva Galperin, *BART Pulls a Mubarak in San Francisco,* Electronic Frontier Foundation Deeplinks Blog, Aug. 12, 2011, https://www.eff.org/deeplinks/2011/08/bart-pulls-mabarak-san-francisco.

27. Thomas J. Johnson & David D. Perlmutter, *Introduction: The Facebook Election,* 13 Mass Communication and Society 554 (2010), http://www.tandfonline.com/doi/abs/10.1080/15205436.2010.517490.

28. The next few pages draw from my article Richard L. Hasen, *Beyond the Margin of Litigation: Reforming U.S. Election Administration to Avoid Electoral Meltdown,* 62 Washington & Lee Law Review 937 (2005).

29. Richard H. Pildes, *The Constitutionalization of Democratic Politics,* 118 Harvard Law Review 28, 82 (2004), http://lsr.nellco.org/cgi/viewcontent.cgi?article=1004&context=nyu_plltwp&sei-redir=1#search=%22pildes%20constitutionalization%20democratic%20politics%22.

30. Steven F. Huefner et al., *From Registration to Recounts Revisited: Developments in the Election Ecosystems of Five Midwestern States* viii (2011), http://moritzlaw.osu.edu/electionlaw/projects/registration-to-recounts/2011edition.pdf.

INDEX

Min -> Courts / election officials = fair
OH -> Not fair (D/R)
W -> who knows - but lack of trust